THOREAU ON BIRDS

EDITED BY

Francis H. Allen

INTRODUCTION BY

John Hay

ILLUSTRATIONS BY

Louis Agassiz Fuertes

BEACON PRESS

Boston

OTHER VOLUMES IN THE CONCORD LIBRARY
SERIES EDITOR: *John Elder*

Eighty Acres: Elegy for a Family Farm
RONALD JAGER

Tarka the Otter
HENRY WILLIAMSON

The Insect World of J. Henri Fabre
EDWIN WAY TEALE, EDITOR

A Land
JACQUETTA HAWKES

In Limestone Country
SCOTT RUSSELL SANDERS

Nature and *Walking*
RALPH WALDO EMERSON AND HENRY DAVID THOREAU

Following the Bloom
DOUGLAS WHYNOTT

Finding Home: Writing on Nature and Culture from Orion *Magazine*
PETER SAUER, EDITOR

The Very Rich Hours: Travels in Orkney, Belize, the Everglades, and Greece
EMILY HIESTAND

Staying Put: Making a Home in a Restless World
SCOTT RUSSELL SANDERS

Thoreau
ON BIRDS

NOTES ON NEW ENGLAND BIRDS FROM THE JOURNALS OF

Henry David Thoreau

Beacon Press
25 Beacon Street
Boston, Massachusetts 02108-2892

Beacon Press books
are published under the auspices of
the Unitarian Universalist Association of Congregations.

99 98 97 96 95 94 93   8 7 6 5 4 3 2 1

Text design by Janis Owens
Engraving of Henry David Thoreau from a limited edition of *Walden*
(Boston: Bibliophile Society, 1909).

Library of Congress Cataloging-in-Publication Data

Thoreau, Henry David, 1817–1862.
    [Journal. Selections]
    Thoreau on birds : notes on New England birds from the Journals of
Henry David Thoreau / edited by Francis H. Allen ; introduction by
John Hay ; illustrations by Louis Agassiz Fuertes.
       p.   cm. — (The Concord library)
    Originally published: Thoreau's bird-lore. Boston : Houghton
Mifflin, 1910. With new introduction.
    Includes index.
    ISBN 0-8070-8520-0 (cloth)
    1. Birds—New England. 2. Birds—New England—Behavior.
I. Allen, Francis H. (Francis Henry), 1866–1947. II. Title.
III. Title: Thoreau's bird-lore. IV. Series.
QL683.N67T525   1993
598.2974—dc20   92-30469

Contents

CONTENTS

Illustrations

The illustrations by Louis Agassiz Fuertes (1874–1927) were furnished by the Department of Library Services, American Museum of Natural History.

{ x }

In his journal entry for 10 May 1854, Thoreau wrote: "In Boston yesterday an ornithologist said significantly, 'If you held the bird in your hand'—but I would rather hold it in my affections." Affections for Thoreau were not the lighthearted emotions a latter-day reader might suppose them to be. Thoreau was not so much concerned with scientific accuracy—with holding the bird in hand—as he was with experiencing a bird's reality.

Francis H. Allen, the editor of this anthology, claimed that Thoreau was more of a describer (by which he meant a descriptive *writer*) than an observer: "He never acquired much skill in the diagnosis of birds seen in the field." It is true that Thoreau was sometimes mistaken when it came to identifying birds and interpreting their habits. But it is too easy for us to criticize him a century of investigation later, after many thousands of bird watchers, students, and scientific teams have studied birds to the last detail, to the latest differentiation between species. In his entries on birds, Thoreau does not care to split the difference between "description" and "observation." He constantly makes measurements of wings, feet, legs, body, as well as of color. Equally characteristically, he simply watches as a hawk lands on the limb of a tree, then flies up again, legs dangling, toward that blue empyrean he was so fond of. Thoreau describes the actions, as he does the minute details of a bird's nest, with the same intense care.

A junco's nest close to the top of Mt. Monadnock "was sunk in the ground by the side of a tuft of grass, and was pretty deep, made of much fine grass and sedge and lined with a little of a delicate bluish hair-like fibre two or three inches long. The eggs were three, of a regular oval form, faint bluish-white, sprinkled with fine pale-brown dots, in two of the three condensed into a ring about the larger end. They had apparently just begun to develop. The nest and tuft were covered by a projecting rock." At that time, apparently, only one such nest had been reported to naturalists, which must have pleased Thoreau.

Thoreau employs physical characteristics in his notes and sketches because of where they lead him—the feather to the air, the seabird to its medium. "A gull of pure white—a wave of foam in the air. How simple and wave-like its outline; the outline of the wings presenting two curves, between which the tail is merely the point of junction,—all wing like a birch scale. . . ." And elsewhere: "The waves rise and dash, taking sides with all waterfowl."

Birds lead Thoreau toward the true nature of their world. Of the green heron, he writes: "It has looked out from its dull eye for so long, standing on one leg, on moon and stars sparkling through silence and dark, and now what a rich experience is its! What says it of stagnant pools, and reeds, and damp night fogs. It would be worth while to look in the eye which has been open and seeing at such hours and in such solitudes. When I behold that dull yellowish-green, I wonder if my own soul is not a bright, invisible green. I would fain lay my eye side by side and learn with it."

Say what you will about poetic fancy, Thoreau's purpose is profoundly realistic: to see in a bird the dimensions of its surroundings. We use the term "our feathered friends" to describe the birds that come to our feeders or perch in our yards, but it doesn't go far toward weaving them into our own lives and experience. Thoreau sees birds as part of a greater and yet nearly unseen neighborhood, as a link in the cosmic surroundings beyond the town limits. Most of his neighbors, however, seemed unaware of this realm. "As I was paddling back at 6 A.M., saw, nearly a half a mile off, a blue heron standing erect on the topmost twig of the great buttonwood on the street in front of Mr. Pritchard's house, while perhaps all within were abed and alseep. Little did they think of it, and how they were presided over."

Thoreau was up early in his self-appointed role of town recorder, or census taker, of all the life that was moving abroad, unnoticed and unattended. He would have the birds, as well as the foxes, snakes, frogs, and snapping turtles to which he was drawn be accepted in his own country. Of the dead body of a great blue heron, shot by a neighbor, he says: "I am glad to recognize him for a native of America,—why not an American citizen?" We are taught, as members of an advanced, technological society, that we have rights to the land superior to those of animals, its original inhabitants. Once again Thoreau's writings serve as bedrock for a very modern and increasingly crucial argument. Why not animals recognized as "citizens," why not rights for the birds?

Beyond the town are other communities and custodians of other dimensions, like the great horned owl: "This is my music each evening. I heard it last evening. It is a sound admirably suited to the swamp and to the twilight woods, suggesting a vast, undeveloped nature which men have not recognized or satisfied. I rejoice that there are owls. They represent the stark, twilight, unsatisfied thoughts I have. Let owls do the idiotic and maniacal hooting for men. This sound faintly suggests the infinite roominess of nature, that there is a world in which owls live. Yet how few are seen, even by the hunters!"

The suggestion of a vaster, unfinished space in the call of an owl carries through all Thoreau's observations. No bird, no life in nature can be separated from its rich world of sense and change. The experience of listening to bird song, or of watching their flight, suggests the "infinite roominess" of natural experience on this planet.

Thoreau was also fascinated by resonance, the sound of wing or song as it was reflected from the walls and surfaces of our earth home. Describing the flight of a nighthawk, he writes: "The nighthawk's ripping sound, heard overhead these days, reminds us that the sky is, as it were, a roof, and that our world is limited on that side, it being reflected as from a roof back to earth. It does not suggest an infinite depth in the sky, but a nearness to the earth, as of a low roof echoing back its sounds."

Thoreau was born in 1817 and died in 1862. The 1850s, the decade in which most of the selections in this anthology were written, also saw the publication of *Walden,* in 1854. This was a period in Thoreau's life when his senses must have been exceptionally keen and alert. As he wrote in *Walden:* "We must learn to reawaken and keep ourselves awake, not by mechanical means, but by an infinite expectation of the dawn, which does not forsake us in our soundest sleep." And being awake he was extraordinarily open to the qualities of what he saw, felt, and listened to, as in this jewel of an entry about the blue jay: "You hear the lisping tinkle of chickadees from time to time, and the unrelenting steel-cold scream of a jay, unmelted, that never flows into a song, a sort of wintry trumpet, screaming cold; hard, tense, frozen music, like the winter sky itself; in the blue livery of winter's hand. It is like a flourish of trumpets in the winter sky. There is no hint of incubation in the jay's scream. Like the creak of a cartwheel."

How could we endure a winter without a blue jay, or, for that matter, the chickadees?

15 December 1885: "This morning it has begun to snow, apparently in earnest. The air is quite thick and the view confined. It is quite still, yet some flakes come down from one side and some from another, crossing each other like warp and woof apparently,

as they are falling in different eddies and currents of air. In the midst of it, I hear and see a few chickadees prying about the twigs of the locusts in the graveyard. They have come into town with the snow. They now and then break into a short, sweet, strain, and then seem suddenly to check themselves, as if they had done it before they thought."

There was nothing so evocative and spontaneous for Thoreau as the song of a bird, and he listened to it, as he watched the bird's passage through the air, as if it were meant to catch his mind: "These sparrows too, are thoughts I have. They come and go; they flit by quickly on their migrations, uttering only a faint *chip*, I know not whither, or why exactly. One will not rest upon its twig for me to scrutinize it. The whole copse will be alive with my rambling thoughts, bewildering me by their very multitude, but they will be all gone directly without leaving me a feather."

The song of the wood thrush touched a depth in Thoreau that no other bird could, and he wrote about it with inspired lyricism. The song was for him original wildness, "a nature which I cannot put my foot through, woods where the wood thrush forever sings, where the hours are early morning ones, and there is dew on the grass and the day is forever improved, where I might have a fertile unknown for a soil about me. I would go after the cows, I would watch the flocks of Admetus there forever, only for my board and clothes. A New Hampshire everlasting and unfallen."

"I doubt," he also wrote, "if they have anything so richly

wild in Europe. So long a civilization must have banished it. It will only be heard in America, perchance, while our star is in the ascendant." When the wood thrush sang, he rejoiced, as did Walt Whitman, in morning in America. He was a man of his age. Follow the birds with Thoreau and you follow a new world.

"I must not lose any of my freedom being a farmer and a landholder. Most who enter on any profession are doomed men. The world might as well sing a dirge over them forthwith."

He would not have his wings clipped by what the world calls business. At the same time, as an independent-minded Yankee, he attended to his business in nature with a practical eye for detail and a total commitment. He was not a hermit, isolated from his neighbors. He had plenty of them, as anyone can guess from reading these pages, where he is often found consulting farmers and other residents about what they have shot, or he has seen. But he was determined to explore a wilderness on home ground which they did not have the time for, where eternal business went on as usual.

John Hay
July 1993

One

DIVING BIRDS

HORNED GREBE

December 26, 1853 Walden still open. Saw in it a small diver, probably a grebe or dobchick, dipper, or what-not, with the markings, as far as I saw, of the crested grebe, but smaller. It had a black head, a white ring about its neck, a white breast, black back, and apparently no tail.[1] It dove and swam a few rods under water, and, when on the surface, kept turning round and round warily and nodding its head the while. This being the only pond hereabouts that is open.

September 27, 1860 Monroe's tame ducks sail along and feed close to me as I am working there. Looking up, I see a little dipper, about one half their size, in the middle of the river, evidently attracted by these tame ducks, as to a place of security. I sit down and watch it. The tame ducks have paddled four or five rods downstream along the shore. They soon detect the dipper three or four

---

[1][From the description it would appear to have been a horned grebe, though the white on the throat and neck of that bird does not form a complete ring. The bird of September, 1860, is more accurately described.]

rods off, and betray alarm by a tittering note, especially when it dives, as it does continually. At last, when it is two or three rods off and approaching them by diving, they all rush to the shore and come out on it in their fear, but the dipper shows itself close to the shore, and when they enter the water again joins them within two feet, still diving from time to time and threatening to come up in their midst. They return up-stream, more or less alarmed, and pursued in this wise by the dipper, who does not know what to make of their fears, and soon the dipper is thus tolled along to within twenty feet of where I sit, and I can watch it at my leisure. It has a dark bill and considerable white on the sides of the head or neck, with black between it, no tufts, and no observable white on back or tail. When at last disturbed by me, it suddenly sinks low (all its body) in the water without diving. Thus it can float at various heights. (So on the 30th I saw one suddenly dash along the surface from the meadow ten rods before me to the middle of the river, and then dive, and though I watched fifteen minutes and examined the tufts of grass, I could see no more of it.)

PIED–BILLED GREBE[1]

October 17, 1855 I saw behind (or rather *in front of*) me as I rowed home a little dipper appear in mid-river, as if I had

[1][Probably most of the "little dippers" which are referred to casually in Thoreau's Journal were of this species, though some were undoubtedly the (in fresh water) rarer horned grebe and others the bufflehead duck.]

passed right over him. It dived while I looked, and I could not see it come up anywhere.

September 9, 1858   Watched a little dipper[1] some ten rods off with my glass, but I could see no white on the breast. It was all black and brownish, and head not enlarged. Who knows how

[1][On the 30th of the same month Thoreau saw a "little dipper" which was "much smaller" than any others he had seen that season and concluded that he had not seen the real little dipper before. What he has to say of this bird of September 9th will apply very well to the pied-billed grebe, however, and the paragraph is placed here for want of a better place.]

many little dippers are sailing and sedulously diving now along the edge of the pickerel-weed and the button-bushes on our river, unsuspected by most? This hot September afternoon all may be quiet amid the weeds, but the dipper, and the bittern, and the yellow-legs, and the blue heron, and the rail are silently feeding there. At length the walker who sits meditating on a distant bank sees the little dipper sail out from amid the weeds and busily dive for its food along their edge. Yet ordinary eyes might range up and down the river all day and never detect its small black head above the water.

LOON

1845–47 (no exact date)   The loon comes in the fall to sail and bathe in the pond,[1] making the woods ring with its wild laughter in the early morning, at rumor of whose arrival all Concord sportsmen are on the alert, in gigs, on foot, two by two, three by three, with patent rifles, patches, conical balls, spy-glass or open hole over the barrel. They seem already to hear the loon laugh; come rustling through the woods like October leaves, these on this side, those on that, for the poor loon cannot be omnipresent; if he dive here, must come up somewhere. The October wind rises, rustling the leaves, ruffling the pond water, so that no loon can be seen rippling the surface. Our sportsmen scour, sweep the pond with spy-glass in vain, making the woods ring with rude [?] charges of

[1] [Walden Pond.]

powder, for the loon went off in that morning rain with one loud, long, hearty laugh, and our sportsmen must beat a retreat to town and stable and daily routine, shop work, unfinished jobs again.

Or in the gray dawn the sleeper hears the long ducking gun explode over toward Goose Pond, and, hastening to the door, sees the remnant of a flock, black duck or teal, go whistling by with outstretched neck, with broken ranks, but in ranger order. And the silent hunter emerges into the carriage road with ruffled feathers at his belt, from the dark pond-side where he has lain in his bower since the stars went out.

And for a week you hear the circling clamor, clangor, of some solitary goose through the fog, seeking its mate, peopling the woods with a larger life than they can hold.

For hours in fall days you shall watch the ducks cunningly tack and veer and hold the middle of the pond, far from the sportsmen on the shore,—tricks they have learned and practiced in far Canada lakes or in Louisiana bayous.

The waves rise and dash, taking sides with all waterfowl.

October 8, 1852 P.M.—Walden. As I was paddling along the north shore, after having looked in vain over the pond for a loon, suddenly a loon, sailing toward the middle, a few rods in front, set up his wild laugh and betrayed himself. I pursued with a paddle and he dived, but when he came up I was nearer than before. He dived again, but I miscalculated the direction he would take, and we were fifty rods apart when he came up, and again he laughed long and loud. He managed very cunningly, and I could not get within half a dozen rods of him. Sometimes he would come up unexpectedly on the opposite side of me, as if he had passed directly under the boat. So long-winded was he, so unweariable, that he would immediately plunge again, and then no wit could divine where in the deep pond, beneath the smooth surface, he might be speeding his way like a fish, perchance passing under the boat. He had time and ability to visit the bottom of the pond in its deepest part. A newspaper authority says a fisherman—giving his name—has caught loon in Seneca Lake, N.Y., eighty feet beneath the surface, with hooks set for trout. Miss Cooper[1] has said the same. Yet he appeared to know his course as surely under water as on the surface, and swam much faster there than he sailed on the surface. It was surprising how serenely he sailed off with unruffled bosom when he came to the surface. It was as well for me to rest on my oars and await his reappearing as to endeavor to calculate where he would come up. When I was straining my eyes over the surface, I would suddenly be startled by his unearthly laugh behind me. But why, after displaying so much cunning, did he betray himself the moment he came to the surface with that loud laugh? His white breast enough betrayed him. He was indeed a silly loon, I thought. Though he took all this pains to avoid me, he never failed to give

[1][Susan Fenimore Cooper, *Rural Hours*, p. 10.]

notice of his whereabouts the moment he came to the surface. After an hour he seemed as fresh as ever, dived as willingly, and swam yet farther than at first. Once or twice I saw a ripple where he approached the surface, just put his head out to reconnoitre, and instantly dived again. I could commonly hear the plash of the water when he came up, and so also detected him. It was commonly a demoniac laughter, yet somewhat like a water-bird, but occasionally, when he had balked me most successfully and come up a long way off, he uttered a long-drawn unearthly howl, probably more like a wolf than any other bird. This was his looning. As when a beast puts his muzzle to the ground and deliberately howls; perhaps the wildest sound I ever heard, making the woods ring; and I concluded that he laughed in derision of my efforts, confident of his own resources. Though the sky was overcast, the pond was so smooth that I could see where he broke the surface if I did not hear him. His white breast, the stillness of the air, the smoothness of the water, were all against him. At length, having come up fifty rods off, he uttered one of those prolonged unearthly howls, as if calling on the god of loons to aid him, and immediately there came a wind from the east and rippled the surface, and filled the whole air with misty rain. I was impressed as if it were the prayer of the loon and his god was angry with me. How surprised must be the fishes to see this ungainly visitant from another sphere speeding his way amid their schools!

I have never seen more than one at a time in our pond, and I believe that that is always a male.[1]

RED-THROATED LOON

November 11, 1858 Goodwin[2] brings me this forenoon a this year's loon, which he just killed on the river,—great northern diver, but a smaller specimen than Wilson describes and somewhat differently marked. It is twenty-seven inches long to end of feet by forty-four and bill three and three quarters to angle of mouth; above blackish-gray with small white spots (two at end of each feather).[3] Beneath, pure white, throat and all, except a dusky bar across the vent. Bill chiefly pale-bluish and dusky. You are struck by its broad, flat, sharp-edged legs, made to cut through the water rather than to walk with, set far back and naturally stretched out backward, its long and powerful bill, conspicuous white throat and breast. Dislodged by winter in the north, it is slowly travelling toward a warmer clime, diving in the cool river this morning, which is now full of light, the trees and bushes on the brink having long since lost their leaves, and the neighboring fields are white with frost. Yet this hardy bird is comfortable and contented there if the sportsman would let it alone.

[1][The sexes are indistinguishable.]
[2][John Goodwin, a Concord gunner and fisherman.]
[3][The size and markings indicate this species in spite of its rarity in fresh water in Massachusetts.]

DOVEKIE
(LITTLE AUK)

July 25, 1860 P.M.—To Mr. Bradshaw's, Wayland, with Ed. Hoar.

I was surprised to see among the birds which Bradshaw has obtained the little auk of Nuttall (*Mergulus alle*,[1] or common sea-dove), which he says that he shot in the fall on the pond of the Assabet at Knight's factory. There were two, and the other was killed with a paddle.

November 19, 1860 Mr. Bradshaw says that he got a little auk in Wayland last week, and heard of two more, one in Weston and the other in Natick. Thinks they came with the storm of the 10th and 11th.

[1][Now called *Alle alle* by the ornithologists.]

GULLS

TERNS

PETRELS

HERRING GULL[1]

April 4, 1852   There are three great gulls sailing in the middle [of Fair Haven]. Now my shouting (perchance) raises one, and, flying low and heavily over the water, with heavy shoulders and sharp beak, it utters its loud mewing or squeaking notes,—some of them like a squeaking pump-handle,—which sound very strange to our woods. It gives a different character to the pond.

April 15, 1852   Thinking of the value of the gull to the scenery of our river in the spring, when for a few weeks they are seen circling about so deliberately and heavily yet gracefully, without

---

[1][Most, if not all, of the large gulls seen by Thoreau at Concord were doubtless of this species.]

{ 10 }

apparent object, beating like a vessel in the air, Gilpin[1] says something to the purpose,—that water-fowl "discover in their flight some determined aim. They eagerly coast the river, or return to the sea; bent on some purpose, of which they never lose sight. But the evolutions of the gull appear capricious, and undirected, both when she flies alone, and, as she often does, in large companies.— The more however her character suffers as a loiterer, the more it is raised in picturesque value, by her continuing longer before the eye; and displaying, in her elegant sweeps along the air, her sharp-pointed wings, and her bright silvery hue.—She is beautiful also, not only on the wing, but when she floats, in numerous assemblies on the water; or when she rests on the shore, dotting either one or the other with white spots; which, minute as they are, are very picturesque: . . . giving life and spirit to a view."

He seems to be describing our very bird. I do not *remember* to have seen them over or in our river meadows when there was not ice there. They come annually a–fishing here like royal hunters, to remind us of the sea and that our town, after all, lies but further up a creek of the universal sea, above the head of the tide. So ready is a deluge to overwhelm our lands, as the gulls to circle hither in the spring freshets. To see a gull beating high over our meadowy flood in chill and windy March is akin to seeing a mackerel schooner on the coast. It is the nearest approach to sailing vessels in our scenery.

[1][William Gilpin, *Remarks on Forest Scenery*, London, 1794.]

I never saw one at Walden. Oh, how it salts our fresh, our sweet-watered Fair Haven[1] all at once to see this sharp-beaked, greedy sea-bird beating over it! For a while the water is brackish to my eyes. It is merely some herring pond, and if I climb the eastern bank I expect to see the Atlantic there covered with countless sails. We are so far maritime, do not dwell beyond the range of the sea-going gull, the littoral birds. Does not the gull come up after those suckers which I see?[2] He is never to me perfectly in harmony with the scenery, but, like the high water, something unusual.

April 19, 1852   What comes flapping low with heavy wing over the middle of the flood? Is it an eagle or a fish hawk? Ah, now he is betrayed, I know not by what motion,—a great gull, right in the eye of the storm. He holds not a steady course, but suddenly he dashes upward even like the surf of the sea which he frequents, showing the under sides of his long, pointed wings, on which do I not see two white spots? He suddenly beats upward thus as if to surmount the airy billows by a slanting course, as the teamster surmounts a slope. The swallow, too, plays thus fantastically and luxuriously and leisurely, doubling some unseen corners in the sky. Here is a gull, then, long after ice in the river. It is a fine sight to see this noble bird leisurely advancing right in the face of the storm.

[1][Fairhaven Pond, or Bay, in the Sudbury River.]
[2][Dead suckers, which he goes on to philosophize about.]

April 7, 1853   A great gull, though it is so fair and the wind northwest, fishing over the flooded meadow. He slowly circles round and hovers with flapping wings in the air over particular spots, repeatedly returning there and sailing quite low over the water, with long, narrow, pointed wings, trembling throughout their length.

March 29, 1854   A gull of pure white,—a wave of foam in the air. How simple and wave-like its outline, the outline of the wings presenting two curves, between which the tail is merely the point of junction,—all wing like a birch scale; tail remarkably absorbed.

March 18, 1855   I see with my glass as I go over the railroad bridge, sweeping the river, a great gull standing far away on the top of a muskrat-cabin which rises just above the water opposite the Hubbard Bath. When I get round within sixty rods of him, ten minutes later, he still stands on the same spot, constantly turning his head to every side, looking out for foes. Like a wooden image of a bird he stands there, heavy to look at; head, breast, beneath, and rump pure white; slate-colored wings tipped with black and extending beyond the tail,—the herring gull. I can see clear down to its webbed feet. But now I advance, and he rises easily, goes off northeastward over the river with a leisurely flight. At Clamshell Hill I sweep the river again, and see, standing midleg deep on the meadow where the water is very shallow with deeper around, another of these wooden images, which is harder to scare. I do not fairly distinguish black tips to its wings. It is ten or fifteen minutes before I get him to rise, and then he goes off in the same leisurely manner, stroking the air with his wings, and now making a great circle back on its course, so you cannot tell which way it is bound. By standing so long motionless in these places they may perchance accomplish two objects, *i.e.*, catch passing fish (suckers?) like a heron and escape the attention of man. Its utmost motion was to plume itself once and turn its head about. If it did not move its head, it would look like a decoy. Our river is quite low for the season, and yet it is here without freshet or easterly storm. It *seems* to take this course on its migrations without regard to the state of the waters.

April 15, 1855 Before we rounded Ball's Hill,—the water now beautifully smooth,—at 2.30 P.M., we saw three gulls sailing on the glassy meadow at least half a mile off, by the oak peninsula,—the plainer because they were against the reflection of the hills. They looked larger than afterward close at hand, as if their whiteness was reflected and doubled. As we advanced into the Great Meadows, making the only ripples in their broad expanse, there being still not a ray of sunshine, only a subdued light through the thinner crescent in the north, the reflections of the maples, of Ponkawtasset and the poplar hill, and the whole township in the southwest, were as perfect as I ever saw. A wall which ran down to the water on the hillside, without any remarkable curve in it, was exaggerated by the reflection into the half of an ellipse. The meadow was expanded to a large lake, the shore-line being referred to the sides of the hills reflected in it. It was a scene worth many such voyages to see. It was remarkable how much light those white gulls, and also a bleached post on a distant shore, absorbed and reflected through that sombre atmosphere,—conspicuous almost as candles in the night. When we got near to the gulls, they rose heavily and flapped away, answering a more distant one, with a remarkable, deliberate, melancholy, squeaking scream, mewing, or piping, almost a squeal. It was a *little* like the loon. Is this sound the origin of the name sea-mew? Notwithstanding the smoothness of the water, we could not easily see black ducks against the reflection of the woods, but heard them rise at a distance before we saw them.

April 22, 1857 A dozen gulls are circling over Fair Haven Pond, some very white beneath, with very long, narrow-pointed, black-tipped wings, almost regular semicircles like the new moon. As they circle beneath a white scud in this bright air, they are almost invisible against it, they are so nearly the same color. What glorious fliers! But few birds are seen; only a crow or two teetering along the water's edge looking for its food, with its large, clumsy head, and on unusually long legs, as if stretched, or its pants pulled up to keep it from the wet, and now flapping off with some large morsel in its bill; or robins in the same place; or perhaps the sweet song of the tree sparrows from the alders by the shore, or of a song sparrow or blackbird. The phœbe is scarcely heard. Not a duck do we see!

March 22, 1858   There is a strong and cool northwest wind. Leaving our boat just below N. Barrett's, we walk down the shore. We see many gulls on the very opposite side of the meadow, near the woods. They look bright-white, like snow on the dark-blue water. It is surprising how far they can be seen, how much light they reflect, and how conspicuous they are. Being strung along one every rod, they made me think of a fleet in line of battle. We go along to the pitch pine hill off Abner Buttrick's, and, finding a sheltered and sunny place, we watch the ducks from it with our glass. There are not only gulls, but about forty black ducks and as many sheldrakes, and, I think, two wood ducks. The gulls appear considerably the largest and make the most show, they are so uniformly light-colored. At a distance, as I have said, they look like snowy masses, and even nearer they have a lumpish look, like a mass of cotton, the head being light as well as the breast. They are seen sailing about in the shallow water, or standing motionless on a clod that just rises above the surface, in which position they have a particularly clumsy look; or one or two may be seen slowly wheeling about above the rest. From time to time the whole flock of gulls suddenly rises and begins circling about, and at last they settle down in some new place and order. With these were at first associated about forty black ducks, pretty close together, sometimes apparently in close single lines, some looking lumpish like decoys of wood, others standing on the bottom and reminding me of penguins. They were constantly diving with great energy, making the water fly apparently two feet upward in a thick shower. Then away they all go, circling about for ten minutes at least before they can decide where to alight.

The black heads and white breasts, which may be goldeneyes, for they are evidently paired, male and female, for the most part,[1]—and yet I thought that I saw the red bill of the sheldrake,—these are most incessantly and skillfully plunging and from time to time apparently pursuing each other. They are much more active, whether diving or swimming about, than you expect ducks to be. Now, perchance, they are seen changing their ground, swimming off, perhaps, two by two, in pairs, very steadily and swiftly, without diving. I see two of these very far off on a bright-blue bay where the waves are running high. They are two intensely white specks, which yet you might mistake for the foaming crest of waves. Now one disappears, but soon is seen again, and then its companion is lost in like manner, having dived.

March 16, 1859 We meet one great gull beating up the course of the river against the wind, at Flint's Bridge. (One says they were seen about a week ago, but there was very little water then.) Its is a very leisurely sort of limping flight, tacking its way along like a

[1]They are sheldrakes [*i.e.*, American mergansers].

sailing vessel, yet the slow security with which it advances suggests a leisurely contemplativeness in the bird, as if it were working out some problem quite at its leisure. As often as its very narrow, long, and curved wings are lifted up against the light, I see a very narrow distinct light edging to the wing where it is thin. Its black-tipped wings. Afterwards, from Ball's Hill, looking north, I see two more circling about looking for food over the ice and water.

March 18, 1859 Rice[1] thinks that he has seen two gulls on the Sudbury meadows,—the white and the gray gulls. He has often seen a man shoot the large gull from Cambridge bridge by heading him off, for the gull flies slowly. He would first run this way, and when the gull turned aside, run that, till the gull passed right over his head, when he shot him. Rice saw Fair Haven Pond still covered with ice, though open along the shore, yesterday. I frequently see the gulls flying up the course of the stream, or of the river valley at least.

March 23, 1859 Then I see come slowly flying from the southwest a great gull, of voracious form, which at length by a sudden and steep descent alights in Fair Haven Pond, scaring up a crow which was seeking its food on the edge of the ice. This shows that the crows get along the meadow's edge also what has washed up.

March 16, 1860 I also see two gulls nearly a mile off. One stands still and erect for three quarters of an hour, or till disturbed,

[1][Israel Rice, a Sudbury farmer living near the river.]

on a little bit of floated meadowcrust which rises above the water,—just room for it to stand on,—with its great white breast toward the wind. Then another comes flying past it, and alights on a similar perch, but which does not rise quite to the surface, so that it stands in the water. Thus they will stand for an hour, at least. They are not of handsome form, but look like great wooden images of birds, bluish-slate and white. But when they fly they are quite another creature.

COMMON TERN
(MACKEREL GULL)

June 21, 1857   At East Harbor River, as I sat on the Truro end of the bridge, I saw a great flock of mackerel gulls, one hundred at least, on a sandy point, whitening the shore there like so many white stones on the shore and in the water, uttering all together their vibrating shrill note. They had black heads, light bluish-slate wings, and light rump and tail and beneath. From time to time all or most would rise and circle about with a clamor, then settle again on the same spot close together.

WILSON'S PETREL
(MOTHER-CAREY'S-CHICKEN)

June 18, 1857   I had shortly before picked up a Mother-Carey's-chicken, which was just washed up dead on the beach.[1] This I carried tied to the tip of my umbrella, dangling out-side. When the inhabitants saw me come up from the beach this stormy day, with this emblem dangling from my umbrella, and saw me set it up in a corner carefully to be out of the way of cats, they may have taken me for a crazy man. . . .

The Mother-Carey's-chicken was apparently about thirteen inches in alar extent, black-brown, with seven primaries, the sec-ond a little longer than the third; rump and vent white, making a sort of ring of white, breast ashy-brown, legs black with yellowish webs, bill black with a protuberance above.

June 22, 1857 It was a thick fog with some rain, and we saw no land nor a single sail, till near Minot's Ledge.[2] The boat stopped and whistled once or twice. The monotony was only relieved by the numerous petrels,[3] those black sea-swallows, incessantly skim-ming over the undulating [surface], a few inches above and parallel with it, and occasionally picking some food from it. Now they dashed past our stern and now across our bows, as if we were sta-tionary, though going at the rate of a dozen knots an hour.

[1][On Cape Cod.]
[2][On the steamer from Provincetown to Boston.]
[3][The season would indicate that these were probably Wilson's petrels, rather than Leach's, which in the latter part of June would be on their breeding-grounds.]

Three

DUCKS

GEESE

AMERICAN MERGANSER
(SHELDRAKE)
(GOOSANDER)

March 29, 1853 Four ducks, two by two, are sailing conspicuously on the river. There appear to be two pairs. In each case one two-thirds white and another grayish-brown and, I think, smaller. They are very shy and fly at fifty rods' distance. Are they whistlers?[1] . . . Would it not be well to carry a spy-glass in order to watch these shy birds such as ducks and hawks? In some respects, methinks, it would be better than a gun. The latter brings them nearer dead, but the former alive. You can identify the species better

[1]These were either mergansers or the golden-eye; I think the former, *i.e. Mergus serrator*, or red-breasted merganser (?), or sheldrake. [Thoreau's "sheldrakes" were doubtless with few exceptions American mergansers (*Mergus americanus*), which species is much commoner in fresh water than the red-breasted. His descriptions indicate this species.]

by killing the bird, because it was a dead specimen that was so minutely described, but you can study the habits and appearance best in the living specimen. These ducks first flew north, or somewhat against the wind (was it to get under weigh?), then wheeled, flew nearer me, and went south up-stream, where I saw them afterward.

April 23, 1854 I had first seen two white ducks far off just above the outlet of the pond, mistaking them for the foaming crest of a wave. These flew soon, perhaps scared by the eagle. I think they were a male and female red-breasted merganser (though I did [not] see the red of the breast), for I saw his *red bill*, and his head was not large with a crest like the golden-eye; very white on breast and sides, the female browner.[1] As ducks often do, they first flew directly and unhesitatingly up the stream, low over the water, for half a mile, then turned and came down, flying thirty or forty feet above the water, the male leading till they were out of sight. This is the way with them, I notice; they first fly in one direction and then go off to alight in another. When they came down the river, the male leading, they were a very good example of the peculiar flight of ducks. They appeared perfectly in a line one behind the other. When they are not they preserve perfect parallelism. This is because of their long necks and feet,—the wings appearing to be attached midway,—and moreover, in this case, of their perfectly level flight, as if learned from skimming over the water.

[1][Certainly mergansers, probably sheldrakes.]

April 6, 1855   You can hear all day, from time to time, in any part of the village, the sound of a gun fired at ducks. Yesterday I was wishing that I could find a dead duck floating on the water, as I had found muskrats and a hare, and now I see something bright and reflecting the light from the edge of the alders five or six rods off. Can it be a duck? I can hardly believe my eyes. I am near enough to see its green head and neck. I am delighted to find a perfect specimen of the *Mergus merganser*,[1] or goosander, undoubtedly shot yesterday by the Fast-Day sportsmen, and I take a small flattened shot from its wing,—flattened against the wing-bone, apparently. The wing is broken, and it is shot through the head.[2] It is a perfectly fresh and very beautiful bird, and as I raise it, I get sight of its long, slender vermilion bill (color of red sealing-wax) and its clean, bright-orange legs and feet, and then of its perfectly smooth and spotlessly pure white breast and belly, tinged with a faint salmon (or tinged with a delicate buff inclining to salmon). . . . My bird is 25⅞ inches long and 35 in alar extent; from point of wing to end of primaries, 11 inches.

It is a great diver and does not mind the cold. It appears admirably fitted for diving and swimming. Its body is flat, and its tail short, flat, compact, and wedge-shaped; its eyes peer out a slight

[1][The American species, of course, now known as *Mergus americanus*.]
[2]The chief wound was in a wing, which was broken. I afterward took three small shot from it, which were flattened against the bill's base and perhaps (?) the quills' shafts.

slit or semi-circle in the skin of the head; and its legs are flat and thin in one direction, and the toes shut up compactly so as to create the least friction when drawing them forward, but their broad webs spread them three and a half inches when they take a stroke. The web is extended three eighths of an inch beyond the inner toe of each foot. There are very conspicuous black teeth-like serrations along the edges of its bill, and this also is roughened so that it may hold its prey securely.

The breast *appeared* quite dry when I raised it from the water.

The head and neck are, as Wilson says, black, glossed with green, but the lower part of the neck pure white, and these colors bound on each other so abruptly that one appears to be sewed on to the other.

It is a perfect wedge from the middle of its body to the end of its tail, and it is only three and a quarter inches deep from back to breast at the thickest part, while the greatest breadth horizontally (at the root of the legs) is five and a half inches. In these respects it reminds me of an otter, which, however, I have never seen.

I suspect that I have seen near a hundred of these birds this spring, but I never got so near one before.

April 7, 1855 In my walk in the afternoon of to-day, I saw from Conantum,[1] say fifty rods distant, two sheldrakes, male and

---

[1][A tract of land on the Sudbury River, so called by Thoreau from the Conant family, who formerly lived there.]

probably female, sailing on A. Wheeler's cranberry meadow. I saw only the white of the male at first, but my glass revealed the female. The male is easily seen a great distance on the water, being a large white mark. But they will let you come only within some sixty rods ordinarily. I observed that they were uneasy at sight of me and began to sail away in different directions. I could plainly see the vermilion bill of the male and his orange legs when he flew (but he *appeared* all white above), and the reddish brown or sorrel of the neck of the female, and, when she lifted herself in the water, as it were preparatory to flight, her white breast and belly. She had a grayish look on the sides. Soon they approached each other again and seemed to be conferring, and then they rose and went off, at first low, down-stream, soon up-stream a hundred feet over the pond, the female leading, the male following close behind, the black at the end of his curved wings very conspicuous. I suspect that about all the conspicuous white ducks I see are goosanders.

I skinned my duck yesterday and stuffed it to-day. It is wonderful that a man, having undertaken such an enterprise, ever persevered in it to the end, and equally wonderful that he succeeded. To skin a bird, drawing backward, wrong side out, over the legs and wings down to the base of the mandibles! Who would expect to see a smooth feather again? This skin was very tender on the breast. I should have done better had I stuffed it at once or turned it back before the skin became stiff. Look out not to cut the ear and eyelid.

But what a pot-bellied thing is a stuffed bird compared even with the fresh dead one I found! It looks no longer like an otter, like a swift diver, but a mere waddling duck. How perfectly the vent of a bird is covered! There is no mark externally.

April 10, 1855   I see afar, more than one hundred rods distant, sailing on Hubbard's meadow, on the smooth water in the morning sun, conspicuous, two male sheldrakes and apparently one female. They glide along, a rod or two apart in shallow water, alternately passing one another and from time to time plunging their heads in the water, but the female (whom only the glass reveals) almost alone diving. I think I saw one male drive the other back. One male with the female kept nearly together, a rod or two ahead of the other.

April 16, 1855   At Flint's,[1] sitting on the rock, we see a great many ducks, mostly sheldrakes, on the pond, which will hardly abide us within half a mile. With the glass I see by their reddish heads that all of one party—the main body—are females. You see little more than their heads at a distance and not much white but on their throats, perchance. When they fly, they look black and white, but not so large nor with that brilliant contrast of black and white which the male exhibits. In another direction is a male by himself, conspicuous, perhaps several. Anon alights near us a flock of golden-eyes—*surely*, with their great black (looking) heads and a

---

[1] [Flint's, or Sandy, Pond, in Lincoln, Mass.]

white patch on the side; short stumpy bills (after looking at the mergansers); much clear black, contrasting with much clear white. Their heads and bills look ludicrously short and parrot-like after the others. Our presence and a boat party on the pond at last drove nearly all the ducks into the deep easterly cove.

We stole down on them carefully through the woods, at last crawling on our bellies, with great patience, till at last we found ourselves within seven or eight rods—as I measured afterward—of the great body of them, and watched them for twenty or thirty minutes with the glass through a screen of cat-briar, alders, etc. There were twelve female sheldrakes close together, and, nearest us, within two rods of the shore, where it was very shallow, two or more constantly moving about within about the diameter of a rod and keeping watch while the rest were trying to sleep,—to catch a nap with their heads in their backs; but from time to time one would wake up enough to plume himself. It seemed as if they must have been broken of their sleep and were trying to make it up, having an arduous journey before them, for we had seen them all disturbed and on the wing within half an hour. They were headed various ways. Now and then they seemed to see or hear or smell us, and uttered a low note of alarm, something like the note of a tree-toad, but very faint, or perhaps a little more wiry and like that of pigeons, but the sleepers hardly lifted their heads for it. How fit that this note of alarm should be made to resemble the croaking of a frog and so not betray them to the gunners! They appeared to sink about midway in the water, and their heads were all a rich reddish brown, their throats white. Now and then one of the watchmen would lift his head and turn his bill directly upward, showing his white throat.

There were some black or dusky ducks in company with them at first, apparently about as large as they, but more alarmed. Their throats looked straw-colored, somewhat like a bittern's, and I saw their shovel bills. These soon sailed further off.

At last we arose and rushed to the shore within three rods of them, and they rose up with a din,—twenty-six mergansers (I think all females), ten black ducks,—and five golden-eyes from a little further off, also another still more distant flock of one of these kinds. The black ducks alone uttered a sound, their usual hoarse *quack*. They all flew in loose array, but the three kinds in separate flocks. We were surprised to find ourselves looking on a company of birds devoted to slumber after the alarm and activity we had just witnessed.

March 1, 1856   It is remarkable that though I have not been able to find any open place in the river almost all winter, except under the further stone bridge and at Loring's Brook,—this winter so remarkable for ice and snow,—Coombs[1] should (as he says) have killed two sheldrakes at the falls by the factory,[2] a place which I had

[1][A Concord man, one of the pigeon-catchers.]
[2][On the Assabet River.]

forgotten, some four or six weeks ago. Singular that this hardy bird should have found this small opening, which I had forgotten, while the ice everywhere else was from one to two feet thick, and the snow sixteen inches on a level. If there is a crack amid the rocks of some waterfall, this bright diver is sure to know it. Ask the sheldrake whether the rivers are completely sealed up.

April 5, 1856 Saw half a dozen white sheldrakes in the meadow, where Nut Meadow Brook was covered with the flood. There were two or three females with them. These ducks would all swim together first a little way to the right, then suddenly turn together and swim to the left, from time to time making the water fly in a white spray, apparently with a wing. Nearly half a mile off I could see their green crests in the sun. They were partly concealed by some floating pieces of ice and snow, which they resembled.

April 24, 1856 A Garfield (I judge from his face) confirmed the story of sheldrakes killed in an open place in the river between the factory and Harrington's, just after the first great snow-storm (which must have been early in January) when the river was all frozen elsewhere. There were three, and they persisted in staying and fishing there. He killed one.

March 27, 1858 P.M.—Sail to Bittern Cliff.

Scare up a flock of sheldrakes just off Fair Haven Hill, the conspicuous white ducks, sailing straight hither and thither. At first they fly low up the stream, but, having risen, come back halfway to us, then wheel and go up-stream. Soon after we scare up a flock of black ducks. We land and steal over the hill through the woods, expecting to find them under Lee's Cliff, as indeed we do, having crawled over the hill through the woods on our stomachs; and there we watched various water-fowl for an hour. There are a dozen sheldrakes (or goosanders) and among them four or five females. They are now pairing. I should say one or two pairs are made. At first we see only a male and female quite on the alert, some way out on the pond, tacking back and forth and looking every way. They keep close together, headed one way, and when one turns the other also turns quickly. The male appears to take the lead. Soon the rest appear, sailing out from the shore into sight. We hear a squeaking note, as if made by a pump, and presently see four or five great herring gulls wheeling about. Sometimes they make a sound like the scream of a hen-hawk. They are shaped somewhat like a very thick white rolling-pin, sharpened at both ends. At length they alight near the ducks.

The sheldrakes at length acquire confidence, come close inshore and go to preening themselves, or it may be they are troubled with lice. They are all busy about it at once, continually thrusting their bills into their backs, still sailing slowly along back and forth offshore. Sometimes they are in two or three straight lines. Now they will all seem to be crossing the pond, but presently you see that they have tacked and are all heading this way again. Among them, or near by, I at length detect three or four whistlers, by their wanting the red bill, being considerably smaller and less white, having a white spot on the head, a black back, and altogether less white, and also keeping more or less apart and not diving when the rest do. Now one half the sheldrakes sail off southward and suddenly go to diving as with one consent. Seven or eight or the whole of the party will be under water and lost at once. In the meanwhile, coming up, they chase one another, scooting over the surface and making the water fly, sometimes three or four making a rush toward one.

*   *   *

The sheldrake has a peculiar long clipper look, often moving rapidly straight forward over the water. It sinks to very various depths in the water sometimes, as when apparently alarmed, showing only its head and neck and the upper part of its back, and at others, when at ease, floating buoyantly on the surface, as if it had taken in more air, showing all its white breast and the white along its sides. Sometimes it lifts itself up on the surface and flaps its wings, revealing its whole rosaceous breast and its lower parts, and looking in form like a penguin. When I first saw them fly upstream I suspected that they had gone to Fair Haven Pond and would alight under the lee of the cliff. So, creeping slowly down through the woods four or five rods, I was enabled to get a fair sight of them, and finally we sat exposed on the rocks within twenty-five rods. They appear not to observe a person so high above them.

It was a pretty sight to see a pair of them tacking about, always within a foot or two of each other and heading the same way, now on this short tack, now on that, the male taking the lead, sinking deep and looking every way. When the whole twelve had come together they would soon break up again, and were continually changing their ground, though not diving, now sailing slowly this way a dozen rods, and now that, and now coming in near the shore. Then they would all go to preening themselves, thrusting their bills into their backs and keeping up such a brisk motion that you could not get a fair sight of one's head. From time to time you heard a slight titter, not of alarm, but perhaps a breeding-note, for they were evidently selecting their mates. I saw one scratch its ear or head with its foot. Then it was surprising to see how, briskly sailing off one side, they went to diving, as if they had suddenly come across a school of minnows. A whole company would disappear at once, never rising high as before. Now for nearly a minute there is not a feather to be seen, and the next minute you see a party of half a dozen there, chasing one another and making the water fly far and wide.

When returning, we saw, near the outlet of the pond, seven or eight sheldrakes standing still in a line on the edge of the ice, and others swimming close by. They evidently love to stand on the ice for a change.

March 30, 1858 Landing at Bittern Cliff, I went round through the woods to get sight of ducks on the pond. Creeping down through the woods, I reached the rocks, and saw fifteen or twenty sheldrakes scattered about. The full-plumaged males, conspicuously black and white and often swimming in pairs, appeared to be the most wary, keeping furthest out. Others, with much less white and duller black, were very busily fishing just north the inlet of the pond, where there is about three feet of water, and others still playing and preening themselves. These ducks, whose tame representatives are so sluggish and deliberate in their motions, were full of activity. A party of these ducks fishing and playing is a very lively scene. On one side, for instance, you will see a party of eight or ten busily diving and most of the time under water, not rising high when they come up, and soon plunging again. The whole surface will be in commotion there, though no ducks may be seen. I saw one come up with a large fish, whereupon all the rest, as they successively came to the surface, gave chase to it, while it held its prey over the water in its bill, and they pursued with a great rush and clatter a dozen or more rods over the surface, making a great furrow in the water, but, there being some trees in the way, I could not see the issue. I saw seven or eight all dive together as with one consent, remaining under half a minute or more. On another side you see a party which seem to be playing and pluming themselves. They will run and dive and come up and dive again every three or four feet, occasionally one pursuing another; will flutter in the water, making it fly, or erect themselves at full length on the surface like a penguin, and flap their wings. This party make an incessant noise. Again you will see some steadily tacking this way or that in the middle of the pond, and often they rest there asleep with their heads in their backs. They readily cross the pond, swimming from this side to that.

April 19, 1858 Rice tells me of winging a sheldrake once just below Fair Haven Pond, and pursuing it in a boat as it swam down the stream, till it went ashore at Hubbard's Wood and crawled into a woodchuck's hole about a rod from the water on a wooded bank. He could see its tail and pulled it out.

March 23, 1859 As we sit there, we see coming, swift and straight, northeast along the river valley, not seeing us and therefore not changing his course, a male goosander, so near that the green reflections of his head and neck are plainly visible. He looks like a paddle-wheel steamer, so oddly painted up, black and white and green, and moves along swift and straight like one. Ere long the same returns with his mate, the red-throated, the male taking the lead.

March 30, 1859 See on Walden two sheldrakes, male and female, as is common. So they have for some time paired. They are a hundred rods off. The male the larger, with his black head and white breast, the female with a red head. With my glass I see the long red bills of both. They swim at first one way near together, then tack and swim the other, looking around incessantly, never quite at their ease, wary and watchful for foes. A man cannot walk down to the shore or stand out on a hill overlooking the pond without disturbing them. They will have an eye upon him. The locomotive-whistle makes every wild duck start that is floating within the limits of the town. I see that these ducks are not here for protection alone, for at last they both dive, and remain beneath about forty pulse-beats,—and again, and again. I think they are looking for fishes. Perhaps, therefore, these divers are more likely to alight in Walden than the black ducks are.

April 2, 1859 From near this cliff, I watch a male sheldrake in the river with my glass. It is very busily pluming itself while it sails about, and from time to time it raises itself upright almost entirely out of water, showing its rosaceous breast. It is some sixty rods off, yet I can see the red bill distinctly when it is turned against its white body. Soon after I see two more, and one, which I think is not a female, is more gray and far less distinctly black and white than the other. I think it is a young male and that it might be called by some a gray duck. However, if you show yourself within sixty rods, they will fly or swim off, so shy are they. Yet in the fall I sometimes get close upon a young bird, which dashes swiftly across or along the river and dives.

April 12, 1859 Saw a duck, apparently a sheldrake, at the northeast end of Cyanean Meadow. It disappeared at last by diving, and I could not find it. But I saw what looked like a ripple made by the wind, which moved slowly down the river at least forty rods toward the shore and there disappeared. Though I saw no bird there, I suspect that the ripple was made by it. Two sheldrakes flew away from this one when first observed. Why did this remain? Was it wounded? Or can those which dart so swiftly across the river and dive be another species and not the young of the season or females of the common one? Is it not, after all, the red-breasted merganser, and did I not see them in Maine?[1]

I see half a dozen sheldrakes very busily fishing around the base of Lupine Hill or Promontory. There are two full-plumaged males and the rest females, or perhaps some of them young males. They are coasting along swiftly with their bodies sunk low and their heads half under, looking for their prey, one behind another, frequently turning and passing over the same ground again. Their crests are very conspicuous, thus:

When one sees a fish he at first swims rapidly after it, and then, if necessary, flies close over the water after it, and this excites all the rest to follow, swimming or flying, and if one seizes the fish, which I suspect is commonly a pickerel, they all pursue the lucky fisher, and he makes the water fly far in his efforts to get away and gulp down his fish. I can see the fish in his bill all the while, and he must swallow it very skillfully and quickly, if at all. I was first attracted

[1][If the males as well as the females had the crests mentioned later the birds were, of course, red-breasted mergansers.]

to them by seeing these great birds rushing, shooting, thus swiftly through the air and water and throwing the water high about them. Sometimes they dive and swim quietly beneath, looking for their game. At length they spy me or my boat, and I hear a faint quack indicative of alarm, and suddenly all arise and go off. In the meanwhile I see two black ducks sailing with them along the shore. These look considerably smaller, and of course carry their heads more erect. They have a raw, gosling look beside the others, and I see their light bills against their dusky necks and heads. At length, when I get near them, I hear their peculiar quack also, and off they go. The sheldrakes appear to be a much more lively bird than the black duck. How different from the waddling domestic duck! The former are all alive, eagerly fishing, quick as thought, as they need to be to catch a pickerel.

February 27, 1860 I had noticed for some time, far in the middle of the Great Meadows, something dazzlingly white, which I took, of course, to be a small cake of ice on its end, but now that I have climbed the pitch pine hill and can overlook the whole meadow, I see it to be the white breast of a male sheldrake, accompanied perhaps by his mate (a darker one). They have settled warily in the very midst of the meadow, where the wind has blown a space of clear water for an acre or two. The aspect of the meadow is skyblue and dark-blue, the former a thin ice, the latter the spaces of open water which the wind has made, but it is chiefly ice still. Thus, as soon as the river breaks up or begins to break up fairly, and the strong wind widening the cracks makes at length open spaces in the ice of the meadow, this hardy bird appears, and is seen sailing in the first widened crack in the ice, where it can come at the water. Instead of a piece of ice I find it to be the breast of the sheldrake, which so reflects the light as to look larger than it is, steadily sailing this way and that with its companion, who is diving from time to time. They have chosen the opening farthest removed from all shores. As I look I see the ice drifting in upon them and contracting their water, till finally they have but a few square rods left, while there are forty or fifty acres near by. This is the first bird of the spring that I have seen or heard of.

March 16, 1860 Saw a flock of sheldrakes a hundred rods off, on the Great Meadows, mostly males with a few females, all intent on fishing. They were coasting along a spit of bare ground that showed itself in the middle of the meadow, sometimes the whole twelve apparently in a straight line at nearly equal distances apart, with each its head under water, rapidly coasting along back and forth, and ever and anon one, having caught something, would be pursued by the others. It is remarkable that they find their finny prey on the middle of the meadow now, and even on the very inmost side, as I afterward saw, though the water is quite low. Of course, as soon as they are seen on the meadows there are fishes there to be caught. I never see them fish thus in the channel. Perhaps the fishes lie up there for warmth already.

March 17, 1860   I see a large flock of sheldrakes, which have probably risen from the pond, go over my head in the woods. A dozen large and compact birds flying with great force and rapidity, spying out the land, eyeing every traveller, fast and far they "steam it" on clipping wings, over field and forest, meadow and flood; now here, and you hear the whistling of their wings, and in a moment they are lost in the horizon. Like swift propellers of the air. Whichever way they are headed, that way their wings propel them. What health and vigor they suggest! The life of man seems slow and puny in comparison,—reptilian.

BLACK DUCK
(DUSKY DUCK)

April 1, 1853   Saw ten black ducks at Clamshell. Had already started two, who probably occupied an outpost. They all went off with a loud and disagreeable quacking like ducks in a poultry-yard, their wings appearing lighter beneath.

March 21, 1854   At sunrise to Clamshell Hill.

River skimmed over at Willow Bay last night. Thought I should find ducks cornered up by the ice; they get behind this hill for shelter. Saw what looked like clods of plowed meadow rising above the ice. Looked with glass and found it to be more than thirty black ducks asleep with their heads in their backs, motionless, and thin ice formed about them. Soon one or two were moving about slowly. There was an open space, eight or ten rods by one or two. At first all within a space of apparently less than a rod in diameter. It was 6.30 A.M., and the sun shining on them, but bitter cold. How tough they are! I crawled far on my stomach and got a near view of them, thirty rods off. At length they detected me and quacked. Some got out upon the ice, and when I rose up all took to flight in a great straggling flock which at a distance looked like crows, in no order. Yet, when you see two or three, the parallelism produced by their necks and bodies steering the same way gives the idea of order.

April 21, 1855   Watched for some time a dozen black ducks on the meadow's edge in a retired place, some on land and some sailing. Fifty rods off and without the glass, they looked like crows feeding on the meadow's edge, with a scarcely perceptible tinge of brown.

February 29, 1856   He[1] loves to recall his hunting days and adventures, and I willingly listen to the stories he has told me half a dozen times already. One day he saw about twenty black ducks on Goose Pond, and stole down on them, thinking to get a shot, but it chanced that a stray dog scared them up before he was ready. He stood on the point of the neck of land between the ponds, and watched them as they flew high toward Flint's Pond. As he looked, he saw one separate from the flock when they had got half-way to

[1][George Minott.]

Flint's Pond, or half a mile, and return straight toward Goose Pond again. He thought he would await him, and give him a shot if he came near enough. As he flew pretty near and rather low, he fired, whereupon the duck rose right up high into the air, and he saw by his motions that he was wounded. Suddenly he dropped, by a slanting fall, into the point of a thick pine wood, and he heard him plainly strike the ground like a stone. He went there and searched for a long time, and was about giving it up, when at length he saw the duck standing, still alive and bleeding, by the side of a stump, and made out to kill him with a stick before he could reach the water.

April 9, 1856 Paddled quite to the head of Pinxter Swamp, where were two black ducks amid the maples, which went off with a hoarse quacking, leaving a feather on the smooth dark water amid the fallen tree-tops and over the bottom of red leaves.

April 14, 1856 There go a couple of ducks, which probably I have started, now scaling far away on motionless pinions, with a slight descent in their low flight, toward some new cove. Anon I scare up two black ducks which make one circle around me, reconnoitring and rising higher and higher, then go down the river. Is it they that so commonly practice this manœuvre?

June 23, 1857 Skinner, the harness-maker, tells me that he found a black duck's nest Sunday before the last, *i.e.* the 14th, with perhaps a dozen eggs in it, a mere hollow on the top of a tussock, four or five feet within a clump of bushes forming an islet (in the spring) in Hubbard's great meadow. He scared up the duck when within a few feet. . . . .

P.M.—Looked for the black duck's nest, but could find no trace of it. Probably the duck led her young to the river as soon as hatched. What with gunners, dogs, pickerel, bullfrogs, hawks, etc., it is a wonder if any of them escape.

June 24, 1857 Melvin[1] thinks there cannot be many black ducks' nests in the town, else his dog would find them, for he will follow their trail as well as another bird's, or a fox. The dog once caught five black ducks here but partly grown.

July 3, 1857 Minott says that old Joe Merriam used to tell of his shooting black ducks in the Dam meadows and what luck he had. One day he had shot a couple of ducks and was bringing them home by the legs, when he came to a ditch. As he had his gun in the other hand, and the ditch was wide, he thought he would toss the ducks over before he jumped, but they had no sooner struck the ground than they picked themselves up and flew away, which discouraged him with respect to duck-shooting.

October 14, 1857 Approaching White Pond by the path, I see on its perfectly smooth surface what I at first mistake for a large raft of dead and black logs and limbs, but it soon elevates itself in the form of a large flock of black ducks, which go off with a loud quacking.

[1][George Melvin, a Concord gunner and fisherman.]

March 31, 1858 I see about a dozen black ducks on Flint's Pond, asleep with their heads in their backs and drifting across the pond before the wind. I suspect that they are nocturnal in their habits and therefore require much rest by day. So do the seasons revolve and every chink is filled. While the waves toss this bright day, the ducks, asleep, are drifting before it across the ponds. Every now and then one or two lift their heads and look about, as if they watched by turns. . . . The leaves are now so dry and loose that it is almost impossible to approach the shore of the pond without being heard by the ducks.

April 2, 1858 See how those black ducks, swimming in pairs far off on the river, are disturbed by our appearance, swimming away in alarm, and now, when we advance again, they rise and fly up-stream and about, uttering regularly a *crack cr-r-rack* of alarm, even for five or ten minutes, as they circle about, long after we have lost sight of them. Now we hear it on this side, now on that.

WOOD DUCK
(SUMMER DUCK)

October 29, 1837 Two ducks, of the summer or wood species, which were merrily dabbling in their favorite basin [at Goose Pond], struck up a retreat on my approach, and seemed disposed to take French leave, paddling off with swan-like majesty. They are first-rate swimmers, beating me at a round pace, and— what was to me a new trait in the duck character—dove every min-

ute or two and swam several feet under water, in order to escape our attention.[1] Just before immersion they seemed to give each other a significant nod, and then, as if by a common understanding, 't was heels up and head down in the shaking of a duck's wing. When they reappeared, it was amusing to observe with what a self-satisfied, darn-it-how-he-nicks-'em air they paddled off to repeat the experiment.

August 6, 1855 At Ball's Hill see five summer ducks, a brood now grown, feeding amid the pads on the opposite side of the river, with a whitish ring, perhaps nearly around neck. A rather shrill squeaking quack when they go off. It is remarkable how much more game you will see if you are in the habit of *sitting* in the fields and woods. As you pass along with a noise it hides itself, but presently comes forth again.

November 9, 1855 Saw in the pool at the Hemlocks what I at first thought was a brighter leaf moved by the zephyr on the surface of the smooth dark water, but it was a splendid male summer duck, which allowed us to approach within seven or eight rods, sailing up close to the shore, and then rose and flew up the curving stream. We soon overhauled it again, and got a fair and long view of it. It was a splendid bird, a perfect floating gem, and Blake,[2] who had never seen the like, was greatly surprised, not knowing that so

---

[1] [Wood ducks do not commonly dive. Thoreau may have been mistaken as to the species.]

[2] [Thoreau's friend Harrison G. O. Blake of Worcester, Mass.]

splendid a bird was found in this part of the world. There it was, constantly moving back and forth by invisible means and wheeling on the smooth surface, showing now its breast, now its side, now its rear. It had a large, rich, flowing, green burnished crest,—a most ample head-dress,—two crescents of dazzling white on the side of the head and the black neck, a pinkish(?)-red bill (with black tip) and similar irides, and a long white mark under and at wing point on sides; the side, as if the form of wing at this distance, light bronze or greenish brown; but, above all, its breast, when it turns into the right light, all aglow with splendid purple (?) or ruby (?) reflections, *like the throat of the hummingbird.* It might not appear so close at hand. This was the most surprising to me. What an ornament to a river to see that glowing gem floating in contact with its waters! As if the hummingbird should recline its ruby throat and its breast on the water. Like dipping a glowing coal in water! It so affected me.

It became excited, fluttered or flapped its wings with a slight whistling noise, and arose and flew two or three rods and alighted. It sailed close up to the edge of a rock, by which it lay pretty still, and finally sailed fast up one side of the river by the willows, etc., off the duck swamp beyond the spring, now and then turning and sailing back a foot or two, while we paddled up the opposite side a rod in the rear, for twenty or thirty rods. At length we went by it, and it flew back low a few rods to where we roused it. It never offered to dive. We came equally near it again on our return. Unless you are thus near, and have a glass, the splendor and beauty of its colors will not be discovered.

★   ★   ★

That duck was all jewels combined, showing different lustres as it turned on the unrippled element in various lights, now brilliant glossy green, now dusky violet, now a rich bronze, now the reflections that sleep in the ruby's grain.

August 3, 1856   Two small ducks (probably wood ducks) flying south. Already grown, and at least looking south!! It reminds me of the swift revolution of the seasons.

August 16, 1858   In my boating of late I have several times scared up a couple of summer ducks of this year, bred in our meadows. They allowed me to come quite near, and helped to people the river. I have not seen them for some days. Would you know the end of our intercourse? Goodwin shot them, and Mrs. ———, who never sailed on the river, ate them. Of course, she knows not what she did. What if I should eat her canary? Thus we share each other's sins as well as burdens. The lady who watches admiringly the matador shares his deed. They belonged to me, as much as to any one, when they were alive, but it was considered of more importance that Mrs. ——— should taste the flavor of them dead than that I should enjoy the beauty of them alive.

July 27, 1860   See, twenty rods or more down-stream, four or five young ducks, which appear already to be disturbed by my boat. So, leaving that to attract their attention, I make my way alongshore in the high grass and behind the trees till I am opposite to them. At a distance they appear simply black and white, as they swim deep,—black backs and white throats. Now I find that they have retreated a little into the pontederia, and are very busily diving, or dipping, not immersing their whole bodies, but their heads and shoulders while their bodies are perfectly perpendicular, just like tame ducks. All of them close together will be in this attitude at the same moment. I now see that the throat, and probably upper part, at least, of breast, is clear-white, and there is a clear line of white above eye and on neck within a line of black; and as they stand on their heads, the tips apparently of their tails (possibly wings??) are conspicuously white or whitish; the upper part, also, is seen to be brownish rather than black. I presume these to be young summer ducks, though so dark; say two-thirds grown.

How easy for the young ducks to hide amid the pickerel-weed along our river, while a boat goes by! and this plant attains its height when these water-fowl are of a size to need its shelter. Thousands of them might be concealed by it along our river, not to speak of the luxuriant sedge and grass of the meadows, much of it so wet as to be inaccessible. These ducks are diving scarcely two feet within the edge of the pickerel-weed, yet one who had not first seen them exposed from a distance would never suspect their neighborhood.

September 17, 1860 See a flock of eight or ten wood ducks on the Grindstone Meadow, with glass, some twenty-five rods off,— several drakes very handsome. They utter a creaking scream as they sail there,—being alarmed,—from time to time, shrill and loud, very unlike the black duck. At last one sails off, calling the others by a short creaking note.

BUFFLE-HEAD
(BUFFLE-HEADED DUCK)

April 19, 1855 From Heywood's Peak I thought I saw the head of a loon in the pond, thirty-five or forty rods distant. Bringing my glass to bear, it seemed sunk very low in the water,— all the neck concealed,—but I could not tell which end was the bill. At length I discovered that it was the whole body of a little duck, asleep with its head in its back, exactly in the middle of the pond. It had a moderate-sized black head and neck, a white breast, and *seemed* dark-brown above, with a white spot on the side of the head, not reaching to the outside, from base of mandibles, and another, perhaps, on the end of the wing, with some black there. It sat drifting round a little, but with ever its breast toward the wind, and from time to time it raised its head and looked round to see if it were safe. I think it was the smallest duck I ever saw. Floating buoyantly asleep on the middle of Walden Pond. Was it not a female of the buffle-headed or spirit duck? I believed the wings looked blacker when it flew, with some white beneath. It floated like a little casket, and at first I doubted a good while if it possessed life, until I saw it raise its head and look around. It had chosen a place for its nap exactly equidistant between the two shores there, and, with its breast to the wind, swung round only as much as a vessel held by its anchors in the stream. At length the cars scared it.

WILD DUCKS (SPECIES UNNAMED)

March 16, 1840   The ducks alight at this season on the windward side of the river, in the smooth water, and swim about by twos and threes, pluming themselves and diving to peck at the root of the lily and the cranberries which the frost has not loosened. It is impossible to approach them within gunshot when they are accompanied by the gull, which rises sooner and makes them restless. They fly to windward first, in order to get under weigh, and are more easily reached by the shot if approached on that side. When preparing to fly, they swim about with their heads erect, and then, gliding along a few feet with their bodies just touching the surface, rise heavily with much splashing and fly low at first, if not suddenly aroused, but otherwise rise directly to survey the danger. The cunning sportsman is not in haste to desert his position, but waits to ascertain if, having got themselves into flying trim, they will not return over the ground in their course to a new resting-place.

April 10, 1852 Took boat at Stedman Buttrick's, a gunner's boat, smelling of muskrats and provided with slats for bushing the boat. Having got into the Great Meadows, after grounding once or twice on low spits of grass ground, we begin to see ducks which we have scared, flying low over the water, always with a striking parallelism in the direction of their flight. They fly like regulars. They are like rolling-pins with wings. A few gulls, sailing like hawks, seen against the woods; crows; white-bellied swallows even here, already, which, I suppose, proves that their insect food is in the air. . . . Ducks most commonly seen flying by twos or threes.

*   *   *

From Carlisle Bridge we saw many ducks a quarter of a mile or more northward, black objects on the water, and heard them laugh something like a loon. Might have got near enough to shoot them. A fine sight to see them rise at last, about fifty of them, apparently black ducks.[1] While they float on the water they appear to preserve constantly their relative distance. Their note not exactly like that of a goose, yet resembling some domestic fowl's cry, you know not what one; like a new species of goose.

[1][Probably not black ducks, to judge by what he says of their note. It seems possible that they might have been brant, though brant are extremely rare in fresh water in New England.]

April 16, 1852   Flight of ducks and partridges earnest but not graceful.

April 17, 1852   These deep withdrawn bays, like that toward Well Meadow, are resorts for many a shy flock of ducks. They are very numerous this afternoon. We scare them up every quarter of a mile. Mostly the whitish duck which Brown thinks the golden-eye (we call them whistlers), and also black ducks, perchance also sheldrakes. They are quite shy; swim rapidly away far into the pond. A flock which we surprised in the smooth bay of Well Meadow divided and showed much cunning, dodging under the shore to avoid us.

October 12, 1852   Paddled on Walden. A rippled surface. Scared up ducks. Saw them first far over the surface, just risen,— two smaller, white-bellied, one larger, black. They circled round as usual, and the first went off, but the black one went round and round and over the pond five or six times at a considerable height and distance, when I thought several times he had gone to the river, and at length settled down by a slanting flight of a quarter of a mile into a distant part of the pond which I had left free; but what beside safety these ducks get by sailing in the middle of Walden I don't know. That black rolling-pin with wings, circling round you half a mile off for a quarter of an hour, at that height, from which he sees the river and Fair Haven all the while, from which he sees so many things, while I see almost him alone. Their wings set so far back. They are not handsome, but wild.

March 18, 1855   Meanwhile a small dark-colored duck, all neck and wings, a winged rolling-pin, went over,—perhaps a teal.

March 27, 1855   The ducks sleep these nights in the shallowest water which does not freeze, and there may be found early in the morning. I think that they prefer that part of the shore which is permanently covered.

April 22, 1856   I raised my sail and, cowering under my umbrella in the stern, wearing the umbrella like a cap and holding the handle between my knees, I steered and paddled, almost perfectly sheltered from the heavy rain. Yet my legs and arms were a little exposed sometimes, in my endeavors to keep well to windward so as to double certain capes ahead. For the wind occasionally drove me on to the western shore. From time to time, from under my umbrella, I could see the ducks spinning away before me, like great bees. For when they are flying low directly from you, you see hardly anything but their vanishing dark bodies, while the rapidly moving wings or paddles, seen edgewise, are almost invisible.

October 22, 1857   As I go through the woods now, so many oak and other leaves have fallen the rustling noise somewhat disturbs my musing. However, Nature in this may have intended some kindness to the ducks, which are now loitering hereabouts on their migration southward, mostly young and inexperienced birds, for, as they are feeding in Goose Pond, for instance, the rustling of the leaves betrays the approach of the sportsman and his dog, or other foe; so perhaps the leaves on the ground protect them more than when on the trees.

March 25, 1858 There are so many sportsmen out that the ducks have no rest on the Great Meadows, which are not half covered with water. They sit uneasy on the water, looking about, without feeding, and I see one man endeavor to approach a flock crouchingly through the meadow for half a mile, with india-rubber boots on, where the water is often a foot deep. This has been going on, on these meadows, ever since the town was settled, and will go on as long as ducks settle here.

March 28, 1858 From Wheeler's ploughed field on the top of Fair Haven Hill, I look toward Fair Haven Pond, now quite smooth. There is not a duck nor a gull to be seen on it. I can hardly believe that it was so alive with them yesterday. Apparently they improve this warm and pleasant day, with little or no wind, to continue their journey northward. The strong and cold northwest wind of about a week past has probably detained them. Knowing that the meadows and ponds were swarming with ducks yesterday, you go forth this particularly pleasant and still day to see them at your leisure, but find that they are all gone. No doubt there are some left, and many more will soon come with the April rains. It is a wild life that is associated with stormy and blustering weather. When the invalid comes forth on his cane, and misses improve the pleasant air to look for signs of vegetation, that wild life has withdrawn itself.

April 13, 1858 Speaking to J. B. Moore[1] about the partridges being run down,[2] he says that he was told by Lexington people some years ago that they found a duck lying dead under the spire of their old meeting-house (since burned) which stood on the Battle-Ground. The weathercock—and it was a cock in this case—was considerably bent, and the inference was that the duck had flown against it in the night.

March 24, 1860 From Holbrook's clearing I see five large dark-colored ducks, probably black ducks, far away on the meadow, with heads erect, necks stretched, on the alert, only one in water. Indeed, there is very little water on the meadows. For length of neck those most wary look much like geese. They appear quite large and heavy. They probably find some sweet grass, etc., where the water has just receded.

There are half a dozen gulls on the water near. They are the large *white* birds of the meadow, the whitest we have. As they so commonly stand above water on a piece of meadow, they are so much the more conspicuous. They are *very* conspicuous to my naked eye a mile off, or as soon as I come in sight of the meadow, but I do not detect the sheldrakes around them till I use my glass, for the latter are not only less conspicuously white, but, as they are fishing, sink very low in the water. Three of the gulls stand to-

[1] [Of Concord.]
[2] [See Chapter 6.]

gether on a piece of meadow, and two or three more are standing solitary half immersed, and now and then one or two circle slowly about their companions.

The sheldrakes appear to be the most native to the river, briskly moving along up and down the side of the stream or the meadow, three-fourths immersed and with heads under water, like cutters collecting the revenue of the river bays, or like pirate crafts peculiar to the stream. They come the earliest and seem to be most at home.

The water is so low that all these birds are collected near the Holt. The inhabitants of the village, poultry-fanciers, perchance, though they be, [know not] these active and vigorous wild fowl (the sheldrakes) pursuing their finny prey ceaselessly within a mile of them, in March and April. Probably from the hen-yard fence with a good glass you can see them at it. They are as much at home on the water as the pickerel is within it. Their serrated bill reminds me of a pickerel's snout. You see a long row of these schooners, black above with a white stripe beneath, rapidly gliding along, and occcasionally one rises erect on the surface and flaps its wings, showing its white lower parts. They are the duck most common and most identified with the stream at this season. They appear to get their food wholly within the water. Less like our domestic ducks.

CANADA GOOSE
(WILD GOOSE)

March 26, 1846 A flock of geese has just got in late, now in the dark flying low over the pond. They came on, indulging at last like weary travellers in complaint and consolation, or like some creaking evening mail late lumbering in with regular anserine clangor. I stood at my door[1] and could hear their wings when they suddenly spied my light and, ceasing their noise, wheeled to the east and apparently settled in the pond.

March 27, 1846 This morning I saw the geese from the door through the mist sailing about in the middle of the pond, but when I went to the shore they rose and circled round like ducks over my head, so that I counted them,—twenty-nine. I after saw thirteen ducks.

March 28, 1852 10.15 P.M.—The geese have just gone over, making a great cackling and awaking people in their beds. They will probably settle in the river. Who knows but they had expected to find the pond open?

April 15, 1852 How indispensable our one or two flocks of geese in spring and autumn! What would be a spring in which that sound was not heard? Coming to unlock the fetters of northern rivers. Those annual steamers of the air.

[1][Of his hut at Walden Pond.]

April 18, 1852 Going through Dennis's field with C.,[1] saw a flock of geese on east side of river near willows. Twelve great birds on the troubled surface of the meadow, delayed by the storm. We lay on the ground behind an oak and our umbrella, eighty rods off, and watched them. Soon we heard a gun go off, but could see no smoke in the mist and rain. And the whole flock rose, spreading their great wings and flew with clangor[2] a few rods and lit in the water again, then swam swiftly toward our shore with out-stretched necks. I knew them first from ducks by their long necks. Soon appeared the man, running toward the shore in vain, in his greatcoat; but he soon retired in vain. We remained close under our umbrella by the tree, ever and anon looking through a peep-hole between the umbrella and the tree at the birds. On they came, sometimes in two, sometimes in three, squads, warily, till we could see the steel-blue and green reflections from their necks. We held the dog close the while,—C., lying on his back in the rain, had him in his arms,—and thus we gradually edged round on the ground in this cold, wet, windy storm, keeping our feet to the tree, and the great wet calf of a dog with his eyes shut so meekly in our arms. We laughed well at our adventure. They swam fast and warily, seeing our umbrella. Occasionally one expanded a gray wing. They showed white on breasts. And not till after half an

[1] [William Ellery Channing, the younger, the Concord poet, Thoreau's most intimate friend and afterwards his biographer.]
[2] The "honk" of the goose.

hour, sitting cramped and cold and wet on the ground, did we leave them.

* * *

Heard the cackling of geese from over the Ministerial Swamp, and soon appeared twenty-eight geese that flew over our heads toward the other river we had left,[1] we now near the black birches. With these great birds in it, the air seems for the first time inhabited. We detect holes in their wings. Their clank expresses anxiety.

April 19, 1852 That last flock of geese yesterday is still in my eye. After hearing their clangor, looking southwest, we saw them just appearing over a dark pine wood, in an irregular waved line, one abreast of the other, as it were breasting the air and pushing it before them. It made you think of the streams of Cayster, etc., etc. They carry weight, such a weight of metal in the air. Their dark waved outline as they disappear. The grenadiers of the air. Man pygmifies himself at sight of these inhabitants of the air. These stormy days they do not love to fly; they alight in some retired marsh or river. From their lofty pathway they can easily spy out the most extensive and retired swamp. How many there must be, that one or more flocks are seen to go over almost every farm in New England in the spring!

[1][That is, the Sudbury River. They were then near the Assabet.]

November 25, 1852 At Walden.—I hear at sundown what I mistake for the squawking of a hen,—for they are firing at chickens hereabouts,[1]—but it proved to be a flock of wild geese going south. This proves how much the voices of all fowls are alike.

November 29, 1852 Geese in river swam as fast as I walked.

March 26, 1853 Saw about 10 A.M. a gaggle of geese, forty-three in number, in a very perfect harrow flying northeasterly. One side of the harrow was a little longer than the other. They appeared to be four or five feet apart. At first I heard faintly, as I stood by Minott's gate, borne to me from the southwest through the confused sounds of the village, the indistinct honking of geese. I was somewhat surprised to find that Mr. Loring at his house should have heard and seen the same flock. I should think that the same flock was commonly seen and heard from the distance of a mile east and west. It is remarkable that we commonly see geese go over in the spring about 10 o'clock in the morning, as if they were accustomed to stop for the night at some place southward whence they reached us at that time. Goodwin saw six geese in Walden about the same time.

November 23, 1853 At 5 P.M. I saw, flying southwest high overhead, a flock of geese, and heard the faint honking of one or two. They were in the usual harrow form, twelve in the shorter line and twenty-four in the longer, the latter abutting on the former at the fourth bird from the front. I judged *hastily* that the interval

[1][A Thanksgiving-Day chicken-shoot.]

between the geese was about double their alar extent, and, as the last is, according to Wilson, five feet and two inches, the former may safely be called eight feet. I hear they were fired at with a rifle from Bunker Hill the other day. This is the sixth flock I have seen or heard of since the morning of the 17th, *i.e.* within a week.

November 18, 1854   Saw sixty geese go over the Great Fields, in one waving line, broken from time to time by their crowding on each other and vainly endeavoring to form into a harrow, honking all the while.

March 20, 1855   Trying the other day to imitate the honking of geese, I found myself flapping my sides with my elbows, as with wings, and uttering something like the syllables *mow-ack* with a nasal twang and twist in my head; and I produced their note so perfectly in the opinion of the hearers that I thought I might possibly draw a flock down.

April 19, 1855   5 A.M.—I hear a faint *honk* and, looking up, see going over the river, within fifty rods, thirty-two geese in the form of a hay-hook, only two in the hook, and they are at least six feet apart. Probably the whole line is twelve rods long. At least three hundred have passed over Concord, or rather within the breadth of a mile, this spring (perhaps twice as many); for I have seen or heard of a dozen flocks, and the two I counted had about thirty each.

November 13, 1855   In mid-forenoon (10.45), seventy or eighty geese, in three harrows successively smaller, flying southwest—pretty well west—over the house. A completely overcast, occasionally drizzling forenoon. I at once heard their clangor and rushed to and opened the window. The three harrows were gradually formed into one great one before they were out of sight, the geese shifting their places without slacking their progress.

November 19, 1855 Speaking of geese, he[1] says that Dr. Hurd told a tough story once. He said that when he went out to the well there came a flock of geese flying so low that they had to rise to clear the well-sweep. M. says that there used to be a great many more geese formerly; he used to hear a great many flocks in a day go "yelling" over. Brant, too, he used to see.

December 13, 1855 Sanborn[2] tells me that he was waked up a few nights ago in Boston, about midnight, by the sound of a flock of geese passing over the city, probably about the same night I heard them here. They go honking over cities where the arts flourish, waking the inhabitants; over State-houses and capitols, where legislatures sit; over harbors where fleets lie at anchor; mistaking the city, perhaps, for a swamp or the edge of a lake, about settling in it, not suspecting that greater geese than they have settled there.

November 8, 1857 A warm, cloudy, rain-threatening morning.

About 10 A.M. a long flock of geese are going over from

---

[1] [George Minott.]
[2] [Mr. F. B. Sanborn of Concord, Thoreau's biographer.]

northeast to southwest, or parallel with the general direction of the coast and great mountain ranges. The sonorous, quavering sounds of the geese are the voice of this cloudy air,—a sound that comes from directly between us and the sky, an aerial sound, and yet so distinct, heavy, and sonorous, a clanking chain drawn through the heavy air. I saw through my window some children looking up and pointing their tiny bows into the heavens, and I knew at once that the geese were in the air. It is always an exciting event. The children, instinctively aware of its importance, rushed into the house to tell their parents. These travellers are revealed to you by the upward-turned gaze of men. And though these undulating lines are melting into the southwestern sky, the sound comes clear and distinct to you as the clank of a chain in a neighboring stithy. So they migrate, not flitting from hedge to hedge, but from latitude to latitude, from State to State, steering boldly out into the ocean of air. It is remarkable how these large objects, so plain when your vision is rightly directed, may be lost in the sky if you look away for a moment,—as hard to hit as a star with a telescope.

It is a sort of encouraging or soothing sound to assuage their painful fears when they go over a town, as a man moans to deaden a physical pain. The direction of their flight each spring and autumn reminds us inlanders how the coast trends. In the afternoon I met Flood, who had just endeavored to draw my attention to a flock of geese in the mizzling air, but encountering me he lost sight of them, while I, at length, looking that way, discerned them, though he could not. This was the third flock to-day. Now if ever, then, we may expect a change in the weather.

November 30, 1857   The air is full of geese. I saw five flocks within an hour, about 10 A.M., containing from thirty to fifty each, and afterward two more flocks, making in all from two hundred and fifty to three hundred at least, all flying southwest over Goose and Walden Ponds. The former was apparently well named Goose Pond. You first hear a faint honking from one or two in the northeast and think there are but few wandering there, but, looking up, see forty or fifty coming on in a more or less broken harrow, wedging their way southwest. I suspect they honk more, at any rate they are more broken and alarmed, when passing over a village, and are seen falling into their ranks again, assuming the perfect harrow form. Hearing only one or two honking, even for the seventh time, you think there are but few till you see them. According to my calculation a thousand or fifteen hundred may have gone over Concord to-day. When they fly low and near, they look very black against the sky.

March 31, 1858   Just after sundown I see a large flock of geese in a perfect harrow cleaving their way toward the northeast, with Napoleonic tactics splitting the forces of winter.

April 1, 1858   I observed night before last, as often before, when geese were passing over in the twilight quite near, though the whole heavens were still light and I knew which way to look by the honking, I could not distinguish them. It takes but a little obscurity to hide a bird in the air. How difficult, even in broadest daylight, to discover again a hawk at a distance in the sky when you have once turned your eyes away!

October 24, 1858   A northeast storm, though not much rain falls to-day, but a fine driving mizzle or "drisk." This, as usual, brings the geese, and at 2.30 P.M. I see two flocks go over. I hear that some were seen two or three weeks ago (??), faintly honking. A great many must go over to-day and also alight in this neighborhood. This weather warns them of the approach of winter, and this wind speeds them on their way. Surely, then, while geese fly overhead we can live here as contentedly as they do at York Factory on Hudson's Bay. We shall perchance be as well provisioned and have as good society as they. Let us be of good cheer, then, and expect the annual vessel which brings the spring to us without fail.

March 24, 1859   C.[1] sees geese go over again this afternoon. How commonly they are seen in still rainy weather like this! He says that when they had got far off they looked like a black ribbon almost perpendicular waving in the air.

March 28, 1859   We see eight geese floating afar in the middle of the meadow, at least half a mile off, plainly (with glass) much

[1][William Ellery Channing, the younger.]

larger than the ducks in their neighborhood and the white on their heads very distinct. When at length they arise and fly off northward, their peculiar *heavy* undulating wings, blue-heron-like and unlike any duck, are very noticeable. The black, sheldrake, etc., move their wings rapidly, and remind you of paddle-wheel steamers. Methinks the wings of the black duck appear to be set very far back when it is flying. The meadows, which are still covered far and wide, are quite alive with black ducks.

When walking about on the low east shore at the Bedford bound, I heard a faint honk, and looked around over the water with my glass, thinking it came from that side or perhaps from a farmyard in that direction. I soon heard it again, and at last we detected a great flock passing over, quite on the other side of us and pretty high up. From time to time one of the company uttered a short note, that peculiarly metallic, clangorous sound. These were in a single undulating line, and, as usual, one or two were from time to time crowded out of the line, apparently by the crowding of those in the rear, and were flying on one side and trying to recover their places, but at last a second short line was formed, meeting the long one at the usual angle and making a figure somewhat like a hay-hook. I suspect it will be found that there is really some advantage in large birds of passage flying in the wedge form and cleaving their way through the air,—that they really do overcome its resistance best in this way,—and perchance the direction and strength of the wind determine the comparative length of the two sides.

The great gulls fly generally up or down the river valley, cutting off the bends of the river, and so do these geese. These fly sympathizing with the river,—a stream in the air, soon lost in the distant sky.

We see these geese swimming and flying at midday and when it is perfectly fair.

If you scan the horizon at this season of the year you are very likely to detect a small flock of dark ducks moving with rapid wing athwart the sky, or see the undulating line of migrating geese against the sky.

Perhaps it is this easterly wind which brings geese, as it did on the 24th.

*   *   *

Undoubtedly the geese fly more numerously over rivers which, like ours, flow northeasterly,—are more at home with the water under them. Each flock runs the gantlet of a thousand gunners, and when you see them steer off from you and your boat you may remember how great their experience in such matters may be, how many such boats and gunners they have seen and avoided between here and Mexico, and even now, perchance (though you, low plodding, little dream it), they see one or two more lying in wait ahead. They have an experienced ranger of the air for their guide. The echo of one gun hardly dies away before they see another pointed at them. How many bullets or smaller shot have sped in vain toward their ranks! Ducks fly more irregularly and shorter distances at a time. The geese rest in fair weather by day only in the midst of our broadest meadow or pond. So they go, anxious and earnest to hide their nest under the pole.[1]

[1][Of course they do not go quite so far north as Thoreau intimates. He was perhaps thinking of the breeding-grounds of the brant.]

HERONS

RAILS

AMERICAN BITTERN
(STAKE-DRIVER)

June 14, 1851   As I proceed along the back road I hear the lark still singing in the meadow, and the bobolink, and the gold robin on the elms, and the swallows twittering about the barns. A small bird chasing a crow high in the air, who is going home at night. All nature is in an expectant attitude. Before Goodwin's house, at the opening of the Sudbury road, the swallows are diving at a tortoise-shell cat, who curvets and frisks rather awkwardly, as if she did not know whether to be scared or not. And now, having proceeded a little way down this road, the sun having buried himself in the low cloud in the west and hung out his crimson curtains, I hear, while sitting by the wall, the sound of the stake-driver at a distance,—like that made by a man pumping in a neighboring farmyard, watering his cattle, or like chopping wood before his door on a frosty morning, and I can imagine like driving a stake in a meadow. The pumper. I immediately went in search of the bird, but, after going a third of a mile, it did not sound much nearer, and the two parts of the sound did not appear to proceed from the same place. What is the peculiarity of these sounds which penetrate so far on the keynote of nature? At last I got near to the brook in the meadow behind Hubbard's wood, but I could not tell if it were further or nearer than that. When I got within half a dozen rods of the brook, it ceased, and I heard it no more. I suppose that I scared it. As before I was further off than I thought, so now I was nearer than I thought. It is not easy to understand how so small a creature can make so loud a sound by merely sucking in or throwing out water with pump-like lungs.[1]

★   ★   ★

It was a sound as of gulping water.

September 20, 1851   I scare up the great bittern in meadow by the Heywood Brook near the ivy. He rises buoyantly as he flies against the wind, and sweeps south over the willow with out-stretched neck, surveying.

---

[1][No water is used in producing the sound. Thoreau had been misinformed by one of his neighbors. See the account in his paper on the "Natural History of Massachusetts" in *Excursions*. For an interesting account of this habit of the bittern's see Mr. Bradford Torrey's paper on "The 'Booming' of the Bittern" in *The Auk* for January, 1889 (vol. vi, pp. 1–8).]

October 5, 1851 The American bittern (*Ardea minor*)[1] flew across the river, trailing his legs in the water, scared up by us. This, according to Peabody,[2] is the boomer (stake-driver). In their sluggish flight they can hardly keep their legs up. Wonder if they can soar.

October 7, 1851 Saw the *Ardea minor* walking along the shore, like a hen with long green legs. Its pencilled throat is so like the reeds and shore, amid which it holds its head erect to watch the passer, that it is difficult to discern it. You can get very near it, for it is unwilling to fly, preferring to hide amid the weeds.

October 12, 1851 Minott calls the stake-driver "belcher-squelcher." Says he has seen them when making the noise. They go *slug-toot, slug-toot, slug-toot.*

June 16, 1852 I hear a stake-driver, like a man at his pump, which sucks,—fit sound for our sluggish river. . . . Most would suppose the stake-driver the sound of a farmer at a distance at his pump, watering his cattle. It oftener sounds like this than like a stake, but sometimes exactly like a man driving a stake in the meadow.

June 20, 1852 The stake-driver is at it in his favorite meadow. I followed the sound. At last I got within two rods, it seeming always to recede and drawing you like a will-o'-the-wisp

[1][Now called *Botaurus lentiginosus.*]
[2][W. B. O. Peabody, *Report on the Birds of Massachusetts.*]

further away into the meadows. When thus near, I heard some lower sounds at the beginning, much more like striking on a stump or a stake, a dry, hard sound; and then followed the gurgling, pumping notes, fit to come from a meadow. This was just within the blueberry and *Pyrus arbutifolia* (choke-berry) bushes, and when the bird flew up alarmed, I went to the place, but could see no water, which makes me doubt if water is necessary to it in making the sound. Perhaps it thrusts its bill so deep as to reach the water where it is dry on the surface. It sounds the more like wood-chopping or pumping, because you seem to hear the echo of the stroke or the reverse motion of the pump-handle. I hear them morning and evening. After the warm weather has come, both morning and evening you hear the bittern pumping in the fens. It does not sound loud near at hand, and it is remarkable that it should be heard so far. Perhaps it is pitched on a favorable key. Is it not a call to its mate? Methinks that in the resemblance of this note to rural sounds, to sounds made by farmers, the protection, the security, of the bird is designed.

July 18, 1852   Again under weigh, we scare up the great bittern amid the pontederia, and, rowing to where he alights, come within three feet of him and scare him up again. He flies sluggishly away, plowing the air with the coulter of his breast-bone, and alighting ever higher up the stream. We scare him up many times in the course of an hour.

August 13, 1852   Saw the head and neck of a great bittern projecting above the meadow-grass, exactly like the point of a stump, only I knew there could be no stump there.

August 31, 1852   The pigeon woodpecker darts across the valley; a catbird mews in the alders; a great bittern flies sluggishly away from his pine tree perch on Tupelo Cliff, digging his way through the air. These and crows at long intervals are all the birds seen or heard.

*   *   *

There goes a great bittern *plodding* home over the meadows at evening, to his perch on some tree by the shore. The rain has washed the leaves clean where he perches. There stands another in the meadow just like a stake, or the point of a stump or root. Its security was consulted both in its form and color. The latter is a sober brown, pale on the breast, as the less exposed side of a root might be; and its attitude is accidental, too, bent forward and *perfectly* motionless. Therefore there is no change in appearance but such as can be referred to the motion of the sailor.

May 13, 1853   Heard a stake-driver in Hubbard's meadow from Corner road. Thus far off, I hear only, or chiefly, the last dry, hard click or stroke part of the note, sounding like the echo from some near wood of a distant stake-driving. Here only this portion of the note, but close by it is more like pumping, when the dry stroke is accompanied by the incessant sound of the pump.

May 27, 1853   Heard a stake-driver yesterday in the rain. It sounded exactly like a man pumping, while another man struck on the head of the pump with an axe, the last strokes sounding peculiarly dry and hard like a forcible echo from the wood-side. One would think all Concord would be built on piles by this time. Very deliberately they drive, and in the intervals are considering the progress of the pile into the soft mud. They are working by the day. He is early and late at his work, building his stake[?]-house, yet did anybody ever see the pile he had driven? He has come back from his Southern tour to finish that job of spile-driving which he undertook last year. It is heavy work—not to be hurried. Only green hands are overhasty.

May 20, 1856   See and hear a stake-driver in the swamp. It took one short pull at its pump and stopped.

June 15, 1857   It was pleasant walking thus[1] at 5 P.M. by solitary sandy paths, through commonly low dry woods of oak or pine, through glistening oak woods (their fresh leaves in the June air), where the yellow-throat (or black-throat?[2]) was heard and the wood thrush sang, and, as I passed a swamp, a bittern boomed. As

[1][In Plymouth, Mass.]
[2][The black-throated bunting, or dickcissel, formerly a common bird in the Cape Cod region of Massachusetts.]

I stood quite near, I heard distinctly two or three dry, hard sucks, as if the bird were drawing up water from the swamp, and then the sounds usually heard, as if ejecting it.

May 28, 1858 From time to time I hear the sound of the bittern, concealed in the grass, indefinitely far or near, and can only guess at the direction, not the distance. I fail to find the nest.

June 17, 1858 The stake-driver comes beating along, like a long, ungainly craft, or a revenue cutter, looking into the harbors, and if it finds a fisherman there, standing out again.

August 19, 1858 We scare up a stake-driver several times. The blue heron has within a week reappeared in our meadows, and the stake-driver begins to be seen oftener, and as early as the 5th I noticed young summer ducks about; the same of hawks, owls, etc. This occurs as soon as the young birds can take care of themselves, and some appear to be very early on the return southward, with the very earliest prospect of fall. Such birds are not only more abundant but, methinks, more at leisure now, having reared their family, and perhaps they are less shy. Yes, bitterns are more frequently seen now to lift themselves from amid the pontederia or flags, and take their sluggish flight to a new resting-place,—bitterns which either have got through the labors of breeding or are now first able to shift for themselves. And likewise blue herons, which have bred or been bred not far from us (plainly), are now at leisure, or are impelled to revisit our slow stream. I have not seen the last since spring.

October 26, 1858 He[1] says that some call the stake-driver "belcher-squelcher," and some, "wollerkertoot." I used to call them "pump-er-gor'." Some say "slug-toot."

November 17, 1858 I am surprised to see a stake-driver fly up from the weeds within a stone's throw of my boat's place. It drops its excrement from thirty feet in the air, and this falling, one part being heavier than another, takes the form of a snake, and suggests that this may be the origin of some of the stories of this bird swallowing a snake or eel which passed through it.

April 17, 1860 Looking off on to the river meadow, I noticed, as I thought, a stout stake aslant in the meadow, three or more rods off, sharp at the top and rather light-colored on one side, as is often the case; yet, at the same time, it occurred to me that a stake-driver often resembled a stake very much, but I thought, nevertheless, that there was no doubt about this being a stake. I took out my glass to look for ducks, and my companion, seeing what I had, and asking if it was not a stake-driver, I suffered my glass at last to rest on it, and I was much surprised to find that it was a stake-driver after all. The bird stood in shallow water near a tussock, perfectly still, with its long bill pointed upwards in the same direction with its body and neck, so as perfectly to resemble a stake aslant. If the bill had made an angle with the neck it would have been betrayed at once. Its resource evidently was to rely on its

[1] [Minott.]

form and color and immobility solely for its concealment. This was its instinct, whether it implies any conscious artifice or not. I watched it for fifteen minutes, and at length it relaxed its muscles and changed its attitude, and I observed a slight motion; and soon after, when I moved toward it, it flew. It resembled more a piece of a rail than anything else,—more than anything that would have been seen here before the white man came. It is a question whether the bird consciously cooperates in each instance with its Maker, who contrived this concealment. I can never believe that this resemblance is a mere coincidence, not designed to answer this very end—which it does answer so perfectly and usefully.

June 6, 1860 Ever and anon we hear a few *sucks* or strokes from the bittern, the stake-driver, wherever we lie to, as if he had taken the job of extending all the fences into the river to keep cows from straying round.

October 16, 1860 Horace Mann[1] tells me that he found in the crop or inside of the stake-driver killed the other day one grasshopper, several thousand-legs one to one and a half inches long, and not much else.

April 16, 1861 He[2] brought me some days ago the contents of a stake-driver's stomach or crop. It is apparently a perch (?), some seven inches long originally, with three or four pebble-

---

[1][The son of the famous educator of that name. He was living in Concord, and he accompanied Thoreau on his journey to Minnesota in the following summer.]
[2][Horace Mann.]

shaped, compact masses of the fur of some very small quadruped, as a meadow mouse, some one fourth inch thick by three fourths in diameter, also several wing-cases of black beetles such as I see on the meadow flood.

GREAT BLUE HERON

1850   John Garfield brought me this morning (September 6th) a young great heron (*Ardea Herodias*), which he shot this morning on a pine tree on the North Branch.[1] It measured four feet, nine inches, from bill to toe and six feet in alar extent, and belongs to a different race from myself and Mr. Frost.[2] I am glad to recognize him for a native of America,—why not an American citizen?

April 19, 1852   Scared up three blue herons in the little pond close by, quite near us. It was a grand sight to see them rise, so slow and stately, so long and limber, with an undulating motion from head to foot, undulating also their large wings, undulating in two directions, and looking warily about them. With this graceful, limber, undulating motion they arose, as if so they got under way, their two legs trailing parallel far behind like an earthy residuum to be left behind. They are large, like birds of Syrian lands, and seemed to oppress the earth, and hush the hillside to silence, as they

[1][The Assabet River.]
[2][Rev. Barzillai Frost, the Concord minister.]

winged their way over it, looking back toward us. It would affect our thoughts, deepen and perchance darken our reflections, if such huge birds flew in numbers in our sky. Have the effect of magnetic passes. They are few and rare. Among the birds of celebrated flight, storks, cranes, geese, and ducks. The legs hang down like a weight which they [?] raise, to pump up as it were with its [*sic*] wings and convey out of danger.

★　　★　　★

To see the larger and wilder birds, you must go forth in the great storms like this. At such times they frequent our neighbor-hood and trust themselves in our midst. A life of fair-weather walks *might* never show you the goose sailing on our waters, or the great heron feeding here. When the storm increases, then these great birds that carry the mail of the seasons lay to. To see wild life you must go forth at a wild season. When it rains and blows, keep-ing men indoors, then the lover of Nature must forth. Then re-turns Nature to her wild estate. In pleasant sunny weather you may catch butterflies, but only when the storm rages that lays prostrate the forest and wrecks the mariner, do you come upon the feeding-grounds of wildest fowl,—of heron and geese.

May 14, 1853　Suddenly there start up from the riverside at the entrance of Fair Haven Pond, scared by our sail, two great blue herons,—slate-color rather,—slowly flapping and undulating, their projecting breast-bones very visible,—or is it possibly their necks bent back?—their legs stuck out straight begind. Getting higher by their flight, they straight come back to reconnoitre us.

Land at Lee's Cliff, where the herons have preceded us and are perched on the oaks, conspicuous from afar, and again we have a fair view of their flight.

★   ★   ★

Again we scare up the herons, who, methinks, will build hereabouts. They were standing by the waterside. And again they alight farther below, and we see their light-colored heads erect, and their bodies at various angles as they stoop to drink. And again they flap away with their great slate-blue wings, necks curled up (?) and legs straight out behind, and, having attained a great elevation, they circle back over our heads, now seemingly black as crows against the sky,—crows with long wings, they might be taken for,—but higher and higher they mount by stages in the sky, till heads and tails are lost and they are mere black wavelets amid the blue, one always following close behind the other. They are evidently mated. It would be worth the while if we could see them oftener in our sky.

August 23, 1853 I see to-day—and may add to yesterday's list—the blue heron launch off from an oak by the river and flap or sail away with lumbering flight; also kingbirds and crows.

September 14, 1854 We see half a dozen herons in this voyage. Their wings are so long in proportion to their bodies that there seems to be more than one undulation to a wing as they are disappearing in the distance, and so you can distinguish them. You see another begin before the first has ended. It is remarkable how common these birds are about our sluggish and marshy river. We must attract them from a wide section of country. It abounds in those fenny districts and meadow pond-holes in which they delight.

April 15, 1855 Returning, we had a fine view of a blue heron, standing erect and open to view on a meadow island, by the great swamp south of the bridge, looking as broad as a boy on the side, and then some sheldrakes sailing in the smooth water beyond. These soon sailed behind points of meadow. The heron flew away, and one male sheldrake flew past us low over the water, reconnoitring, large and brilliant black and white. When the heron takes to flight, what a change in size and appearance! It is *presto change!* There go two great undulating wings pinned together, but the body and neck must have been left behind somewhere.

August 5, 1855 As I was paddling back at 6 A.M., saw, nearly half a mile off, a blue heron standing erect on the topmost twig of the great buttonwood on the street in front of Mr. Prichard's house,[1] while perhaps all within were abed and asleep. Little did they think of it, and how they were presided over. He looked at first like a spiring twig against the sky, till you saw him flap his

---

[1][In the centre of the village of Concord.]

wings. Presently he launched off and flew away over Mrs. Brooks's house.

October 29, 1855 Returning, I scare up a blue heron from the bathing-rock this side the Island. It is whitened by its droppings, in great splotches a foot or more wide. He has evidently frequented it to watch for fish there.

November 1, 1855 As I pushed up the river past Hildreth's, I saw the blue heron (probably of last Monday) arise from the shore and disappear with heavily-flapping wings around a bend in front; the greatest of the bitterns (*Ardeæ*), with heavily-undulating wings, low over the water, seen against the woods, just disappearing round a bend in front; with a great slate-colored expanse of wing, suited to the shadows of the stream, a tempered blue as of the sky and dark water commingled. This is the aspect under which the Musketaquid[1] might be represented at this season: a long, smooth lake, reflecting the bare willows and button-bushes, the stubble, and the wool-grass on its tussock, a muskrat-cabin or two conspicuous on its margin amid the unsightly tops of pontederia, and a bittern disappearing on undulating wing around a bend.

April 26, 1856 A blue heron sails away from a pine at Holden Swamp shore and alights on the meadow above. Again he flies, and alights on the hard Conantum side, where at length I detect

[1][The Concord River. See note, p. 89.]

him standing far away stake-like (his body concealed), eying me and depending on his stronger vision.

August 16, 1858   A blue heron, with its great undulating wings, prominent cutwater, and leisurely flight, goes over southwest, cutting off the bend of the river west of our house.

August 19, 1858   When I see the first heron, like a dusky blue wave undulating over our meadows again, I think, since I saw them going northward the other day, how many of these forms have been added to the landscape, complete from bill to toe, while, perhaps, I have idled! I see two herons. A small bird is pursuing the heron as it does a hawk. Perhaps it is a blackbird and the herons gobble up their young!

September 18, 1858   Near the pond[1] we scare up twenty or thirty ducks, and at the pond three blue herons. They are of a hoary blue. One flies afar and alights on a limb of a large white pine near Well Meadow Head, bending it down. I see him standing there with outstretched neck.

August 14, 1859   When I reached the upper end of this weedy bar, at about 3 P.M., this warm day, I noticed some light-colored object in mid-river, near the other end of the bar. At first I thought of some large stake or board standing amid the weeds there, then of a fisherman in a brown holland sack, referring him to the shore beyond. Supposing it the last, I floated nearer and nearer till I saw

[1][Fairhaven Pond.]

plainly enough the motions of the person, whoever it was, and that it was no stake. Looking through my glass thirty or forty rods off, I thought certainly that I saw C.,[1] who had just bathed, making signals to me with his towel, for I referred the object to the shore twenty rods further. I saw his motions as he wiped himself,—the movements of his elbows and his towel. Then I saw that the person was nearer and therefore smaller, that it stood on the sand-bar in mid-stream in shallow water and must be some maiden in a bathing-dress,—for it was the color of brown holland web,—and a very peculiar kind of dress it seemed. But about this time I discovered with my naked eye that it was a blue heron standing in very shallow water amid the weeds of the bar and pluming itself. I had not noticed its legs at all, and its head, neck, and wings, being constantly moving, I had mistaken for arms, elbows, and towel of a bather, and when it stood stiller its shapely body looked like a peculiar bathing-dress. I floated to within twenty-five rods and watched it at my leisure. Standing on the shallowest part of the bar at that end, it was busily dressing its feathers, passing its bill like a comb down its feathers from base to tip. From its form and color, as well as size, it was singularly distinct. Its great spear-shaped head and bill was very conspicuous, though least so when turned toward me (whom it was eying from time to time). It coils its neck away upon its back or breast as a sailor might a rope, but occasionally

[1][W. E. Channing.]

stretches itself to its full height, as tall as a man, and looks around and at me. Growing shy, it begins to wade off, until its body is partly immersed amid the weeds,—potamogetons,—and then it looks more like a goose. The neck is continually varying in length, as it is doubled up or stretched out, and the legs also, as it wades in deeper or shallower water.

Suddenly comes a second, flying low, and alights on the bar yet nearer to me, almost high and dry. Then I hear a note from them, perhaps of warning,—a short, coarse, frog-like purring or eructating sound. You might easily mistake it for a frog. I heard it half a dozen times. It was not very loud. Anything but musical. The last proceeds to plume himself, looking warily at me from time to time, while the other continues to edge off through the weeds. Now and then the latter holds its neck as if it were ready to strike its prey,—stretched forward over the water,—but I saw no stroke. The arch may be lengthened or shortened, single or double, but the great spear-shaped bill and head are ever the same. A great hammer or pick, prepared to transfix fish, frog, or bird. At last, the water becoming too deep for wading, this one takes easily to wing—though up to his body in water—and flies a few rods to the shore. It rather flies, then, than swims. It was evidently scared. These were probably birds of this season. I saw some distinct ferruginous on the angle of the wing. There they stood in the midst of the open river, on this shallow and weedy bar in the sun, the leisurely sentries, lazily pluming themselves, as if the day were too long for them. They gave a new character to the stream. Adjutant they were to my idea of the river, these two winged men.

You have not seen our weedy river, you do not know the significance of its weedy bars, until you have seen the blue heron wading and pluming itself on it. I see that it was made for these shallows, and they for it. Now the heron is gone from the weedy shoal, the scene appears incomplete. Of course, the heron has sounded the depth of the water on every bar of the river that is fordable to it. The water there is not so many feet deep, but so many heron's tibiæ. Instead of a foot rule you should use a heron's leg for a measure. If you would know the depth of the water on these few shoalest places of Musketaquid, ask the blue heron that wades and fishes there. In some places a heron can wade across.

How long we may have gazed on a particular scenery and think that we have seen and known it, when, at length, some bird or quadruped comes and takes possession of it before our eyes, and imparts to it a wholly new character! The heron uses these shallows as I cannot. I give them up to him.

October 10, 1860   Horace Mann shows me the skeleton of a blue heron. The neck is remarkably strong, and the bill. The latter is 5 + inches long to the feathers above and 6½ to the gape. A stake-driver which he has, freshly killed, has a bill 3 inches long above and 4⅛ to the gape and between ⅝ and ⅝ deep vertically at the base. This bird weighs a little over two pounds, being quite large and fat. Its nails are longer and less curved than those of the heron.

The sharp bill of the heron, like a stout pick, wielded by that long and stout neck, would be a very dangerous weapon to encounter. He has made a skeleton of the fish hawk which was brought to me within a month. I remark the great eye-sockets, and the claws, and perhaps the deep, sharp breast-bone. Including its strong hooked bill it is clawed at both ends, harpy-like.

GREEN HERON
(GREEN BITTERN)

June 11, 1840[1] We stole noiselessly down the stream, occasionally driving a pickerel from the covert of the pads, or a bream from her nest, and the small green bittern would now and then sail away on sluggish wings from some recess of the shore. With its patient study by rocks and sandy capes, has it wrested the whole of her secret from Nature yet? It has looked out from its dull eye for so long, standing on one leg, on moon and stars sparkling through silence and dark, and now what a rich experience is its! What says it of stagnant pools, and reeds, and damp night fogs? It would be worth while to look in the eye which has been open and seeing at such hours and in such solitudes. When I behold that dull yellowish green, I wonder if my own soul is not a

[1][Under this date Thoreau enters in his Journal some notes of the Concord and Merrimac excursion of August and September, 1839.]

bright, invisible green. I would fain lay my eye side by side with its and learn of it.

June 25, 1854   A green bittern, apparently, awkwardly alighting on the trees and uttering its hoarse, *zarry* note, *zskeow-zskeow-zskeow*.

July 12, 1854   I see a green bittern wading in a shallow muddy place, with an awkward teetering fluttering pace.

August 2, 1856   A green bittern comes, noiselessly flapping, with stealthy and inquisitive looking to this side the stream and then that, thirty feet above the water. This antediluvian bird, creature of the night, is a fit emblem of a dead stream like this Musketi-cook.[1] This especially is the bird of the river. There is a sympathy between its sluggish flight and the sluggish flow of the stream,— its slowly lapsing flight, even like the rills of Musketicook and my own pulse sometimes.

August 1, 1858   Edward Bartlett[2] and another brought me a green bittern, this year's bird, apparently full grown but not full plumaged, which they caught near the pool on A. Heywood's land behind Sleepy Hollow. They caught it in the woods on the hillside.

---

[1][The Concord River. *Musketaquid* was the Indian name for Concord. On his Maine woods excursion in 1853, Thoreau had asked some Indians what it meant, "but they changed it to *Musketicook*, and repeated that, and Tahmunt said that it meant Dead Stream, which is probably true. *Cook* appears to mean stream, and perhaps *quid* signifies the place or ground."]

[2][One of Thoreau's boy friends in Concord.]

It had not yet acquired the long feathers of the neck. The neck was bent back on itself an inch or more,—that part being bare of feathers and covered by the long feathers from above,—so that it did not appear very long until stretched out. This doubling was the usual condition and not apparent, but could be felt by the hand. So the green bitterns are leaving the nest now.

VIRGINIA RAIL
(MEADOW-HEN)

June 16, 1853 Coming down the river, heard opposite the new houses, where I stopped to pluck the tall grass, a sound as of young blackbirds amid the button-bushes. After a long while gazing, standing on the roots of the button-bushes, I detected a couple of meadow or mud hens (*Rallus Virginianus*) gliding about under the button-bushes over the mud and through the shallow water, and uttering a squeaking or squawking note, as if they had a nest there or young. Bodies about the size of a robin; short tail; wings and tail white-edged; bill about one and a half inches long, orange beneath in one bird; brown, deepening into black spots above; turtle-dove color on breasts and beneath; ashy about eyes and cheeks. Seemed not willing to fly, and for a long time unwilling to pass me, because it must come near to keep under the button-bushes.

SORA
(CAROLINA RAIL)

October 3, 1858   One brings me this morning a
Carolina rail alive, this year's bird evidently from its marks. He
saved it from a cat in the road near the Battle-Ground. On being
taken up, it pecked a little at first, but was soon quiet. It staggers
about as if weak on my windowsill and pecks at the glass, or stands
with its eyes shut, half asleep, and its back feathers hunched up.
Possibly it is wounded. I suspect it may have been hatched here. Its
feet are large and spreading, qualifying it to run on mud or pads.
Its crown is black, but chin white, and its back feathers are distinctly edged with white in streaks.

RAIL (UNIDENTIFIED)

July 16, 1860   Standing amid the pipes of the Great
Meadow, I hear a very sharp creaking *peep*, no doubt from a rail
quite near me, calling to or directing her young, who are meanwhile uttering a very faint, somewhat similar peep, which you
would not hear if not very much inclined to hear it, in the grass
close around me. Sometimes the old bird utters two short, sharp
creaks. I look sharp, but can see nothing of them. She sounds now
here, now there, within two or three rods of me, incessantly running in the grass. I had already heard, more distant, a more prolonged note from some water-fowl, perhaps a plover, if not possibly a male rail, hereabouts.

AMERICAN COOT

April 24, 1856   Goodwin shot, about 6 P.M., and brought to me a cinereous coot (*Fulica Americana*) which was flying over the willows at Willow Bay, where the water now runs up.

It measures fourteen inches to end of tail; eighteen and one half to end of legs. Tail projects a half-inch beyond closed wings. Alar extent twenty-six inches. (These dimensions are somewhat stretched.) Above it is a bluish slate, passing into olive behind the wings, the primaries more brownish. Beneath, ash-color or pale slate. Head and neck, uniform deep black. Legs, clear green in front, passing into lead-color behind and on the lobes. Edging of wings, white; also the tips of the secondaries for one fourth of an inch, and a small space under the tail. Wings beneath, very light, almost silvery, slate. Vent, for a small space, black. Bill, bluish-white, with a chestnut bar near tip, and corresponding chestnut spot on each side of lower mandible and a somewhat diamond-shaped chestnut spot at base in front. No noticeable yellow on bill. Irides, reddish. No noticeable whitish spot beneath eyes; only bare lid. Legs and feet are very neat; talons very slender, curving, and sharp, the middle ones ½ inch+ long. Lobes chiefly on the inner side of the toes. Legs bare half an inch above the joint. From its fresh and tender look I judge it to be a last year's bird. It is quite lousy.

SHORE-BIRDS

WOODCOCK

October 27, 1851   Saw a woodcock[1] feeding, probing the mud with its long bill, under the railroad bridge within two
feet of me for a long time. Could not scare it far away. What a dis-
proportionate length of bill! It is a sort of badge they [wear] as a
punishment for greediness in a former state.

July 9, 1852   Nowadays I scare up the woodcock (?) by
shaded brooks and springs in the woods. It has a carry-legs flight
and goes off with a sort of whistle.

December 17, 1856   At Clamshell, to my surprise, scare up
either a woodcock or a snipe. I think the former, for I plainly saw
considerable red on the breast, also a light stripe along the neck. It
was feeding alone, close to the edge of the hill, where it is springy
and still soft, almost the only place of this character in the neighborhood, and though I started it three times, it each time flew but
little way, round to the hillside again, perhaps the same spot it had

[1]Or snipe?

left a moment before, as if unwilling to leave this unfrozen and comparatively warm locality. It was a great surprise this bitter cold day, when so many springs were frozen up, to see this hardy bird loitering still. Once alighted, you could not see it till it arose again.

November 21, 1857 Just above the grape-hung birches, my attention was drawn to a singular-looking dry leaf or parcel of leaves on the shore about a rod off. Then I thought it might be the dry and yellowed skeleton of a bird with all its ribs; then the shell of a turtle, or possibly some large dry oak leaves peculiarly curved and cut; and then, all at once, I saw that it was a woodcock, perfectly still, with its head drawn in, standing on its great pink feet. I had, apparently, noticed only the yellowish-brown portions of the plumage, referring the dark-brown to the shore behind it. May it not be that the yellowish-brown markings of the bird correspond somewhat to its skeleton? At any rate with my eye steadily on it from a point within a rod, I did not for a considerable time suspect it to be a living creature. Examining the shore after it had flown with a whistling flight, I saw that there was a clear space of mud between the water and the edge of ice-crystals about two inches wide, melted so far by the lapse of the water, and all along the edge of the ice, for a rod or two at least, there was a hole where it had thrust its bill down, probing, every half-inch, frequently closer. Some animal life must be collected at that depth just in that narrow space, savory morsels for this bird.

I was paddling along slowly, on the lookout for what was to be seen, when my attention was caught by a strange-looking leaf or bunch of leaves on the shore, close to the water's edge, a rod distant. I thought to myself, I may as well investigate that, and so pushed slowly toward it, my eyes resting on it all the while. It then looked like a small shipwrecked hulk and, strange to say, like the bare skeleton of a fowl that has been picked and turned yellowish, resting on its breast-bone, the color of a withered black or red oak leaf. Again I thought it must be such a leaf or cluster of leaves peculiarly curved and cut or torn on the upper edges.

The chubby bird dashed away zigzag, carrying its long

tongue-case carefully before it, over the witch-hazel bushes. This is its walk,—the portion of the shore, the narrow strip, still kept open and unfrozen between the water's edge and the ice. The sportsman might discover its neighborhood by these probings.

WILSON'S SNIPE

February 27, 1853 Mr. Herbert is strenuous that I say "ruffed grouse" for "partridge" and "hare" for "rabbit." He says of the snipe, "I am myself satisfied that the sound is produced by the fact that the bird, by some muscular action or other, turns the quill-feathers edge-wise, as he drops plumb through the air; and that while in this position, during his accelerated descent, the vibration of the feathers and the passage of the air between them gives utterance to this wild humming sound."

April 10, 1854 There are many snipes now feeding in the meadows, which you come close upon, and then they go off with hoarse *cr-r-r-ack cr-r-r-ack*. They dive down suddenly from a considerable height sometimes when they alight.

April 18, 1854 Scared up snipes on the meadow's edge, which go off with their strange zigzag, crazy flight and a distressed sound,—*craik craik* or *cr-r-ack cr-r-rack*. One booms now at 3 P.M. They circle round and round, and zigzag high over the meadow, and finally alight again, descending abruptly from that height.

April 20, 1854 The sound of the snipes, winnowing that evening air now at starlight, visible but for an instant high over the meadows, is heard far into the village,—*hoo hoo hoo hoo hoo hoo*, rising higher and higher or dying away as they circle round,—a ghostly sound.

April 15, 1856   At the same time, I hear a part of the hovering note of my first snipe, circling over some distant meadow, a mere waif, and all is still again. A-lulling the watery meadows, fanning the air like a spirit over some far meadow's bay.

April 25, 1856   I landed on Merrick's pasture near the rock, and when I stepped out of the boat and drew it up, a snipe flew up, and lit again seven or eight rods off. After trying in vain for several minutes to see it on the ground there, I advanced a step and, to my surprise, scared up two more, which had squatted on the bare meadow all the while within a rod, while I drew up my boat and made a good deal of noise. In short, I scared up twelve, one or two at a time, within a few rods, which were feeding on the edge of the meadow just laid bare, each rising with a sound like *squeak squeak*, hoarsely. That part of the meadow seemed all alive with them. It is almost impossible to see one on the meadow, they squat and run so low, and are so completely the color of the ground. They rise from within a rod, fly half a dozen rods, and then drop down on the bare open meadow before your eyes, where there seems not stubble enough to conceal them, and are at once lost as completely as if they had sunk into the earth. I observed that some, when finally scared from this island, flew off rising quite high, one a few rods behind the other, in their peculiar zigzag manner, rambling about

high over the meadow, making it uncertain where they would settle, till at length I lost sight of one and saw the other drop down
almost perpendicularly into the meadow, as it appeared.

March 29, 1858 At the first pool I also scared up a snipe. It
rises with a single *cra-a-ck* and goes off with its zigzag flight, with
its bill presented to the earth, ready to charge bayonets against the
inhabitants of the mud.

April 9, 1858 I hear the booming of snipe this evening, and
Sophia[1] says she heard them on the 6th. The meadows having been
bare so long, they may have begun yet earlier. Persons walking up
or down our village street in still evenings at this season hear this
singular *winnowing* sound in the sky over the meadows and know
not what it is. This "booming" of the snipe is our regular village
serenade. I heard it this evening for the first time, as I sat in the
house, through the window. Yet common and annual and remarkable as it is, not one in a hundred of the villagers hears it, and hardly
so many know what it is. Yet the majority know of the Germanians
who have only been here once. Mr. Hoar was almost the only inhabitant of this street whom I had heard speak of this note, which
he used annually to hear and listen for in his sundown or evening
walks.

April 2, 1859 As I go down the street just after sunset, I hear
many snipe to-night. This sound is annually heard by the villagers,

[1][His sister.]

but always at this hour, *i.e.* in the twilight,—a hovering sound high in the air,—and they do not know what to refer it to. It is very easily imitated by the breath. A sort of shuddering with the breath. It reminds me of calmer nights. Hardly one in a hundred hears it, and perhaps not nearly so many know what creature makes it. Perhaps no one dreamed of snipe an hour ago, but the air seemed empty of such as they; but as soon as the dusk begins, so that a bird's flight is concealed, you hear this peculiar spirit-suggesting sound, now far, now near, heard through and above the evening din of the village. I did not hear one when I returned up the street half an hour later.

GREATER YELLOW-LEGS
(TELLTALE)

October 25, 1853 P.M.—Sailed down river to the pitch pine hill behind Abner Buttrick's, with a strong northwest wind, and cold.

Saw a telltale on Cheney's shore, close to the water's edge. I am not quite sure whether it is the greater or lesser, but am inclined to think that all I have seen are the lesser.[1] It was all white below and dark above, with a pure white tail prettily displayed in flying. It kept raising its head with a jerk as if it had the St. Vitus's dance. It

---

[1][The date and the note would indicate that the bird was probably the greater yellow-legs, not the lesser.]

would alight in the water and swim like a little duck. Once, when I went ashore and started it, it flew so as to bring a willow between it and me, and alighted quite near, much nearer than before, to spy me. When it went off, it uttered a sharp *te-te-te-te-te*, flying with quivering wings, dashing about. I think that the storm of yesterday and last night brought it up.

May 31, 1854   Saw a greater telltale, and this is the only one[1] I have seen probably; distinguished by its size. It is very watchful, but not timid, allowing me to come quite near, while it stands on the lookout at the water's edge. It keeps nodding its head with an awkward jerk, and wades in the water to the middle of its yellow legs; goes off with a loud and sharp *phe phe phe phe*, or something like that. It acts the part of the telltale, though there are no birds here, as if it were with a flock. Remarkable as a sentinel for other birds.

SOLITARY SANDPIPER

September 24, 1855   I suppose it was the solitary sandpiper (*Totanus solitarius*)[2] which I saw feeding at the water's edge on Cardinal Shore, like a snipe. It was very tame; we did not scare it even by shouting. I walked along the shore to within twenty-five feet of it, and it still ran toward me in feeding, and

[1][That is, the only species of telltale.]
[2][Now known as *Helodromas solitarius*.]

when I flushed it, it flew round and alighted between me and C.,[1] who was only three or four rods off. It was about as large as a snipe; had a bluish dusky bill about an inch and a quarter long, apparently straight, which it kept thrusting into the shallow water with a nibbling motion, a perfectly white belly, dusky-green legs; bright brown and black above, with duskier wings. When it flew, its wings, which were uniformly dark, hung down much, and I noticed no white above, and heard no note.

UPLAND PLOVER

June 15, 1860 As I stood there I heard that peculiar hawk-like (for rhythm) but more resonant or clanging kind of scream which I may have heard before this year, plover-like, indefinitely far,—over the Clamshell plain. After proceeding half a dozen rods toward the hill, I heard the familiar willet note of the upland plover and, looking up, saw one standing erect—like a large telltale, or chicken with its head stretched up—on the rail fence. After a while it flew off southwest and low, then wheeled and went a little higher down the river. Of pigeon size, but quick quivering wings. Finally rose higher and flew more or less zigzag, as if uncertain where it would alight, and at last, when almost out of sight, it pitched down into a field near Cyrus Hubbard's.

[1][Channing.]

SPOTTED SANDPIPER
(PEETWEET)

August 22, 1853   A peetweet flew along the shore and uttered its peculiar note. Their wings appear double as they fly by you, while their bill is cumbrously carried pointing downward in front.

June 14, 1855   Looked at the peetweet's nest which C.[1] found yesterday. It was very difficult to find again in the broad open meadow; no nest but a mere hollow in the dead cranberry leaves, the grass and stubble ruins, under a little alder. The old bird went off at last from under us; low in the grass at first and with *wings up*, making a worried sound which attracted other birds. I frequently noticed others afterward flying low over the meadow and alighting and uttering this same note of alarm. There were only four eggs in this nest yesterday,[2] and to-day, to C.'s surprise, there are the two eggs which he left and a young peetweet beside; a gray pinch of down with a black centre to its back, but already so old and precocious that it runs with its long legs swiftly off from squatting beside the two eggs, and hides in the grass. We have some trouble to catch it. How came it here with these eggs, which will not be hatched for some days? C. saw nothing of it yesterday. J. Farmer[3]

[1] [C. in Thoreau's Journal always stands for his friend Channing.]
[2] [Channing had taken two of them.]
[3] [Jacob Farmer, of Concord, a farmer by occupation and an observer of wild creatures.]

says that young peetweets run at once like partridges and quails, and that they are the only birds he knows that do. These eggs were not addled (I had opened one, C. another). Did this bird come from another nest, or did it belong to an earlier brood? Eggs white, with black spots here and there all over, dim at great end.

May 4, 1856   See a peetweet on Dove Rock,[1] which just peeps out. As soon as the rocks begin to be bare the peetweet comes and is seen teetering on them and skimming away from me.

July 6, 1856   In A. Hosmer's ice-bared meadow south of Turnpike, hear the distressed or anxious *peet* of a peetweet, and see it hovering over its young, half-grown, which runs beneath and suddenly hides securely in the grass when but a few feet from me.

September 18, 1858   I notice that the wing of the peetweet, which is about two inches wide, has a conspicuous and straight-edged white bar along its middle on the under side for half its length. It is seven eighths of an inch wide and, being quite parallel with the darker parts of the wing, it produces that singular effect in its flying which I have noticed. This line, by the way, is not mentioned by Wilson, yet it is, perhaps, the most noticeable mark of the bird when flying! The under side of the wings is commonly slighted in the description, though it is at least as often seen by us as the upper.

May 2, 1859   A peetweet and its mate at Mantatuket Rock. The river seems really inhabited when the peetweet is back and

[1][In the Assabet.]

those little light-winged millers (?). This bird does not return to our stream until the weather is decidedly pleasant and warm. He is perched on the accustomed rock. Its note peoples the river, like the prattle of children once more in the yard of a house that has stood empty.

May 8, 1860 The simple *peep peep* of the peetweet, as it flies away from the shore before me, sounds hollow and rather mournful, reminding me of the seashore and its wrecks, and when I smell the fresh odor of our marshes the resemblance is increased.

PLOVER

1850 As I was stalking over the surface of this planet in the dark to-night, I started a plover resting on the ground and heard him go off with whistling wings.

Six

QUAIL

GROUSE

BOB-WHITE
(QUAIL)

July 21, 1851 The quail, invisible, whistles, and who attends?

January 17, 1856 Henry Shattuck tells me that the quails come almost every day and get some saba beans within two or three rods of his house,—some which he neglected to gather. Probably the deep snow drives them to it.

February 7, 1857 Hayden the elder tells me that the quails have come to his yard every day for almost a month and are just as tame as chickens. They come about his wood-shed, he supposes to pick up the worms that have dropped out of the wood, and when it storms hard gather together in the corner of the shed. He walks within, say, three or four feet of them without disturbing them. They come out of the woods by the graveyard, and sometimes they go down toward the river. They will be about his yard the greater part of the day; were there yesterday, though it was so warm, but now probably they can get food enough elsewhere. They go just the same to Poland's, across the road. About ten years ago there was a bevy of fifteen that used to come from the same woods, and one day, they being in the barn and scared by the cat, four ran into the hay and died there. The former do not go to the houses further from the woods. Thus it seems in severe winters the quails venture out of the woods and join the poultry of the farmer's yard, if it be near the edge of the wood. It is remarkable that this bird, which thus half domesticates itself, should not be found wholly domesticated before this.

RUFFED GROUSE
(PARTRIDGE)

1850   The fire stopped within a few inches of a partridge's nest to-day, June 4th, whom we took off in our hands and found thirteen creamy-colored eggs. I started up a woodcock when I went to a rill to drink, at the westernmost angle of R. W. E.'s[1] wood-lot.

June 13, 1851   I heard partridges drumming to-night as late as 9 o'clock. What singularly space penetrating and filling sound! Why am I never nearer to its source?

[1][Ralph Waldo Emerson's.]

July 16, 1851 Some thoughtless and cruel sportsman has killed twenty-two young partridges not much bigger than robins, against the laws of Massachusetts and humanity.

September 23, 1851 The partridge and the rabbit,—they still are sure to thrive like true natives of the soil, whatever revolutions occur. If the forest is cut off, many bushes spring up which afford them concealment, and they become more numerous than ever.

December 21, 1851 Who ever saw a partridge soar over the fields? To every creature its own nature. They are very wild; but are they scarce? Or can you exterminate them for that?

February 18, 1852 I find the partridges among the fallen pinetops on Fair Haven these afternoons, an hour before sundown, ready to commence budding in the neighboring orchard.

April 22, 1852 Our dog sends off a partridge with a whir, far across the open field and the river, like a winged bullet.

May 1, 1852 A partridge bursts away from under the rock below me on quivering wings, like some moths I have seen.

June 27, 1852 I meet the partridge with her brood in the woods, a perfect little hen. She spreads her tail into a fan and beats the ground with her wings fearlessly within a few feet of me, to attract my attention while her young disperse, but they keep up a faint, wiry kind of peep, which betrays them, while she mews and squeaks as if giving them directions.

October 15, 1852 The flight of a partridge, leaving her lair (?) on the hillside only a few rods distant, with a gentle whirring sound, is like the blowing of rocks at a great distance. Perhaps it produces the same kind of undulations in the air.

April 6, 1853   Hear the faint, swelling, far-off beat of a partridge.

May 11, 1853   I hear the distant drumming of a partridge. Its beat, however distant and low, falls still with a remarkably forcible, almost painful, impulse on the ear, like veritable little drumsticks on our tympanum, as if it were a throbbing or fluttering in our veins or brows or the chambers of the ear, and belonging to ourselves,—as if it were produced by some little insect which had made its way up into the passages of the ear, so penetrating is it. It is as palpable to the ear as the sharpest note of a fife. Of course, that bird can drum with its wings on a log which can go off with such a powerful whir, beating the air. I have seen a thoroughly frightened hen and cockerel fly almost as powerfully, but neither can sustain it long. Beginning slowly and deliberately, the partridge's beat sounds faster and faster from far away under the boughs and through the aisles of the wood until it becomes a regular roll, but is speedily concluded. How many things shall we not see and be and do, when we walk there where the partridge drums!

June 12, 1853   Going up Pine Hill, disturbed a partridge and her brood. She ran in deshabille directly to me, within four feet, while her young, not larger than a chicken just hatched, dispersed, flying along a foot or two from the ground, just over the bushes, for a rod or two. The mother kept close at hand to attract my attention, and mewed and clucked and made a noise as when a hawk is in sight. She stepped about and held her head above the bushes and clucked just like a hen. What a remarkable instinct that which keeps the young so silent and prevents their peeping and betraying themselves! The wild bird will run almost any risk to save her young. The young, I believe, make a fine sound at first in dispersing, something like a cherry-bird.

November 8, 1853 The partridges go off with a whir, and then sail a long way level and low through the woods with that impetus they have got, displaying their neat forms perfectly.

January 31, 1854 Many tracks of partridges there along the meadow-side in the maples, and their droppings where they appear to have spent the night about the roots and between the stems of trees. I think they eat the buds of the azalea. And now, with a mew, preluding a whir, they go off before me. Coming up, I follow her tracks to where she eased herself for lightness, and immediately after are five or six parallel cuts in the snow, where her wing struck when she lifted herself from the ground, but no trace more.

April 25, 1854 The first partridge drums in one or two places, as if the earth's pulse now beat audibly with the increased flow of life. It slightly flutters all Nature and makes her heart palpitate.

July 6, 1854 Disturbed two broods of partridges this afternoon,—one a third grown, flying half a dozen rods over the bushes, yet the old, as anxious as ever, rushing to me with the courage of a hen.

January 25, 1855   In the partridge-tracks the side toes are more spread than in crows; and I believe the hind one is not so long. Both trail the middle toe.

January 31, 1855   As I skated near the shore under Lee's Cliff, I saw what I took to be some scrags or knotty stubs of a dead limb lying on the bank beneath a white oak, close by me. Yet while I looked directly at them I could not but admire their close resemblance to partridges. I had come along with a rapid whir and suddenly halted right against them, only two rods distant, and, as my eyes watered a little from skating against the wind, I was not convinced that they were birds till I had pulled out my glass and deliberately examined them. They sat and stood, three of them, perfectly still with their heads erect, some darker feathers like ears, methinks, increasing their resemblance to scrabs [*sic*], as where a small limb is broken off. I was much surprised at the remarkable stillness they preserved, instinctively relying on the resemblance to the ground for their protection, *i.e.* withered grass, dry oak leaves, dead scrags, and broken twigs. I thought at first that it was a dead oak limb with a few stub ends or scrabbs [*sic*] sticking up, and for some time after I had noted the resemblance to birds, standing only two rods off, I could not be sure of their character on account of their perfect motionlessness, and it was not till I brought my glass to bear on them and saw their eyes distinctly, steadily glaring on me, their necks and every muscle tense with anxiety, that I was convinced. At length, on some signal which I did not perceive, they went with a whir, as if shot, off over the bushes.

February 12, 1855 I see at Warren's Crossing where, last night perhaps, some partridges rested in this light, dry, deep snow. They must have been almost completely buried. They have left their traces at the bottom. They are such holes as would be made by crowding their bodies in backwards, slanting-wise, while perhaps their heads were left out. The dog scared them out of similar holes yesterday in the open orchard.

February 13, 1855 The tracks of partridges are more remarkable in this snow than usual, it is so light, being at the same time a foot deep. I see where one has waddled along several rods, making a chain-like track about three inches wide (or two and a half), and at the end has squatted in the snow, making a perfectly smooth and regular oval impression, like the bowl of a spoon, five inches wide. Then, six inches beyond this, are the marks of its wings where it struck the snow on each side when it took flight. It must have risen at once without running. In one place I see where one, after running a little way, has left four impressions of its wings on the snow on each side extending eighteen or twenty inches and twelve or fifteen in width. In one case almost the entire wing was distinctly impressed, eight primaries and five or six secondaries. In one place, when alighting, the primary quills, five of them, have marked the snow for a foot. I see where many have dived into the snow, apparently last night, on the side of a shrub oak hollow. In four places they have passed quite underneath it for more than a foot; in one place, eighteen inches. They appear to have dived or burrowed into it, then passed along a foot or more underneath and squatted there, perhaps, with their heads out, and have invariably left much dung at the end of this hole. I scared one from its hole only half a rod in front of me now at 11 A.M.

*   *   *

To resume the subject of partridges, looking further in an open place or glade amid the shrub oaks and low pitch pines, I found as many as twenty or thirty places where partridges had lodged in the snow, apparently the last night or the night before. You could see commonly where their bodies had first struck the snow and furrowed it for a foot or two, and six inches wide, then entered and gone underneath two feet and rested at the further end, where the manure is left. Is it not likely that they remain quite under the snow there, and do not put their heads out till ready to start? In many places they walked along before they went under the snow. They do not go under deep, and the gallery they make is mostly filled up behind them, leaving only a thin crust above. Then invariably, just beyond this resting-place, you could see the marks made by their wings when they took their departure:

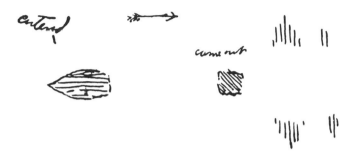

These distinct impressions made by their wings, in the pure snow, so common on all hands, though the bird that made it is gone and there is no trace beyond, affect me like some mystic Oriental symbol,—the winged globe or what-not,—as if made by a spirit. In some places you would see a furrow and hollow in the snow where there was no track for rods around, as if a large snowball or a cannon-ball had struck it, where apparently the birds had not paused in their flight. It is evidently a regular thing with them thus to lodge in the snow. Their tracks, when perfectly distinct, are seen to be almost in one straight line thus, trailing the middle toe:

about five inches apart. In one place I saw where one had evidently trailed the tips of the wings, making two distinct lines five or six inches apart, one on each side the foot-tracks; probably made by a male.

February 16, 1855 I find in the leavings of the partridges numerous ends of twigs. They are white with them, some half an inch long and stout in proportion. Perhaps they are apple twigs. The bark (and bud, if there was any) has been entirely digested, leaving the bare, white, hard wood of the twig. Some of the ends of apple twigs looked as if they had been bitten off. It is surprising what a quantity of this wood they swallow with their buds. What a hardy bird, born amid the dry leaves, of the same color with them, that, grown up, lodges in the snow and lives on buds and twigs! Where apple buds are just freshly bitten off they do not seem to have taken so much twig with them.

February 22, 1855 He[1] had seen a partridge drum standing on a wall. Said it stood very upright and produced the sound by striking its wings together behind its back, as a cock often does, but did not strike the wall nor its body. This he is sure of, and declares that he is mistaken who affirms the contrary, though it were Audubon himself. Wilson says he "begins to strike with his stiffened wings" while standing on a log, but does not say what he strikes, though one would infer it was either the log or his body. Peabody says he beats his body with his wings.[2]

---

[1] [Mr. Jacob Farmer.]
[2] [It is now known that the ruffed grouse in drumming simply beats the air with

December 14, 1855 Suddenly I heard the screwing mew and then the whir of a partridge on or beneath an old decaying apple tree which the pines had surrounded. There were several such, and another partridge burst away from one. They shoot off swift and steady, showing their dark-edged tails, almost like a cannon-ball. I saw one's track under an apple tree and where it had pecked a frozen-thawed apple.

February 4, 1856 I see that the partridges feed quite extensively on the sumach berries, *e.g.* at my old house.[1] They come to them after every snow, making fresh tracks, and have now stripped many bushes quite bare.

February 8, 1856 E. Garfield says that he saw the other day where a fox had caught in the snow three partridges and eaten two. He himself last winter caught two, on the hillside south of Fair Haven, with his hands. They flew before him and dived into the snow, which was about a foot deep, going twice their length into it. He thrust his hand in and caught them. Puffer said that his companion one night speared a partridge on the alders on the south side the pond.

February 11, 1856 Saw a partridge by the riverside, opposite Fair Haven Hill, which at first I mistook for the top of a fence-post

his wings, which do not strike his body or the log or each other. In *Bird-Lore* for Nov.-Dec., 1908 (vol. x, pp. 246–249) Mr. E. J. Sawyer describes the drumming and shows a photograph of a bird taken in the act. The same magazine for March-April, 1909 (vol. xi, p. 77), shows a photograph by Dr. C. F. Hodge of one of his tame grouse in the act of drumming.]

[1][His hut at Walden Pond.]

above the snow, amid some alders. I shouted and waved my hand four rods off, to see if it was one, but there was no motion, and I thought surely it must be a post. Nevertheless I resolved to investigate. Within three rods, I saw it to be indeed a partridge, to my surprise, standing perfectly still, with its head erect and neck stretched upward. It was as complete a deception as if it had designedly placed itself on the line of the fence and in the proper place for a post. It finally stepped off daintily with a teetering gait and head up, and took to wing.

May 24, 1856 [Humphrey Buttrick][1] has known a partridge to fly at once from one to two miles after being wounded (tracked them by the blood) without alighting. Says he has caught as many as a dozen partridges in his hands. He lies right down on them, or where he knows them to be, then passes his hands back and forth under his body till he feels them. You must not lift your body at all or they will surely squeeze out, and when you feel one must be sure you get hold of their legs or head, and not feathers merely.[2]

June 11, 1856 A partridge with young in the Saw Mill Brook path. Could hardly tell what kind of creature it was at first, it made such a noise and fluttering amid the weeds and bushes. Finally ran off with its body flat and wings somewhat spread.

---

[1][A Concord man.]
[2][These must have been *young* partridges, of course.]

March 8, 1857   A partridge goes off from amid the pitch pines. It lifts each wing so high above its back and flaps so low, and withal so rapidly, that they present the appearance of a broad wheel, almost a revolving sphere, as it whirs off like a cannon-ball shot from a gun.

April 29, 1857   Sweet-fern at entrance of Ministerial Swamp. A partridge there drums incessantly. C. says it makes his heart beat with it, or he feels it in his breast.

July 25, 1857   As we were returning over the track[1] where I had passed but a few moments before, we started a partridge with her young partly from beneath the wooden rails. While the young hastened away, she sat within seven feet of us and plumed herself, perfectly fearless, without making a noise or ruffling her feathers as they do in our neighborhood, and I thought it would be a good opportunity to observe whether she flew as quietly as other birds when not alarmed. We observed her till we were tired, and when we compelled her to get out of our way, though she took to wing as easily as if we had not been there and went only two or three rods, into a tree, she flew with a considerable *whir*, as if this were unavoidable in a rapid motion of the wings.

October 20, 1857   Melvin says he has caught partridges in his hands. If there's only one hole, knows they've not gone out. Sometimes shoots them through the snow.

[1][On the Northeast Carry, Moosehead Lake, Maine.]

November 20, 1857   I see a partridge on the ground under a white oak by Tarbell's black birches, looking just like a snag. This is the second time I have seen them in such a place. Are they not after acorns?

November 28, 1857   P.M.—Around Ebby Hubbard's wood-lot.

On the hillside above his swamp, near the Ministerial land, I found myself walking in one of those shelf-like hillside paths made by Indians, hunters, cows, or what-not, and it was beset with fresh snares for partridges. . . . Upright twigs are stuck in the ground across the path, a foot or more in height and just close enough together to turn a partridge aside, leaving a space about four inches wide in the middle, and some twigs are stretched across above to prevent the birds hopping over. Then a sapling about an inch in diameter or less is bent over, and the end caught under one of the twigs which has a notch or projection on one side, and a free-running noose, attached to the sapling, hangs in the opening and is kept spread by being hung on some very slight nicks in the two twigs. This seems to suppose the bird to be going one way only, but perhaps if it cannot escape one way it will turn and try to go back, and so spring the trap.

I saw one that was sprung with nothing in it, another whose slip-noose was blown or fallen one side, and another with a partridge still warm in it. It was a male bird hanging dead by the neck, just touching its toes to the ground. It had a collar or ruff about its neck, of large and conspicuous black feathers with a green reflection. This black is peculiar to the male, the female's being brown. Its feet, now clinched in its agony, were the strangest-looking pale blue, with a fine fringe, of scales or the like, on each side of each toe. The small black feathers were centred with gray spots. The scapulars were darker brown, dashed with large clear pale-brown spots; the breast-feathers light with light-brown marks. The tail-feathers had each a broad black bar, except the middle one, which was more mixed or grayish there. The bands of the females are said to be more brown, as is their collar. There were a few droppings of the bird close by the snare in two instances. Were they dropped after it was caught? Or did they determine the locality of the snare?

These birds appear to run most along the sides of wooded banks around swamps. At least these paths and snares occur there oftenest. I often scare them up from amid or near hemlocks in the woods.

The general color of the bird is that of the ground and dry leaves on it at present. The bird hanging in the snare was very inconspicuous. I had gone close by it once without noticing it. Its wings are short and stout and look as if they were a little worn by striking the ground or bushes, or perhaps in drumming. I observed a bare bright-red or scarlet spot over each eye.

April 12, 1858 Returning on the railroad, the noon train down passed us opposite the old maid Hosmer's house. In the woods just this side, we came upon a partridge standing on the track, between the rails over which the cars had just passed. She had evidently been run down, but, though a few small feathers were scattered along for a dozen rods beyond her, and she looked a little ruffled, she was apparently more disturbed in mind than body. I took her up and carried her one side to a safer place. At first she made no resistance, but at length fluttered out of my hands and ran two or three feet. I had to take her up again and carry and drive her further off, and left her standing with head erect as at first, as if beside herself. She was not lame, and I suspect no wing was broken. I did not suspect that this swift wild bird was ever run down by the cars. We have an account in the newspapers of every cow and calf that is run over, but not of the various wild creatures who meet with that accident. It may be many generations before the partridges learn to give the cars a sufficiently wide berth.

April 22, 1859   Scare up partridges feeding about the green springy places under the edge of hills. See them skim or scale away for forty rods along and upward to the woods, into which they swiftly scale, dodging to right and left and avoiding the twigs, yet without once flapping the wings after having launched themselves.

December 24, 1859   I saw the tracks of a partridge more than half an inch deep in the ice, extending from this island[1] to the shore, she having walked there in the slosh. They were quite perfect and

---

[1][An island in Flint's Pond whereon were some remarkably large blueberry bushes which Thoreau has been describing.]

reminded me of bird-tracks in stone. She may have gone there to bud on these blueberry trees. I saw where she spent the night at the bottom of the largest clump, in the snow.

This blueberry grove must be well known to the partridges; no doubt they distinguish their tops from afar.

January 22, 1860 I scare a partridge that was eating the buds and ends of twigs of the *Vaccinium vacillans* on a hillside.

April 19, 1860 Toward night, hear a partridge drum. You will hear at first a single beat or two far apart and have time to say, "There is a partridge," so distinct and deliberate is it often, before it becomes a rapid roll.

June 14, 1860 A brood of little partridges in the woodpaths. The old bird utters a loud wiry, mewing sound of alarm, the young a very fine sharp sound like cherry-birds.

June 27, 1860 2 P.M.—Up Assabet to Farmer's.

See on the open grassy bank and shore, just this side the Hemlocks, a partridge with her little brood. Being in my boat, I went within three rods, and they were hardly scared at all. The young were but little bigger than chickens four or five days old, yet could fly two or three rods. The partridge now takes out her brood to feed, all the country over; and what an extensive range they have!—not confined to a barnyard.

PIGEONS

PASSENGER PIGEON
(WILD PIGEON)[1]

August 1845 I sit here at my window like a priest
of Isis, and observe the phenomena of three thousand years ago,
yet unimpaired. The tantivy of wild pigeons, an ancient race of
birds, gives a voice to the air, flying by twos and threes athwart my
view or perching restless on the white pine boughs occasionally; a
fish hawk dimples the glassy surface of the pond and brings up a
fish; and for the last half-hour I have heard the rattle of railroad cars
conveying travellers from Boston to the country.

1850[2] The fire reached the base of the cliff and then rushed
up its sides. The squirrels ran before it in blind haste, and three pigeons dashed into the midst of the smoke.

---

[1][On account of the interest attaching to this bird, once so abundant and now
nearly or quite extinct, practically every reference to it in Thoreau's Journal, however seemingly trivial, is here reproduced.]

[2][Though this was written in 1850, the fire referred to had happened some years
earlier.]

July 21, 1851   Some pigeons here are resting in the thickest of the white pines during the heat of the day, migrating, no doubt. They are unwilling to move for me. Flies buzz and rain about my hat, and the dead twigs and leaves of the white pine, which the choppers have left here, exhale a dry and almost sickening scent. A cuckoo chuckles, half throttled, on a neighboring tree, and now, flying into the pine, scares out a pigeon, which flies with its handsome tail spread, dashes this side and that between the trees helplessly, like a ship carrying too much sail in midst of a small creek, some great admiral having no room to manœuvre,—a fluttering flight.

September 12, 1851   Saw a pigeon-place on George Heywood's cleared lot,—the six dead trees set up for the pigeons to alight on, and the brush house close by to conceal the man. I was rather startled to find such a thing going now in Concord. The pigeons on the trees looked like fabulous birds with their long tails and their pointed breasts. I could hardly believe they were alive and not some wooden birds used for decoys, they sat so still; and, even when they moved their necks, I thought it was the effect of art. As they were not catching then, I approached and scared away a dozen birds who were perched on the trees, and found that they were freshly baited there, though the net was carried away, perchance to some other bed. The smooth sandy bed was covered with buckwheat, wheat or rye, and acorns. Sometimes they use corn, shaved off the ear in its present state with a knife. There were left the sticks with which they fastened the nets. As I stood there, I heard a rush-ing sound and, looking up, saw a flock of thirty or forty pigeons dashing toward the *trees*, who suddenly whirled on seeing me and circled round and made a new dash toward the bed, as if they would fain alight if I had not been there, then steered off. I crawled into the bough house and lay awhile looking through the leaves, hoping to see them come again and feed, but they did not while I stayed. This net and bed belong to one Harrington of Weston, as I hear. Several men still take pigeons in Concord every year; by a method, methinks, extremely old and which I seem to have seen pictured in some old book of fables or symbols, and yet few in Concord know exactly how it is done. And yet it is all done for money and because the birds fetch a good price, just as the farmers raise corn and potatoes. I am always expecting that those engaged in such a pursuit will be somewhat less grovelling and mercenary than the regular trader or farmer, but I fear that it is not so.

May 9, 1852 Saw pigeons in the woods, with their inquisi-tive necks and long tails, but few representatives of the great flocks that once broke down our forests.

September 2, 1852 Small flocks of pigeons are seen these days. Distinguished from doves by their sharper wings and bodies.

March 29, 1853 He[1] saw two pigeons to-day. *Prated* [*sic*] for them; they came near and then flew away.

[1][Dugan, of Concord.]

March 30, 1853   A range-pole on the side of Mt. Tabor,[1] twenty-odd feet long and ten or twelve from the ground, slanted upward on three forked posts like a rafter, a bower[2] being opposite the lower end two rods off, and this end of the pole full of shot.

August 9, 1853   Saw pigeons the other day (August 5).

September 2, 1853   Hear the sharp *quivet* of pigeons at the Thrush Alley clearing. Mistook it for a jay at first, but saw the narrow, swift-flying bird soon.

December 15, 1853   He[3] had ten live pigeons in a cage under his barn. He used them to attract others in the spring. The reflections from their necks were very beautiful. They made me think of shells cast up on a beach. He placed them in a cage on the bed and could hear them prate at the house. . . . The turtle doves[4] plagued him, for they were restless and frightened the pigeons.

March 19, 1854   Goodwin killed a pigeon yesterday.

July 18, 1854   Brooks has let out some of his pigeons, which stay about the stands or perches to bait others. Wild ones nest in his woods quite often. He begins to catch them the middle of August.

[1][A hill near Beaver Pond in Lincoln.]
[2][A pigeon-stand.]
[3][Mr. George Brooks of Concord.]
[4][Mourning doves.]

August 15, 1854 Crossed from top of Annursnack to top of Strawberry Hill[1] past a pigeon-bed.

*   *   *

In the meanwhile we came upon another pigeon-bed, where the pigeons were being baited, a little corn, etc., being spread on the ground, and, [as?] at the first, the bower was already erected.

September 5, 1854 Saw two pigeons, which flew about his pond and then lit on the elms over his house. He[2] said they had come to drink from Brooks's, as they often did.

September 12, 1854 I scare pigeons from Hubbard's oaks beyond. How like the creaking of trees the slight sounds they make! Thus they are concealed. Not only their *prating* or *quivet* is like a sharp creak, but I heard a sound from them like a dull grating or cracking of bough on bough.

*   *   *

On a white oak beyond Everett's orchard by the road, I see quite a flock of pigeons; their blue-black droppings and their feathers spot the road. The bare limbs of the oak apparently attracted them, though its acorns are thick on the ground. These are found whole in their crops. They swallow them whole. I should think

[1][In Acton.]
[2][Samuel Barrett, who had a sawmill and a gristmill on Spencer Brook, a tributary of the Assabet.]

from the droppings that they had been eating berries. I hear that Wetherbee caught ninety-two dozen last week.

April 16, 1855   In the meanwhile heard the *quivet* through the wood, and, looking, saw through an opening a small compact flock of pigeons flying low about.

April 26, 1855   Going over Ponkawtasset, hear a golden-crested (?) wren,[1]—the robin's note, etc.,—in the tops of the high wood; see myrtle-birds and half a dozen pigeons. The *prate* of the last is much like the creaking of a tree. They lift their wings at the same moment as they sit. There are said to be many about now. See their warm-colored breasts.

April 27, 1855   Heard a singular sort of screech, somewhat like a hawk, under the Cliff, and soon some pigeons flew out of a pine near me.

May 26, 1855   Saw a beautiful blue-backed and long-tailed pigeon sitting daintily on a low white pine limb.

September 2, 1856   A few pigeons were seen a fortnight ago. I have noticed none in all walks, but G. Minott, whose mind runs on them so much, but whose age and infirmities confine him to his wood-shed on the hillside, saw a small flock a fortnight ago. I rarely pass at any season of the year but he asks if I have seen any pigeons. One man's mind running on pigeons, he will sit thus in

---

[1][He afterwards learned that this bird with the robin-like notes in its song was the ruby-crowned wren, or kinglet, not the golden-crowned.]

the midst of a village, many of whose inhabitants never see nor dream of a pigeon except in the pot, and where even naturalists do not observe them, and he, looking out with expectation and faith from morning till night, will surely see them.

September 16, 1856   See a flock of pigeons dash by. From a stout breast they taper straightly and slenderly to the tail. They have been catching them a while.

May 14, 1857   Abel Hosmer[1] tells me that he has collected and sown white pine seed, and that he has found them in the crop of pigeons. (?)

September 30, 1857   Minott said he had seen a couple of pigeons go over at last, as he sat in his shed. At first he thought they were doves, but he soon saw that they were pigeons, they flew so straight and fast.

September 9, 1858   R.[2] says that he has caught pigeons which had ripe grapes in their crops long before any were ripe here, and that they came from the southwest.

September 13, 1858   A small dense flock of wild pigeons dashes by over the side of the hill, from west to east,—perhaps from Wetherbee's to Brooks's, for I see the latter's pigeon-place. They make a dark slate-gray impression.

[1][A Concord farmer.]
[2][Israel Rice, the Sudbury farmer.]

September 23, 1858   Met a gunner from Lynn on the beach,[1] who had several pigeons which he had killed in the woods by the shore. Said that they had been blown off the mainland.

May 7, 1859   I frequently see pigeons dashing about in small flocks, or three or four at a time, over the woods here.[2] Theirs is a peculiarly swift, dashing flight.

September 9, 1859   I start many pigeons now in a sprout-land.

September 13, 1859   It is a wonder how pigeons can swallow acorns whole, but they do.

September 14, 1859   They are catching pigeons nowadays. Coombs has a stand west of Nut Meadow, and he says that he has just shot fourteen hawks there, which were after the pigeons.

September 15, 1859   P.M.—To Annursnack.

Dense flocks of pigeons hurry-skurry over the hill. Pass near Brooks's pigeon-stands. There was a flock perched on his poles, and they sat so still and in such regular order there, being also the color of the wood, that I thought they were wooden figures at first. They were perched not only in horizontal straight lines one above the other, which the cross-bars required, but at equal distances apart on these perches, which must be their own habit; and it struck me that they made just such a figure seen against the sky as pi-

[1][On the south shore of Rockport, Mass.]
[2][In Acton, adjoining Concord on the west.]

geonholes cut in a doves' house do, *i.e.* a more or less triangular figure, and possibly the seeing them thus perched might have originally suggested this arrangement of the holes.

Pigeons dart by on every side,—a dry slate color, like weather-stained wood (the weather-stained birds), fit color for this aerial traveller, a more subdued and earthy blue than the sky, as its field (or path) is between the sky and the earth,—not black or brown, as is the earth, but a terrene or slaty blue, suggesting their aerial resorts and habits.

September 21, 1859 I sat near Coombs's pigeon-place by White Pond. The pigeons sat motionless on his bare perches, from time to time dropping down into the bed and uttering a *quivet* or two. Some stood on the perch; others squatted flat. I could see their dove-colored breasts. Then all at once, being alarmed, would take flight, but ere long return in straggling parties. He tells me that he has fifteen dozen baited, but does not intend to catch any more at present, or for two or three weeks, hoping to attract others. Rice says that white oak acorns pounded up, shells and all, make the best bait for them.

September 28, 1859 The white pine seed is very abundant this year, and this must attract more pigeons. Coombs tells me that he finds the seed in their crops. Also that he found within a day or two a full-formed egg with shell in one.

November 8, 1859 Coombs says that quite a little flock of pigeons bred here last summer. He found one nest in a small white pine near his pigeon-stand (where he baited them in the summer), so low he could put his hand in it (!?).

January 23, 1860 Minott says that pigeons alight in great flocks on the tops of hemlocks in March, and he thinks they eat the seed. (But he also thought for the same reason that they ate the white pine seed at the same season, when it is not there! They might find a little of the last adhering to the pitch.)

June 14, 1860 See a pigeon.[1]

September 4, 1860 Saw flocks of pigeons the 2d and 3d.

MOURNING DOVE
(TURTLE DOVE)

July 12, 1852 The turtle dove flutters before you in shady wood-paths, or looks out with extended neck, losing its balance, slow to leave its perch.

September 27, 1852 It must have been a turtle dove that eyed me so near, turned its head sideways to me for a fair view, looking with a St. Vitus twitching of its neck, as if to recover its balance on an unstable perch,—that is their way.

May 27, 1858 Ed. Emerson[2] shows me an egg of a bittern (*Ardea minor*) from a nest in the midst of the Great Meadows, which four boys found, scaring up the bird, last Monday, the 24th.

[1][In the western part of Concord.]
[2][Edward Waldo Emerson, son of Ralph Waldo Emerson, then a boy of thirteen.]

It was about a foot wide on the top of a tussock, where the water around was about one foot deep. I will measure the egg.[1] They were a little developed. Also an egg of a turtle dove, one of two in a nest in a pitch pine, about six feet from the ground, in Sleepy Hollow Cemetery, by the side of a frequented walk, on a fork on a nearly horizontal limb. The egg is milk-white, elliptical, one and three sixteenths inches long by seven eighths wide.

May 28, 1858   I get the nest of the turtle dove above named, it being deserted and no egg left. It appears to have been built on the foundation of an old robin's nest and consists of a loose wisp of straw and pinweed, the seedy ends projecting, ten inches long, laid across the mud foundation of the robin's nest, with a very slight depression. Very loose and coarse material is artificially disposed, without any lining or architecture. It was close to a frequented path of the cemetery and within reach of the hand.

December 30, 1860   Eben Conant's sons tell me that there has been a turtle dove associating with their tame doves and feeding in the yard from time to time for a fortnight past. They saw it to-day.

[1]It is clay-colored, one and seven eighths inches long by one and nine sixteenths, about the same size at each end.

Eight

HAWKS
EAGLES

MARSH HAWK
(FROG HAWK)
(HEN-HARRIER)

April 24, 1852   The sparrows, frogs, rabbits, etc., are made to resemble the ground for their protection; but so is the hawk that preys on them; but he is of a lighter color beneath, that creeping things over which he hovers may confound him with the sky. The marsh hawk is not easily distinguished from the meadow or the stems of the maples.

July 29, 1853   I see three or four (apparently) young marsh hawks, but full grown, circling and tumbling about not much above the ground and playing with one another. They are quite a reddish brown. They utter a squeak (not a shrill scream), much like a small bird or animal.

April 23, 1855   See a frog hawk beating the bushes regularly. What a peculiarly formed wing! It should be called the kite. Its wings are very narrow and pointed, and its form in front is a remarkable curve, and its body is not heavy and buzzard-like. It occasionally hovers over some parts of the meadow or hedge and circles back over it, only rising enough from time to time to clear the trees and fences.

May 14, 1855   See a male hen-harrier skimming low along the side of the river, often within a foot of the muddy shore, looking for frogs, with a very compact flock of small birds, probably swallows, in pursuit. Occasionally he alights and walks or hops flutteringly a foot or two over the ground.

November 5, 1855   At Hubbard's Crossing I see a large male hen-harrier skimming over the meadow, its deep slate somewhat sprinkled or mixed with black; perhaps young. It flaps a little and then sails straight forward, so low it must rise at every fence. But I perceive that it follows the windings of the meadow over many fences.

April 8, 1856   The marsh hawks[1] flew in their usual irregular low tacking, wheeling, and circling flight, leisurely flapping and beating, now rising, now falling, in conformity with the contour of the ground. The last I think I have seen on the same beat in former years. He and his race must be well acquainted with the Musketicook and its meadows. No sooner is the snow off than he is back to his old haunts, scouring that part of the meadows that is

---

[1][Two seen that afternoon.]

bare, while the rest is melting. If he returns from so far to these meadows, shall the sons of Concord be leaving them at this season for slight cause?

April 22, 1856   A marsh hawk, in the midst of the rain, is skimming along the shore of the meadow, close to the ground, and, though not more than thirty rods off, I repeatedly lose sight of it, it is so nearly the color of the hillside beyond. It is looking for frogs.

May 20, 1856   Two marsh hawks, male and female, flew about me a long time, screaming,—the female largest, with ragged wings,—as I stood on the neck of the peninsula. This induced me to climb four pines, but I tore my clothes, got pitched all over, and found only a squirrel; yet they have, no doubt, a nest thereabouts.[1]

May 14, 1857   See a pair of marsh hawks, the smaller and lighter-colored male, with black tips to wings, and the large brown female, sailing low over J. Hosmer's sprout-land and screaming, apparently looking for frogs or the like. Or have they not a nest near? They hover very near me. The female, now so near, sails very grandly, with the outer wing turned or tilted up when it circles, and the bars on its tail when it turns, etc., reminding me of a great brown moth. Sometimes alone; and when it approaches its mate it utters a low, grating note like *cur-r-r*. Suddenly the female holds

---

[1][Later, as will be seen, he learned that marsh hawks' nests are not to be looked for in trees.]

straight toward me, descending gradually. Steadily she comes on, without swerving, until only two rods off, then wheels.

October 28, 1857   I look up and see a male marsh hawk with his clean-cut wings, that has just skimmed past above my head,—not at all disturbed, only tilting his body a little, now twenty rods off, with demi-semi-quaver of his wings. He is a very neat flyer.

April 19, 1858   Spend the day hunting for my boat, which was stolen. As I go up the riverside, I see a male marsh hawk hunting. He skims along exactly over the edge of the water, on the meadowy side, not more than three or four feet from the ground and winding with the shore, looking for frogs, for in such a tortuous line do the frogs sit. They probably know about what time to expect his visits, being regularly decimated. Particular hawks farm particular meadows. It must be easy for him to get a breakfast. Far as I can see with a glass, he is still tilting this way and that over the water-line.

May 2, 1858   If I were to be a frog hawk for a month I should soon know some things about the frogs. How patiently they skim the meadows, occasionally alighting, and fluttering as if it were difficult ever to stand still on the ground. I have seen more of them than usual since I too have been looking for frogs.

May 30, 1858   P.M.—To hen-harrier's nest and to Ledum Swamp.

Edward Emerson shows me the nest which he and another

discovered. It is in the midst of the low wood, sometimes inundated, just southwest of Hubbard's Bath, the island of wood in the meadow. The hawk rises when we approach and circles about over the wood, uttering a note singularly like the common one of the flicker. The nest is in a more bushy or open place in this low wood, and consists of a large mass of sedge and stubble with a very few small twigs, as it were accidentally intermingled. It is about twenty inches in diameter and remarkably flat, the slight depression in the middle not exceeding three quarters of an inch. The whole opening amid the low bushes is not more than two feet in diameter. The thickness of it raises the surface about four inches above the ground. The inner and upper part is uniformly rather fine and pale-brown sedge. There are two dirty, or rather dirtied, white eggs left (of four that were), one of them one and seven tenths inches long, and not "spherical," as Brewer says, but broad in proportion to length.[1]

June 8, 1858 The marsh hawk's eggs are not yet hatched. She rises when I get within a rod and utters that peculiar cackling or scolding note, much like, but distinct from, that of the pigeon woodpecker. She keeps circling over the nest and repeatedly stoops within a rod of my head in an angry manner. She is not so large as a hen-hawk, and is much more slender. She will come sailing

---

[1]Another is one and seven eighths inches long by one and a half inches.

swiftly and low over the tops of the trees and bushes, etc., and then stoop as near to my head as she dares, in order to scare me away. The primaries, of which I count but five, are very long and loose, or distant, like fingers with which she takes hold of the air, and form a very distinct part of the wing, making an angle with the rest. Yet they are not broad and give to the wing a long and slender appearance. The legs are stretched straight back under the tail.[1] I see nothing of the male, nor did I before. A red-wing and a kingbird are soon in pursuit of the hawk, which proves, I think, that she meddles with their nests or themselves. She circles over me, scolding, as far as the edge of the wood, or fifteen rods.

June 17, 1858 P.M.—To hawk's nest.

One egg is hatched since the 8th, and the young bird, all down, with a tinge of fawn or cinnamon, lies motionless on its breast with its head down and is already about four inches long! An hour or two after, I see the old hawk pursue a stake-driver which was flying over this spot, darting down at him and driving him off.

August 8, 1858 Saw yesterday a this year's (?) marsh hawk, female, flying low across the road near Hildreth's. I took it to be a young bird, it came so near and looked so fresh. It is a fine rich-brown, full-breasted bird, with a long tail. Some hens in the grass

---

[1][This is the habitual manner of carrying the legs in flight among the birds of prey and some other orders. See Dr. C. W. Townsend's paper in the *Auk*, April, 1909, vol. xxvi, p. 109.]

beneath were greatly alarmed and began to run and fly with a cackling to the shelter of a corn-field. They which did not see the hawk
and were the last to stir expressed the most alarm. Meanwhile the
hawk sails low and steadily over the field away, not thinking of disturbing them.

October 9, 1858 Methinks hawks are more commonly seen
now,—the slender marsh hawk for one. I see four or five in different places. I watch two marsh hawks which rise from the woods
before me as I sit on the Cliff, at first plunging at each other, gradually lifting themselves as they come round in their gyrations,
higher and higher, and floating toward the southeast. Slender dark
motes they are at last, almost lost to sight, but every time they
come round eastward I see the light of the westering sun reflected
from the under sides of their wings.

November 20, 1858 He[1] says that a marsh hawk had his nest
in his meadow several years, and though he shot the female three
times, the male with but little delay returned with a new mate. He
often watched these birds, and saw that the female could tell when
the male was coming a long way off. He thought that he fed her and
the young all together (?). She would utter a scream when she perceived him, and, rising into the air (before or after the scream?), she
turned over with her talons uppermost, while he passed some three

[1][Martial Miles, a Concord farmer.]

rods above, and caught without fail the prey which he let drop, and then carried it to her young. He had seen her do this many times, and always without failing.

March 24, 1860   I see a male frog hawk beating a hedge, scarcely rising more than two feet from the ground for half a mile, quite below the level of the wall within it. How unlike the hen-hawk in this!

May 8, 1860   How the marsh hawk circles or skims low, round and round over a particular place in a meadow, where, perhaps, it has seen a frog, screaming once or twice, and then alights on a fence-post! How it crosses the causeway between the willows, at a gap in them with which it is familiar, as a hen knows a hole in a fence! I lately saw one flying over the road near our house.

May 29, 1860   We next proceeded to the marsh hawk's nest from which the eggs were taken a fortnight ago and the female shot. It was in a long and narrow cassandra swamp northwest of the lime-kiln and some thirty rods from the road, on the side of a small and more open area some two rods across, where were few if any bushes and more [?] sedge with the cassandra. The nest was on a low tussock, and about eighteen inches across, made of dead birch twigs around and a pitch pine plume or two, and sedge grass at bottom, with a small cavity in the middle.

The female was shot and eggs taken on the 16th; yet here was the male, hovering anxiously over the spot and neighborhood and scolding at us. Betraying himself from time to time by that peculiar *clacking* note reminding you of a pigeon woodpecker. We thought it likely that he had already got another mate and a new nest near by. He would not quite withdraw though fired at, but still would return and circle near us. They are said to find a new mate very soon.

July 3, 1860   Looked for the marsh hawk's nest (of June 16th) in the Great Meadows.[1] It was in the very midst of the sweet-gale (which is three feet high), occupying an opening only a foot or two across. We had much difficulty in finding it again, but at last nearly stumbled on to a young hawk. There was one as big as my fist, resting on the bare, flat nest in the sun, with a great head, staring eyes, and open gaping or panting mouth, yet mere down, grayish-white down, as yet; but I detected another which had crawled a foot one side amid the bushes for shade or safety, more than half as large again, with small feathers and a yet more angry, hawk-like look. How naturally anger sits on the young hawk's head! It was 3.30 P.M., and the old birds were gone and saw us not. Meanwhile their callow young lie panting under the sweet-gale and rose bushes in the swamp, waiting for their parents to fetch them food.

SHARP-SHINNED HAWK

May 4, 1855   Sitting in Abel Brooks's Hollow, see a small hawk go over high in the air, with a long tail and distinct

[1][This was another nest than that described under May 29.]

from wings. It advanced by a sort of limping flight yet rapidly, not circling nor tacking, but flapping briskly at intervals and then gliding straight ahead with rapidity, controlling itself with its tail. It seemed to be going a journey. Was it not the sharp-shinned, or *Falco fuscus?*[1]

July 21, 1858 P.M.—To Walden, with E. Bartlett and E. Emerson.

The former wished to show me what he thought an owl's nest he had found. Near it, in Abel Brooks's wood-lot, heard a note and saw a small hawk fly over. It was the nest of this bird. Saw several of the young flitting about and occasionally an old bird. The nest was in a middling-sized white pine, some twenty feet from the ground, resting on two limbs close to the main stem, on the south side of it. It was quite solid, composed entirely of twigs about as big round as a pipe-stem and less; was some fifteen inches in diameter and one inch deep, or nearly flat, and perhaps five inches thick. It was very much dirtied on the sides by the droppings of the young. As we were standing about the tree, we heard again the note of a young one approaching. We dropped upon the ground, and it alighted on the edge of the nest; another alighted near by, and a third a little further off. The young were apparently as big as the old, but still lingered about the nest and returned to it. I could hear them coming some distance off. Their note was a kind of peeping

[1][The sharp-shinned hawk is now known as *Accipiter velox.*]

squeal, which you might at first suspect to be made by a jay; not very loud, but as if to attract the old and reveal their whereabouts. The note of the old bird, which occasionally dashed past, was somewhat like that of the marsh hawk or pigeon woodpecker, a cackling or clattering sound, chiding us. The old bird was anxious about her inexperienced young, and was trying to get them off. At length she dashed close past us, and appeared to fairly strike one of the young, knocking him off his perch, and he soon followed her off. I saw the remains of several birds lying about in that neighborhood, and saw and heard again the young and old thereabouts for several days thereafter. A young man killed one of the young hawks, and I saw it. It was the *Falco fuscus*, the American brown or slate-colored hawk. Its length was thirteen inches; alar extent, twenty-three. The tail reached two or more inches beyond the closed wings. Nuttall says the upper parts are "a deep slate-color" (these were very dark brown); also that the nest is yet unknown. But Wilson describes his *F. velox* (which is the same as Nuttall's *F. fuscus*) as "whole upper parts very dark brown," but legs, greenish-yellow (these were yellow). The toes had the peculiar pendulous lobes which W. refers to. As I saw it in the woods, I was struck by its dark color above, its tawny throat and breast, brown-spotted, its clean, slender, long yellow legs, feathered but little below the knee, its white vent, its wings distinctly and rather finely dark-barred beneath, short, black, much curved bill, and slender black sharp claws. Its tail with a dark bar near edge beneath. In hand I found it had the white spots on scapulars of the *F. fuscus*, and had not the white bars on tail of the *F. Pennsylvanicus*.[1] It also had the fine sharp shin.

COOPER'S HAWK

May 29, 1860 We proceeded to the Cooper's hawk nest in an oak and pine wood (Clark's) north of Ponkawtasset. I found a fragment of one of the eggs which he[2] had thrown out. Farmer's egg, by the way, was a dull or dirty white, *i.e.* a rough white with large dirty spots, perhaps in the grain, but not surely, of a regular oval form and a little larger than his marsh hawk's egg. I climbed to the nest, some thirty to thirty-five feet high in a white pine, against the main stem. It was a mass of bark-fibre and sticks about two and a half feet long by eighteen inches wide and sixteen high. The lower and main portion was a solid mass of fine bark-fibre such as a red squirrel uses. This was surrounded and surmounted by a quantity of dead twigs of pine and oak, etc., generally the size of a pipe-stem or less. The concavity was very slight, not more than an inch and a half, and there was nothing soft for a lining, the bark-fibres being several inches beneath the twigs, but the bottom was floored for a diameter of six inches or more with flakes of white oak and pitch pine bark one or two inches long each,

[1] [The broad-winged hawk, now called *Buteo platypterus*.]
[2] [Jacob Farmer, who had found the nest and shot the female hawk May 16, saving one of the eggs.]

a good handful of them, and on this the eggs had lain. We saw nothing of the hawk.

RED–TAILED HAWK
(HEN–HAWK)

March 26, 1853   Up the Assabet, scared from his perch a stout hawk,—the red-tailed undoubtedly, for I saw very plainly the cow-red when he spread his wings from off his tail (and rump?). I rowed the boat three times within gunshot before he flew, twice within four rods, while he sat on an oak over the water,—I think because I had two ladies with me, which was as good as bushing the boat. Each time, or twice at least, he made a motion to fly before he started. The ends of his primaries looked very ragged against the sky. This is the hen-hawk of the farmer, the same, probably, which I have scared off from the Cliff so often. It was an interesting eagle-like object, as he sat upright on his perch with his back to us, now and then looking over his shoulder, the broad-backed, flat-headed, curve-beaked bird.

April 4, 1853   At Conantum End I saw a red-tailed hawk launch himself away from an oak by the pond at my approach,—a heavy flier, flapping even like the great bittern at first,—heavy forward.

April 30, 1855   I hear from far the scream of a hawk circling over the Holden woods and swamp. This accounts for those two men with guns just entering it. What a dry, shrill, angry scream! I see the bird with my glass resting upon the topmost plume of a tall white pine. Its back, reflecting the light, looks white in patches; and now it circles again. It is a red-tailed hawk. The tips of its wings are curved upward as it sails. How it scolds at the men beneath! I see its open bill. It must have a nest there. Hark! there goes a gun, and down it tumbles from a rod or two above the wood. So I thought, but was mistaken. In the meanwhile, I learn that there is a nest there, and the gunners killed one this morning, which I examined. They are now getting the young. Above it was brown, but not at all reddish-brown except about head. Above perhaps I should call it brown, and a dirty white beneath; wings above thickly barred with darker, and also wings beneath. The tail of twelve reddish feathers, once black-barred near the end. The feet pale-yellow and very stout, with srong, sharp black claws. The head and neck were remarkably stout, and the beak short and curved from the base. Powerful neck and legs. The claws pricked me as I handled it. It measured one yard and three eighths plus from tip to tip, *i.e.* four feet and two inches. Some ferruginous on the neck; ends of wings nearly black.

May 1, 1855   Went to Garfield's for the hawk of yesterday. It was nailed to the barn *in terrorem* and as a trophy. He gave it to me with an egg. He called it the female, and probably was right, it was so large. He tried in vain to shoot the male, which I saw circling about just out of gunshot and screaming, while he robbed the nest. He climbed the tree when I was there yesterday afternoon, the tallest white pine or other tree in its neighborhood, over a swamp, and found two young, which he thought not more than a fortnight old,—with only down, at least no feathers,—and one addled egg, also three or four white-bellied or deer mouse (*Mus leucopus*[1]), a perch, and a sucker,[2] and a gray rabbit's skin. He had seen squirrels, etc., in other nests. These fishes were now stale. I found the remains of a partridge under the tree. The reason I did not see my hawks at Well Meadow last year was that he found and broke up their nest there, containing five eggs.

The hawk measures exactly 22½ inches in length and 4 feet 4½ inches in alar extent, and weighs 3¼ pounds. The ends of closed wings almost two inches short of end of tail. General color *above* of wings and back an olivaceous brown, thickly barred with waving lines of very dark brown, there being a much broader bar next to the tip of the secondaries and tertiaries; and the first five primaries are nearly black toward the ends. A little white appears, especially on the tertiaries. The wing-coverts and scapulars glossed with purple reflections. The twelve tail-feathers (which MacGillivray says is the number in all birds of prey, *i.e.* the *Falconinæ* and *Striginæ*) showing five and three quarters inches a clear brown red, or rather fox-color, above, with a narrow dark band within half an inch of the end, which is tipped with dirty white. A slight

---

[1] [Now known as *Peromyscus leucopus noveboracensis*.]
[2] I think these must have been dead fish they found.

inclination to dusky bars near the end of one side feather. Lower tail-coverts for nearly an inch white, barred with fox-color. Head and neck a paler, inclining to ferruginous, brown. *Beneath:* Breast and wing-linings brown and white, the feathers of first centred with large dark-brown hastate spots, and the wing-linings streaked with ferruginous. Wings white, barred with dusky. "Vent and femorals," as Nuttall says, "pale ochreous." Tail white, softened by the superior color. I do not perceive that the abdomen is barred.

Bill very *blue* black, with a *short, stout* curved tip,—curving from the cere more than a quarter of a circle, extends not quite a quarter of an inch beyond the lower mandible,—and is proportionally stouter *at tip* than in any of *his Falconinæ*, judging from plates of heads; whole visible, including cere, $1\frac{1}{8}$ inches long, and 1 inch deep at base; cere yellowish-green.

Tarsus and toes very pale yellow; claws blue-black. As MacGillivray says of *Buteo*, claws flattened beneath, "that of the middle toe with an inner sharp edge." (He says, as I *gather*, that all the diurnal birds of prey of Great Britain, *i.e. Falconinæ*, have claws either flattened or concave beneath, except *Pandion*, the inner edge of the middle one being more or less sharp, but least so in *Circus*, or harrier.) Tarsus feathered in front one third the way down. The toes for length stand in this order,—the first (or hind), second, fourth, third, the first being the shortest; for stoutness thus,—one, two, three, four. Claws for stoutness follow the same order with the toes. Utmost spread of toes and claws 4½ inches. A considerable web between third and fourth toes.[1] Toes with papillæ not rigid beneath.

The wing extends nearly two feet from the body, and is 10¾ inches wide; from flexure is 15¾ inches. When fully expanded it has a rounded outline and a ragged appearance owing to the separation of the first five or six primaries, as I noticed the male bird while resting. The first primary short; they stand, first and eighth, seventh, sixth, second, fifth, third, fourth. The fifth and third are about the same length, and the fourth only a quarter of an inch longer than the third. As in the *Buteo vulgaris* of MacGillivray, found in Europe and in our north, the four first primaries "abruptly cut out on the inner web"; the second, third, fourth, and fifth, but *not* the first and sixth, "slightly so on the outer." There are ten primaries and there are fourteen secondaries. (MacGillivray says the primaries of the *Falconinæ* are ten, the secondaries from thirteen to eighteen.) The wing, I see, naturally opens at the primaries.

This is evidently very closely allied to the *Buteo vulgaris*, but apparently the wings are not so long compared with the tail, and there is a difference in the comparative length and stoutness of the toes; the feet of this are not "*bright* yellow," and the upper mandible

---

[1] In this respect *Circus* and *Falco* much the same; *Aquila* and *Pernis* and *Milvus* have several short webs; *Haliaëtus*, *Pandion*, and *Accipiter* are free.

is much stouter and more recurved at tip, judging from his plate of the head and his description. It is recurved as much as his osprey's.

The ear looked like a large round hole in the side of the head behind the eye.

The egg is a very dirty brownish white, with brown spots about the smaller end, though one end is about as large as the other. It is larger than a hen's egg,—2⅜ inches by 2.

*　　*　　*

Early in spring I occasionally see hen-hawks perched about river, and approach quite near them, but never at any other time.

This hawk's flesh had a very disagreeable rank scent, as I was cutting it up, though fresh,—cutting off the wings, etc., etc.

September 14, 1855 P.M.—To Hubbard's Close.

I scare from an oak by the side of the Close a young hen-hawk, which, launching off with a scream and a heavy flight, alights on the topmost plume of a large pitch pine in the swamp northward, bending it down, with its back toward me, where it might be mistaken for a plume against the sky, the light makes all things so black. It has a red tail; black primaries; scapulars and wing-coverts gray-brown; back showing much white and whitish head. It keeps looking round, first this side then that, warily.

October 28, 1857 I hear the scream of a hen-hawk, soaring and circling onward. I do not often see the marsh hawk thus. What a regular figure this fellow makes on high, with his broad tail and broad wings! Does he perceive me, that he rises higher and circles to one side? He goes round now one full circle without a flap, tilting his wing a little; then flaps three or four times and rises higher. Now he comes on like a billow, screaming. Steady as a planet in its orbit, with his head bent down, but on second thought that small sprout-land seems worthy of a longer scrutiny, and he gives one circle backward over it. His scream is somewhat like the whinnering of a horse, if it is not rather a *split squeal.*[1] It is a hoarse, tremulous breathing forth of his winged energy. But why is it so regularly repeated at that height? Is it to scare his prey, that he may see by its motion where it is, or to inform its mate or companion of its whereabouts? Now he crosses the at present broad river steadily, deserving to have one or two rabbits at least to swing about him. What majesty there is in this small bird's flight! The hawks are large-souled.

March 23, 1859 As we entered Well Meadow, we saw a hen-hawk perch on the topmost plume of one of the tall pines at the head of the meadow. Soon another appeared, probably its mate, but we looked in vain for a nest there. It was a fine sight, their soaring above our heads, presenting a perfect outline and, as they came round, showing their rust-colored tails with a whitish rump, or, as they sailed away from us, that slight teetering or quivering motion

[1][The note described is evidently that of the red-tailed hawk rather than that of the other "hen-hawk," the red-shouldered.]

of their dark-tipped wings seen edgewise, now on this side, now that, by which they balanced and directed themselves. These are

the most eagle-like of our common hawks. They very commonly perch upon the very topmost plume of a pine, and, if motionless, are rather hard to distinguish there.

HEN-HAWKS
(SPECIES UNIDENTIFIED)[1]

September 7, 1851 There were two hen-hawks soared and circled for our entertainment, when we were in the woods on that Boon Plain[2] the other day, crossing each other's or-

[1][The term "hen-hawk" is applied in New England ordinarily to the large buzzard hawks, or buteos,—the red-tailed hawk (*Buteo borealis*) and the red-shouldered hawk (*B. lineatus*). Thoreau, however, seems never to have identified the latter species except in the case of a dead bird brought to him Jan. 12, 1859, and Mr. William Brewster, the ornithologist, who has known the Concord country intimately for many years, informs the editor that the red-tailed hawk was up to about 1888 the common hen-hawk there, though it is now almost entirely superseded by the red-shouldered. It seems probable, therefore, that most of Thoreau's hen-hawks were red-tails, as was certainly the case with many which he describes.]

[2][In Stow, Mass., near Concord.]

bits from time to time, alternating like the squirrels of the morning,[1] till, alarmed by our imitation of a hawk's shrill cry, they gradually inflated themselves, made themselves more aerial, and rose higher and higher into the heavens, and were at length lost to sight; yet all the while earnestly looking, scanning the surface of the earth for a stray mouse or rabbit.

June 8, 1853   As I stood by this pond, I heard a hawk scream, and, looking up, saw a pretty large one circling not far off and incessantly screaming, as I at first supposed to scare and so discover its prey, but its screaming was so incessant and it circled from time to time so near me, as I moved southward, that I began to think it had a nest near by and was angry at my intrusion into its domains. As I moved, the bird still followed and screamed, coming sometimes quite near or within gunshot, then circling far off or high into the sky. At length, as I was looking up at it, thinking it the only living creature within view, I was singularly startled to behold, as my eye by chance penetrated deeper into the blue,—the abyss of blue above, which I had taken for a solitude,—its mate silently soaring at an immense height and seemingly indifferent to me. We are surprised to discover that there can be an eye on us on that side, and so little suspected,—that the heavens are full of eyes, though they look so blue and spotless. Then I knew it was the female that circled and screamed below. At last the latter rose gradu-

---

[1] [Two caged squirrels revolving their cylinder alternately.]

ally to meet her mate, and they circled together there, as if they could not possibly feel any anxiety on my account. When I drew nearer to the tall trees where I suspected the nest to be, the female descended again, swept by screaming still nearer to me just over the tree-tops, and finally, while I was looking for the orchis in the swamp, alighted on a white pine twenty or thirty rods off. (The great fringed orchis just open.) At length I detected the nest about eighty feet from the ground, in a very large white pine by the edge of the swamp. It was about three feet in diameter, of dry sticks, and a young hawk, apparently as big as its mother, stood on the edge of the nest looking down at me, and only moving its head when I moved. In its imperfect plumage and by the slow motion of its head it reminded me strongly of a vulture, so large and gaunt. It appeared a tawny brown on its neck and breast, and dark brown or blackish on wings. The mother was light beneath, and apparently lighter still on rump.

June 9, 1853 I have come with a spy-glass to look at the hawks. They have detected me and are already screaming over my head more than half a mile from the nest. I find no difficulty in looking at the young hawk (there appears to be one only, standing on the edge of the nest), resting the glass in the crotch of a young oak. I can see every wink and the color of its iris. It watches me more steadily than I it, now looking straight down at me with both eyes and outstretched neck, now turning its head and looking with one eye. How its eye and its whole head express anger! Its anger is more in its eye than in its beak. It is quite hoary over the eye and on the chin. The mother meanwhile is incessantly circling about and above its charge and me, farther or nearer, sometimes withdrawing a quarter of a mile, but occasionally coming to alight for a moment almost within gunshot, on the top of a tall white pine; but I hardly bring my glass fairly to bear on her, and get sight of her angry eye through the pine-needles, before she circles away again. Thus for an hour that I lay there, screaming every minute or oftener with open bill. Now and then pursued by a kingbird or a blackbird, who appear merely to annoy it by dashing down at its back. Meanwhile the male is soaring, apparently quite undisturbed, at a great height above, evidently not hunting, but amusing or recreating himself in the thinner and cooler air, as if pleased with his own circles, like a geometer, and enjoying the sublime scene. I doubt if he has his eye fixed on any prey, or the earth. He probably descends to hunt.

June 12, 1853 I forgot to say that I visited my hawk's nest, and the young hawk was perched now four or five feet above the nest, still in the shade. It will soon fly. Now, then, in secluded pine woods, the young hawks sit high on the edges of their nests or on the twigs near by in the shade, waiting for their pinions to grow, while their parents bring to them their prey. Their silence also is remarkable, not to betray themselves, nor will the old bird go to the nest while you are in sight. She pursues me half a mile when I withdraw.

June 13, 1853 9 A.M.—To Orchis Swamp.

Find that there are two young hawks; one has left the nest and is perched on a small maple seven or eight rods distant. This one appears much smaller than the former one. I am struck by its large, naked head, so vulture-like, and large eyes, as if the vulture's were an inferior stage through which the hawk passed. Its feet, too, are large, remarkably developed, by which it holds to its perch securely like an old bird, before its wings can perform their office. It has a buff breast, striped with dark brown. Pratt, when I told him of this nest, said he would like to carry one of his rifles down there. But I told him that I should be sorry to have them killed. I would rather save one of these hawks than have a hundred hens and chickens. It was worth more to see them soar, especially now that they are so rare in the landscape. It is easy to buy eggs, but not to buy hen-hawks. My neighbors would not hesitate to shoot the last pair of hen-hawks in the town to save a few of their chickens! But such economy is narrow and grovelling. It is unnecessarily to sacrifice the greater value to the less. I would rather never taste chickens' meat nor hens' eggs than never to see a hawk sailing through the upper air again. This sight is worth incomparably more than a chicken soup or a boiled egg. So we exterminate the deer and substitute the hog. It was amusing to observe the swaying to and fro of the young hawk's head to counterbalance the gentle motion of the bough in the wind.

May 4, 1858 As I sit there by the swamp-side this warm summery afternoon, I hear the crows cawing hoarsely, and from time to time see one flying toward the top of a tall white pine. At length I distinguish a hen-hawk perched on the top. The crow repeatedly stoops toward him, now from this side, now from that, passing near his head each time, but he pays not the least attention to it.

November 9, 1858 Now the young hen-hawks, full-grown but inexperienced, still white-breasted and brown (not red)-tailed, swoop down after the farmer's hens, between the barn and the house, often carrying one off in their clutches, and all the rest of the pack half fly, half run, to the barn. Unwarrantably bold, one ventures to stoop before the farmer's eyes. He clutches in haste his trusty gun, which hangs, ready loaded, on its pegs; he pursues warily to where the marauder sits teetering on a lofty pine, and when he is sailing scornfully away he meets his fate and comes fluttering head forward to earth. The exulting farmer hastes to secure his trophy. He treats the proud bird's body with indignity. He carries it home to show to his wife and children, for the hens were his wife's special care. He thinks it one of his best shots, full thirteen rods. This gun is "an *all-fired* good piece"—nothing but robin-shot. The body of the victim is delivered up to the children and the dog and, like the body of Hector, is dragged so many times round Troy.

But alas for the youthful hawk, the proud bird of prey, the tenant of the skies! We shall no more see his wave-like outline against a cloud, nor hear his scream from behind one. He saw but a pheasant in the field, the food which nature has provided for him, and stooped to seize it. This was his offense. He, the native of these skies, must make way for those bog-trotters from another land, which never soar. The eye that was conversant with sublimity, that looked down on earth from under its sharp projecting brow, is closed; the head that was never made dizzy by any height is brought low; the feet that were not made to walk on earth now lie useless along it. With those trailing claws for grapnels it dragged the lower sky. Those wings which swept the sky must now dust the chimney-corner, perchance. So weaponed, with strong beak and talons, and wings, like a war-steamer, to carry them about. In vain were the brown-spotted eggs laid, in vain were ye cradled in the loftiest pine of the swamp. Where are your father and mother? Will they hear of your early death? before ye had acquired your full plumage, they who nursed and defended ye so faithfully?

November 11, 1858　The tail-coverts of the young hen-hawk, *i.e.* this year's bird, at present are white, very handsomely barred or watered with dark brown in an irregular manner, somewhat as

above, the bars on opposite sides of the midrib alternating in an agreeable manner. Such natural objects have suggested the "watered" figures or colors in the arts. Few mortals ever look down on the tail-coverts of a young hen-hawk, yet these are not only beautiful, but of a peculiar beauty, being differently marked and colored (to judge from Wilson's account of the old) from those of the old bird. Thus she finishes her works above men's sight.

January 12, 1859 Farmer says that he saw what he calls the common hen-hawk, one soaring high with apparently a chicken in its claws, while a young hawk circled beneath, when former suddenly let drop the chicken, but the young failing to catch, he shot down like lightning and caught and bore off the falling chicken before it reached the earth.

February 16, 1859 The hen-hawk and the pine are friends. The same thing which keeps the hen-hawk in the woods, away from the cities, keeps me here. That bird settles with confidence on a white pine top and not upon your weathercock. That bird will not be poultry of yours, lays no eggs for you, forever hides its nest. Though willed, or *wild*, it is not willful in its wildness. The unsympathizing man regards the wildness of some animals, their strangeness to him, as a sin; as if all their virtue consisted in their tamableness. He has always a charge in his gun ready for their extermination. What we call wildness is a civilization other than our own. The hen-hawk shuns the farmer, but it seeks the friendly shelter and support of the pine. It will not consent to walk in the barn-yard, but it loves to soar above the clouds. It has its own way and is beautiful, when we would fain subject it to our will. So any surpassing work of art is strange and wild to the mass of men, as is genius itself. No hawk that soars and steals our poultry is wilder than genius, and none is more persecuted or above persecution. It can never be poet laureate, to say "Pretty Poll" and "Polly want a cracker."

March 15, 1860 A hen-hawk sails away from the wood southward. I get a very fair sight of it sailing overhead. What a perfectly regular and neat outline it presents! an easily recognized figure anywhere. Yet I never see it represented in any books. The exact correspondence of the marks on one side to those on the other, as the black or dark tip of one wing to the other, and the dark line midway the wing. I have no idea that one can get as correct an idea of the form and color of the under sides of a hen-hawk's wings by spreading those of a dead specimen in his study as by looking up at a free and living hawk soaring above him in the fields. The penalty for obtaining a petty knowledge thus dishonestly is that it is less interesting to men generally, as it is less significant. Some, seeing and admiring the neat figure of the hawk sailing two or three hundred feet above their heads, wish to get nearer and hold it in their hands, perchance, not realizing that they can see it best at this distance, better now, perhaps, than ever they will again. What is an eagle in captivity, screaming in a courtyard? I am not the wiser respecting eagles for having seen one there. I do not wish to know the length of its entrails.

How neat and all compact this hawk! Its wings and body are all one piece, the wings apparently the greater part, while its body is a mere fullness or protuberance between its wings, an inconspicuous pouch hung there. It suggests no insatiable maw, no corpulence, but looks like a larger moth, with little body in proportion to its wings, its body naturally more etherealized as it soars higher.

These hawks, as usual, begin to be common about the first of March, showing that they were returning from their winter quarters.

April 22, 1860 See now hen-hawks, a pair, soaring high as for pleasure, circling ever further and further away, as if it were midsummer. The peculiar flight of a hawk thus fetches the year about. I do not see it soar in this serene and leisurely manner very early in the season, methinks.

ROUGH-LEGGED HAWK

March 29, 1858 As I sit two thirds the way up the sunny side of the pine hill, looking over the meadows, which are now almost completely bare, the crows, by their swift flight and scolding, reveal to me some large bird of prey hovering over the river. I perceive by its markings and size that it cannot be a hen-hawk, and now it settles on the topmost branch of a white maple, bending it down. Its great armed and feathered legs dangle helplessly in the air for a moment, as if feeling for the perch, while its body is tipping this way and that. It sits there facing me some forty or fifty rods off, pluming itself but keeping a good lookout. At this distance and in this light, it appears to have a rusty-brown head and breast and is white beneath, with rusty leg-feathers and a tail black beneath. When it flies again it is principally black varied with white, regular light spots on its tail and wings beneath, but chiefly a conspicuous white space on the forward part of the back; also some of the upper side of the tail or tail-coverts is white. It has broad, ragged, buzzard-like wings, and from the white of its back, as well as the shape and shortness of its wings and its not having a gull-like body, I think it must be an eagle.[1] It lets itself down with its legs somewhat helplessly dangling, as if feeling for something on the bare meadow, and then gradually flies away, soaring and circling higher and higher until lost in the downy clouds. This lofty soaring is at least a grand recreation, as if it were nourishing sublime ideas. I should like to know why it soars higher and higher so,

[1] [Thoreau was evidently thinking only of distinguishing the bird from the fish hawk with its long and narrow wings. The description answers very well to that of the rough-legged hawk, the only New England species with fully feathered legs except the much rarer golden eagle, which lacks the white markings described. Neither of the eagles has short wings, while the wings of the rough-legged hawk are notably broad and buzzard-like.]

whether its thoughts are really turned to earth, for it seems to be more nobly as well as highly employed than the laborers ditching in the meadow beneath or any others of my fellow-townsmen.

BALD EAGLE
(WHITE-HEADED EAGLE)

April 8, 1854   Saw a large bird sail along over the edge of Wheeler's cranberry meadow just below Fair Haven, which I at first thought a gull, but with my glass found it was a hawk and had a perfectly white head and tail and broad or blackish wings. It sailed and circled along over the low cliff, and the crows dived at it in the field of my glass, and I saw it well, both above and beneath, as it turned, and then it passed off to hover over the Cliffs at a greater height. It was undoubtedly a white-headed eagle. It was to the eye but a large hawk.

April 23, 1854   Saw my white-headed eagle again, first at the same place, the outlet of Fair Haven Pond. It was a fine sight, he is mainly—*i.e.* his wings and body—so black against the sky, and they contrast so strongly with his white head and tail. He was first flying low over the water; then rose gradually and circled westward toward White Pond. Lying on the ground with my glass, I could watch him very easily, and by turns he gave me all possible views of himself. When I observed him edgewise I noticed that the tips of his wings curved upward slightly the more, like a stereotyped undulation. He rose very high at last, till I almost lost him in the clouds, circling or rather *looping* along westward, high over river and wood and farm, effectually concealed in the sky. We who live this plodding life here below never know how many eagles fly over us. They are concealed in the empyrean. I think I have got the worth of my glass now that it has revealed to me the white-headed eagle.[1] Now I see him edgewise like a black ripple in the air, his white head still as ever turned to earth, and now he turns his under side to me, and I behold the full breadth of his broad black wings, somewhat ragged at the edges.

August 22, 1858   At Baker Farm a large bird rose up near us, which at first I took for a hen-hawk, but it appeared larger. It screamed the same, and finally soared higher and higher till it was almost lost amid the clouds, or could scarcely be distinguished except when it was seen against some white and glowing cumulus. I think it was at least half a mile high, or three quarters, and yet I distinctly heard it scream up there each time it came round, and with my glass saw its head steadily bent toward the ground, looking for its prey. Its head, seen in a proper light, was distinctly whitish, and I suspect it may have been a white-headed eagle.[2] It did not once flap its wings up there, as it circled and sailed, though I watched it for nearly a mile. How fit that these soaring birds should be haughty and fierce, not like doves to our race!

[1] [He had bought a spy-glass a few weeks before.]
[2] [The eagle is so very much larger than any of our hawks that it seems doubtful if this bird could have been one.]

August 29, 1858 Ah! what a voice was that hawk's or eagle's of the 22d! Think of hearing, as you walk the earth, as usual in leaden shoes, a fine, shrill scream from time to time, which you would vainly endeavor to refer to its true source if you had not watched the bird in its upward flight. It comes from yonder black spot on the bosom of a cloud. I should not have suspected that sound to have issued from the bosom of a cloud if I had not seen the bird. What motive can an eagle have for screaming among the clouds, unobserved by terrestrial creatures? We walk invested by sound,—the cricket in the grass and the eagle in the clouds. And so it circled over, and I strained my eyes to follow it, though my ears heard it without effort.

SPARROW HAWK
September 24, 1851 A sparrow hawk,[1] hardly so big as a nighthawk, flew over high above my head,—a pretty little graceful fellow, too small and delicate to be rapacious.

FISH HAWK
March 27, 1842 Cliffs.—Two little hawks have just come out to play, like butterflies rising one above the other in endless alternation far below me. They swoop from side to side in the

[1][Thoreau at this time had made but little acquaintance with the hav.ks, and this bird was probably not very exactly identified as to species.]

broad basin of the tree-tops, with wider and wider surges, as if swung by an invisible pendulum. They stoop down on this side and scale up on that.

Suddenly I look up and see a new bird, probably an eagle, quite above me, laboring with the wind not more than forty rods off. It was the largest bird of the falcon kind I ever saw. I was never so impressed by any flight. She sailed the air, and fell back from time to time like a ship on her beam ends, holding her talons up as if ready for the arrows. I never allowed before for the grotesque attitudes of our national bird.[1]

The eagle must have an educated eye.

March 31, 1842 I cannot forget the majesty of that bird at the Cliff. It was no sloop or smaller craft hove in sight, but a ship of the line, worthy to struggle with the elements. It was a great presence, as of the master of river and forest. His eye would not have quailed before the owner of the soil; none could challenge his rights. And then his retreat, sailing so steadily away, was a kind of advance. How is it that man always feels like an interloper in nature, as if he had intruded on the domains of bird and beast?[2]

April 14, 1852 A fish hawk is calmly sailing over all, looking for his prey. The gulls are all gone now, though the water is high,

[1][See the next note.]
[2][This bird appears to have been a fish hawk, not an eagle. At least in his paper on the "Natural History of Massachusetts," included in *Excursions*, Thoreau uses the same terms in writing of the fish hawk.]

but I can see the motions of a muskrat on the calm sunny surface a great way off. So perfectly calm and beautiful, and yet no man looking at it this morning but myself. It is pleasant to see the zephyrs strike the smooth surface of the pond from time to time, and a darker shade ripple over it.

The streams break up; the ice goes to the sea. Then sails the fish hawk overhead, looking for his prey.

October 22, 1852   When I approached the pond[1] over Heywood's Peak, I disturbed a hawk (a fish hawk?) on a white pine by the water watching for his prey, with long, narrow, sharp wings and a white belly. He flew slowly across the pond somewhat like a gull. He is the more picturesque object against the woods or water for being white beneath.

November 17, 1854   I think it must have been a fish hawk which I saw hovering over the meadow and my boat (a raw cloudy afternoon), now and then sustaining itself in one place a hundred feet or more above the water, intent on a fish, with a hovering or fluttering motion of the wings somewhat like a kingfisher. Its wings were very long, slender, and curved in outline of front edge. I think there was some white on rump. It alighted near the top of an oak within rifle-shot of me and my boat, afterward on the tiptop of a maple by waterside, looking very large.

[1][Walden Pond.]

April 15, 1855 The Great Meadows are covered, except a small island in their midst, but not a duck do we see there. On a low limb of a maple on the edge of the river, thirty rods from the present shore, we saw a fish hawk eating a fish. Sixty rods off we could see his white crest. We landed, and got nearer by stealing through the woods. His legs looked long as he stood up on the limb with his back to us, and his body looked black against the sky and by contrast with the white of his head. There was a dark stripe on the side of the head. He had got the fish under his feet on the limb, and would bow his head, snatch a mouthful, and then look hastily over his right shoulder in our direction, then snatch another mouthful and look over his left shoulder. At length he launched off and flapped heavily away. We found at the bottom of the water beneath where he sat numerous fragments of the fish he had been eating, parts of the fins, entrails, gills, etc., and some was dropped on the bough. From one fin which I examined, I judged that it was either a sucker or a pout. There were small leaches adhering to it.

In the meanwhile, as we were stealing through the woods, we heard the pleasing note of the pine warbler, bringing back warmer weather, and we heard one honk of a goose, and, looking up, saw a large narrow harrow of them steering northeast. Half a mile further we saw another fish hawk, upon a dead limb midway up a swamp white oak over the water, at the end of a small island. We paddled directly toward him till within thirty rods. A crow came scolding to the tree and lit within three feet, looking about as large, compared with the hawk, as a crow blackbird to a crow, but he paid no attention to him. We had a very good view of him, as he sat sideways to us, and of his eagle-shaped head and beak. The white feathers of his head, which were erected somewhat, made him look like a copple-crowned hen. When he launched off, he uttered a clear whistling note,—*phe phe, phe phe, phe phe,—somewhat* like that of a telltale, but more round and less shrill and rapid, and another, perhaps his mate, fifty rods off, joined him. They flew heavily, as we looked at them from behind, more like a blue heron and bittern than I was aware of, their long wings undulating slowly to the tip, like the heron's, and the bodies seeming sharp like a gull's and unlike a hawk's.

In the water beneath where he was perched, we found many fragments of a pout,—bits of red gills, entrails, fins, and some of the long flexible black feelers,—scattered for four or five feet. This pout appeared to have been quite fresh, and was probably caught alive. We afterward started one of them from an oak over the water a mile beyond, just above the boat-house, and he skimmed off very low over the water, several times striking it with a loud sound heard plainly sixty rods off at least; and we followed him with our eyes till we could only see faintly his undulating wings against the sky in the western horizon. You could probably tell if any were about by looking for fragments of fish under the trees on which they would perch.

May 12, 1855 From beyond the orchard saw a large bird far over the Cliff Hill, which, with my glass, I soon made out to be a fish hawk advancing. Even at that distance, half a mile off, I distinguished its gull-like body,—pirate-like fishing body fit to dive,—and that its wings did not curve upward at the ends like a hen-hawk's (at least I could not see that they did), but rather hung down. It came on steadily, bent on fishing, with long and *heavy* undulating wings, with an easy, sauntering flight, over the river to the pond, and hovering over Pleasant Meadow a long time, hovering from time to time in one spot, when more than a hundred feet high, then making a very short circle or two and hovering again, then sauntering off against the woodside. At length he reappeared, passed downward over the shrub oak plain and alighted on an oak (of course now bare), standing this time apparently lengthwise on the limb. Soon took to wing again and went to fishing down the stream a hundred feet high. When just below Bittern Cliff, I observed by its motions that it observed something. It made a broad circle of observation in its course, lowering itself somewhat; then, by one or two steep sidewise flights, it reached the water, and, as near as intervening trees would let me see, skimmed over it and endeavored to clutch its prey in passing. It failed the first time, but probably succeeded the second. Then it leisurely winged its way to a tall bare tree on the east side of the Cliffs, and there we left it apparently pluming itself. It had a very white belly, and indeed appeared all white beneath its body. I saw broad black lines between the white crown and throat.

*   *   *

Returning over Conantum, I directed my glass toward the dead tree on Cliffs, and was surprised to see the fish hawk still sitting there, about an hour after he first alighted; and now I found that he was eating a fish, which he had under his feet on the limb and ate as I have already described. At this distance his whole head looked white with his breast.

May 14, 1855   Under the dead pine on which the fish hawk sat on the 12th *inst.*, a half-mile from the river, I find a few fish bones—one, I am pretty sure from comparison, the jaw of a pout. So that in three instances, the only ones observed this year, they were feeding on pouts. Probably the mice, etc., had picked up the rest of his droppings. Thus these inhabitants of the interior get a taste of fish from time to time,—crumbs from the fish hawk's table.

April 6, 1856   As I am going along the Corner road by the meadow mouse brook, hear and see, a quarter of a mile northwest, on those conspicuous white oaks near the river in Hubbard's second grove, the crows buffeting some intruder. The crows had betrayed to me some large bird of the hawk kind which they were buffeting. I suspected it before I looked carefully. I saw several crows on the oaks, and also what looked to my naked eye like a cluster of the palest and most withered oak leaves with a black base about as big as a crow. Looking with my glass, I saw that it was a great bird. The crows sat about a rod off, higher up, while another crow was occasionally diving at him, and all were cawing. The great bird was just starting. It was chiefly a dirty white with great broad wings with black tips and black on other parts, giving it the appearance of dirty white, barred with black. I am not sure whether it was a white-headed eagle or a fish hawk. There appeared much more white than belongs to either, and more black than the fish hawk has. It rose and wheeled, flapping several times, till it got under way; then, with its rear to me, presenting the least surface, it moved off steadily in its orbit over the woods northwest, with the slightest possible undulation of its wings,—a noble planetary motion, like Saturn with its ring seen edgewise. It is so rare that we see a large body self-sustained in the air. While crows sat still and silent and confessed their lord. Through my glass I saw the outlines of this sphere against the sky, trembling with life and power as it skimmed the topmost twigs of the wood toward some more solitary oak amid the meadows. To my naked eye it showed only so much black as a crow in its talons might. Was it not the white-headed eagle in the state when it is called the sea eagle?[1] Perhaps its neck-feathers were erected.

[1] [Wilson, in his *American Ornithology*, gave an account of the "sea eagle," which he suspected to be the young of the bald eagle.]

April 14, 1856 See from my window a fish hawk flying high west of the house, cutting off the bend between Willow Bay and the meadow, in front of the house, between one vernal lake and another. He suddenly wheels and, straightening out his long, narrow wings, makes one circle high above the last meadow, as if he had caught a glimpse of a fish beneath, and then continues his course down the river.

P.M.—Sail to hill by Bedford line.

Wind southwest and pretty strong; sky overcast; weather cool. Start up a fish hawk from near the swamp white oaks southwest of the Island, undoubtedly the one of the morning. I now see that this is a much darker bird, both above and beneath, than that bird of the 6th. It flies quite low, surveying the water, in an undulating, buoyant manner, like a marsh hawk, or still more a nighthawk, with its long curved wings. He flies so low westward that I lose sight of him against the dark hillside and trees.

April 16, 1856 As I walk along the bank of the Assabet, I hear the *yeep yeep yeep yeeep yeeep yeep*, or perhaps *peop*, of a fish hawk, repeated *quite fast*, but not so shrill and whistling as I think I have heard it, and directly I see his long curved wings undulating over Pinxter Swamp, now flooded.

August 25, 1856 I cross the meadows in the face of a thunderstorm rising very dark in the north. There were several boats out, but their crews soon retreated homeward before the approaching storm. It came on rapidly, with vivid lightning striking the northern earth and heavy thunder following. Just before, and in the shadow of, the cloud, I saw, advancing majestically with wide circles over the meadowy flood, a fish hawk and, apparently, a black eagle (maybe a young white-head). The first, with slender curved wings and silvery breast, four or five hundred feet high, watching the water while he circled slowly southwesterly. What a vision that could detect a fish at that distance! The latter, with broad black wings and broad tail, thus:

hovered only about one hundred feet high; evidently a different species, and what else but an eagle? They soon disappeared southwest, cutting off a bend. The thunder-shower passed off to the southeast.

October 26, 1857 A storm is a new, and in some respects more active, life in nature. Larger migrating birds make their appearance. They, at least, sympathize with the movements of the watery element and the winds. I see two great fish hawks (*possibly* blue herons) slowly beating northeast against the storm, by what a curious tie circling ever near each other and in the same direction, as if you might expect to find the very motes in the air to be paired; two long undulating wings conveying a feathered body through the misty atmosphere, and this inseparably associated with another planet of the same species. I can just glimpse their undulating lines. Damon and Pythias they must be. The waves beneath, which are of kindred form, are still more social, multitudinous, ἀνήριθμον. Where is my mate, beating against the storm with me? They fly according to the valley of the river, northeast or southwest.

I start up snipes also at Clamshell Meadow. This weather sets the migratory birds in motion and also makes them bolder.

April 25, 1858 P.M.—To Assabet.

Approaching the Island, I hear the *phe phe, phe phe, phe phe, phe phe, phe*, the sharp whistling note, of a fish hawk, and, looking round, see him just afterward launching away from one of the swamp white oaks southwest of the Island. There is about half a second between each note, and he utters them either while perched or while flying. He shows a great proportion of wing and some white on back. The wings are much curved. He sails along some eighty feet above the water's edge, looking for fish, and alights again quite near. I see him an hour afterward about the same spot.

April 28, 1858 I see the fish hawk again [two or three indecipherable words] Island. As it flies low, directly over my head, I see that its body is white beneath, and the white on the forward side of the wings beneath, if extended across the breast, would form a regular crescent. Its wings do not form a regular curve in front, but an abrupt angle. They are loose and broad at tips. This bird goes fishing slowly down one side of the river and up again on the other, forty to sixty feet high, continually poising itself almost or quite stationary, with its head to the northwest wind and looking down,

flapping its wings enough to keep its place, sometimes stationary for about a minute. It is not shy. This boisterous weather is the time to see it.

May 1, 1858 Suddenly a large hawk sailed over from the Assabet, which at first I took for a hen-harrier, it was so neat a bird and apparently not very large. It was a fish hawk, with a very conspicuous white crown or head and a uniform brown above elsewhere; beneath white, breast and belly. Probably it was the male, which is the smaller and whiter beneath. A wedge-shaped tail. He alighted on a dead elm limb on Prichard's ground, and at this distance, with my glass, I could see some dark of head above the white of throat or breast. He was incessantly looking about as if on his guard. After fifteen minutes came a crow from the Assabet and alighted cawing, about twenty rods from him, and ten minutes later another. How alert they are to detect these great birds of prey! They do not thus pursue ordinary hawks, and their attendance alone might suggest to unskillful observers the presence of a fish hawk or eagle. Some crows up the Assabet evidently knew that he was sitting on that elm far away. He sailed low almost directly over my boat, fishing. His wings had not obviously that angular form which I thought those of another had the other day.

April 7, 1859 Standing under the north side of the hill, I hear the rather innocent *phe phe, phe phe, phe phe, phe'* of a fish hawk (for it is not a scream, but a rather soft and innocent note), and, looking up, see one come sailing from over the hill. The body looks quite short in proportion to the spread of the wings, which are quite dark or blackish above. He evidently has something in his talons. We soon after disturb him again, and, at length, after circling around over the hill and adjacent fields, he alights in plain sight on one of the half-dead white oaks on the top of the hill, where probably he sat before. As I look through my glass, he is perched on a large dead limb and is evidently standing on a fish (I had noticed something in his talons as he flew), for he stands high and uneasily, finding it hard to keep his balance in the wind. He is disturbed by our neighborhood and does not proceed at once to eat his meal. I see the tail of the fish hanging over the end of the limb. Now and then he pecks at it. I see the white on the crown of the hawk. It is a very large black bird as seen against the sky. Soon he sails away again, carrying his fish, as before, horizontally beneath his body, and he circles about over the adjacent pasture like a hawk hunting, though he can only be looking for a suitable place to eat his fish or waiting for us to be gone.

Looking under the limb on which he was perched, we find a piece of the skin of a sucker (?) or some other scaly fish which a hawk had dropped there long since. No doubt many a fish hawk has taken his meal on that sightly perch.

It seems, then, that the fish hawk which you see soaring and sailing so leisurely about over the land—for this one soared quite high into the sky at one time—may have a fish in his talons all the while and only be waiting till you are gone for an opportunity to eat it on his accustomed perch.

October 5, 1860　I see a fish hawk, skimming low over it,[1] suddenly dive or stoop for one of those little fishes that rise to the surface so abundantly at this season. He then sits on a bare limb over the water, ready to swoop down again on his finny prey, presenting, as he sits erect, a long white breast and belly and a white head. No doubt he well knows the habits of these little fishes which dimple the surface of Walden at this season, and I doubt if there is any better fishing-ground for him to resort to. He can easily find a perch overlooking the lake and discern his prey in the clear water.

HAWKS (SPECIES UNNAMED)

September 25, 1851　In these cooler, windier, crystal days the note of the jay sounds a little more native. Standing on the Cliffs, I see them flitting and screaming from pine to pine be-

---

[1][Walden Pond.]

neath, displaying their gaudy blue pinions. Hawks, too, I perceive, sailing about in the clear air, looking white against the green pines, like the seeds of the milkweed. There is almost always a pair of hawks. Their shrill scream, that of the owls, and wolves are all related.

October 9, 1851 The circling hawk steers himself through the air like the skater, without a visible motion.

December 20, 1851 Saw a large hawk circling over a pine wood below me, and screaming, apparently that he might discover his prey by their flight. Travelling ever by wider circles. What a symbol of the thoughts, now soaring, now descending, taking larger and larger circles, or smaller and smaller! It flies not directly whither it is bound, but advances by circles, like a courtier of the skies. No such noble progress! How it comes round, as with a wider sweep of thought! But the majesty is in the imagination of the beholder, for the bird is intent on its prey. Circling and ever circling, you cannot divine which way it will incline, till perchance it dives down straight as an arrow to its mark. It rises higher above where I stand, and I see with beautiful distinctness its wings against the sky,—primaries and secondaries, and the rich tracery of the outline of the latter (?), its inner wings, or wing-linings, within the outer,—like a great moth seen against the sky. A will-o'-the-wind. Following its path, as it were, through the vortices of the air. The poetry of motion. Not as preferring one place to another, but enjoying each as long as possible. Most gracefully so surveys new scenes and revisits the old. As if that hawk were made to be the symbol of my thought, how bravely he came round over those parts of the wood which he had not surveyed, taking in a new segment, annexing new territories! Without "heave-yo!" it trims its sail. It goes about without the creaking of a block. That America yacht of the air that never makes a tack, though it rounds the globe itself, takes in and shakes out its reefs without a flutter,—its sky-scrapers all under its control. Holds up one wing, as if to admire, and sweeps off this way, then holds up the other and sweeps that. If there are two concentrically circling, it is such a regatta as Southampton waters never witnessed.[1]

Flights of imagination, Coleridgean thoughts. So a man is said to soar in his thought, ever to fresh woods and pastures new. Rises as in thought.

★　　★　　★

What made the hawk mount? Did you perceive the manœuvre? Did he fill himself with air? Before you were aware of it, he had mounted by his spiral path into the heavens.

April 22, 1852　Saw four hawks soaring high in the heavens over the Swamp Bridge Brook. At first saw three; said to myself there must be four, and found the fourth. Glad are they, no doubt, to be out after being confined by the storm.

---

[1][The yacht *America* had in the preceding August won her famous cup in a race round the Isle of Wight.]

April 29, 1852 I discover a hawk over my head by his shadow on the ground; also small birds.

June 15, 1852 I hear the scream of a great hawk, sailing with a ragged wing against the high wood-side, apparently to scare his prey and so detect it,—shrill, harsh, fitted to excite terror in sparrows and to issue from his split and curved bill. I see his open bill the while against the sky. Spit with force from his mouth with an undulatory quaver imparted to it from his wings or motion as he flies. A hawk's ragged wing will grow whole again, but so will not a poet's.

August 31, 1852 I saw a small hawk fly along under the hillside and alight on the ground, its breast and belly pure downy white. It was a very handsome bird. Though they are not fitted to walk much on the ground, but to soar, yet its feet, which are but claws to seize its prey and hold to its perch, are handsome appendages, and it is a very interesting sight on the ground. Yet there is a certain unfitness in so fair a breast, so pure white, made to breast nothing less pure than the sky or clouds, coming so nearly in contact with the earth. Never bespattered with the mud of earth. That was the impression made on me,—of a very pure breast, accustomed to float on the sky, in contact with the earth. It stood quite still, watching me, as if it was not easy for it to walk.

September 16, 1852 What makes this such a day for hawks? There are eight or ten in sight from the Cliffs, large and small, one or more with a white rump. I detected the transit of the first by his shadow on the rock, and I look toward the sun for him. Though he is made light beneath to conceal him, his shadow betrays him. A hawk must get out of the wood, must get above it, where he can sail. It is narrow dodging for him amid the boughs. He cannot be a hawk there, but only perch gloomily. Now I see a large one—perchance an eagle, I say to myself!—down in the valley, circling and circling, higher and wider. This way he comes. How beautiful does he repose on the air, in the moment when he is directly over you, and you see the form and texture of his wings! How light he must make himself, how much earthy heaviness expel, before he can thus soar and sail! He carries no useless clogs there with him. They are out by families; while one is circling this way, another circles that. Kites without strings. Where is the boy that flies them? Are not the hawks most observed at this season?

March 30, 1853 The motions of a hawk correcting the flaws in the wind by raising his shoulder from time to time, are much like those of a leaf yielding to them. For the little hawks are hunting now. You have not to sit long on the Cliffs before you see one.

March 2, 1855 Heard two hawks scream. There was something truly March-like in it, like a prolonged blast or whistling of the wind through a crevice in the sky, which, like a cracked blue saucer, overlaps the woods. Such are the first rude notes which prelude the summer's quire, learned of the whistling March wind.

October 22, 1855   I sat on a bank at the brook crossing, beyond the grove, to watch a flock of *seringos*,[1] perhaps Savannah
sparrows, which, with some *F. hyemalis*[2] and other sparrows, were
actively flitting about amid the alders and dogwood. . . . Suddenly
a pigeon hawk[3] dashed over the bank very low and within a rod of
me, and, striking its wings against the twigs with a clatter close to
a sparrow, which escaped, it alighted amid the alders in front,
within four rods of me. It was attracted by the same objects which
attracted me. It sat a few moments, balancing itself and spreading
its tail and wings,—a chubby little fellow. Its back appeared a sort
of deep chocolate-brown. Every sparrow at once concealed itself,
apparently deep in the bushes next the ground. Once or twice he
dashed down there amid the alders and tried to catch one. In a few
minutes he skimmed along the hedge by the path and disappeared
westward. But presently, hearing the sound of his wings amid the
bushes, I looked up and saw him dashing along through the willows and then out and upward high over the meadow in pursuit of
a sparrow (perhaps a seringo). The sparrow flew pretty high and
kept doubling. When it flew direct, the hawk gained, and got
within two or three feet of it; but when it doubled, it gained on the
hawk; so the latter soon gave up the chase, and the little bird flew

[1][See note to Savannah Sparrow, Chapter 15.]
[2][*Fringilla hyemalis*, the slate-colored junco or snowbird, now known as *Junco hyemalis*.]
[3]Was I sure?

off high over my head, with a panting breath and a rippling ricochet flight, toward the high pine grove. When I passed along the
path ten minutes after, I found that all those sparrows were still hid
under the bushes by the ditch-side, close to the ground, and I saw
nothing of them till I scared them out by going within two or three
feet. No doubt they warned each other by a peculiar note. What a
corsair the hawk is to them!—a little fellow hardly bigger than a
quail.

February 29, 1856 [Minott] told again of the partridge hawk
striking down a partridge which rose before him and flew across
the run in the beech woods, –how suddenly he did it,––and he,
hearing the fluttering of the partridge, came up and secured it,
while the hawk kept out of gunshot.

September 27, 1857 As I sit there I see the shadow of a hawk
flying above and behind me. I think I see more hawks nowadays.
Perhaps it is both because the young are grown and their food, the
small birds, are flying in flocks and are abundant. I need only sit still
a few minutes on any spot which overlooks the river meadows, before I see some black circling mote beating along, circling along the
meadow's edge, now lost for a moment as it turns edgewise in a peculiar light, now reappearing further or nearer.

OWLS

LONG-EARED OWL

June 24, 1857   Went to Farmer's Swamp to look for the screech owl's[1] nest Farmer had found. You go about forty-five rods on the first path to the left in the woods and then turn to the left a few rods. I found the nest at last near the top of a middling-sized white pine, about thirty feet from the ground. As I stood by the tree, the old bird dashed by within a couple of rods, uttering a peculiar mewing sound, which she kept up amid the bushes, a blackbird in close pursuit of her. I found the nest empty, on one side of the main stem but close to it, resting on some limbs. It was made of twigs rather less than an eighth of an inch thick and was almost flat above, only an inch lower in the middle than at the edge, about sixteen inches in diameter and six or eight inches thick, with the twigs in the midst, and beneath was mixed sphagnum and sedge from the swamp beneath, and the lining or flooring was

---

[1][The situation of the nest and Thoreau's description of the notes indicate a long-eared owl rather than a screech owl.]

coarse strips of grape-vine bark; the whole pretty firmly matted together. How common and important a material is grape-vine bark for birds' nests! Nature wastes nothing. There were white droppings of the young on the nest and one large pellet of fur and small bones two and a half inches long. In the meanwhile, the old bird was uttering that hoarse worried note from time to time, somewhat like a partridge's, flying past from side to side and alighting amid the trees or bushes. When I had descended, I detected one young one two-thirds grown perched on a branch of the next tree, about fifteen feet from the ground, which was all the while staring at me with its great yellow eyes. It was gray with gray horns and a dark beak. As I walked past near it, it turned its head steadily, always facing me, without moving its body, till it looked directly the opposite way over its back, but never offered to fly. Just then I thought surely that I heard a puppy faintly barking at me four or five rods distant amid the bushes, having tracked me into the swamp,—*what what, what what what.* It was exactly such a noise as the barking of a very small dog or perhaps a fox. But it was the old owl, for I presently saw her making it. She repeated [*sic*] perched quite near. She was generally reddish-brown or partridge-colored, the breast mottled with dark brown and fawn-color in downward strings [*sic*], and had plain fawn-colored thighs.

SHORT-EARED OWL

December 8, 1853   At midday (3 P.M.) saw an owl fly from toward the river and alight on Mrs. Richardson's front-yard fence. Got quite near it, and followed it to a rock on the heap of dirt at Collier's cellar. A rather dark brown owl above (with a decided owl head (and eyes), though not very broad), with longitudinal tawny streaks (or the reverse), none transverse, growing lighter down the breast, and at length clear rusty yellowish or cream-color beneath and about feathered feet. Wings large and long, with a distinct large black spot beneath; bill and claws, I think, black. Saw no ears. Kept turning its head and great black eyes this way and that when it heard me, but appeared not to see me. Saw my shadow better, for I ap[proached] on the sunny side. I am inclined to think it the short-eared owl, though I could see no ears, though it reminded me of what I had read of the hawk owl.[1] It was a foot or more long and spread about three feet. Flew somewhat flappingly, yet hawk-like. Went within two or three rods of it.

BARRED OWL

December 14, 1858   I see at Derby's shop a barred owl (*Strix nebulosa*),[2] taken in the woods west of the factory on the

[1][The description is that of the short-eared owl, except that the eyes of that species are yellow, not black. The pupils may have been dilated, however, so as to give a general impression of black eyes.]

[2][Now *Strix varia.*]

11th, found (with its wing broke [*sic*]) by a wood-chopper. It measures about three and a half feet in alar extent by eighteen to twenty inches long, or *nearly* the same as the cat owl, but is small and without horns. It is very mild and quiet, bears handling perfectly well, and only snaps its bill with a loud sound at the sight of a cat or dog. It is apparently a female, since it is large and has white spots on the wings. The claws are quite dark rather than dark horn-color. It hopped into the basin of the scales, and I was surprised to find that it weighed only one pound and one ounce. It may be thin-fleshed on account of its broken wing, but how light-bodied these flyers are! It has no yellow iris like the cat owl, and has the bristles about its yellow bill which the other has not. It has a very smooth and handsome round head, a brownish gray. Solemnity is what they express,—fit representatives of the night.[1]

S A W - W H E T   O W L
(A C A D I A N   O W L)

January 6, 1859 Miles had hanging in his barn a little owl (*Strix Acadica*)[2] which he caught alive with his hands about a week ago. He had forced it to eat, but it died. It was a funny little

---

[1][Thoreau had once before seen a live barred owl, and he gives an account of it in the chapter on "Winter Visitors" in *Walden*. This account does not appear in the published *Journal*. It was probably written in one of those early journals which were destroyed in the preparation of the *Week* and *Walden*.]

[2][Now *Cryptoglaux acadica*.]

brown bird, spotted with white, seven and a half inches long to the end of the tail, or eight to the end of the claws, by nineteen in alar extent,—not so long by considerable as a robin, though much stouter. This one had three (not two)[1] *white* bars on its tail, but no noticeable white at the tip. Its cunning feet were feathered quite to the extremity of the toes, looking like whitish (or tawny-white) mice, or as when one pulls stockings over his boots. As usual, the white spots on the upper sides of the wings are smaller and a more distinct white, while those beneath are much larger, but a subdued, satiny white. Even a bird's wing has an upper and under side, and the last admits only of more subdued and tender colors.

SCREECH OWL

August, 1845 After the evening train has gone by and left the world to silence and to me, the whip-poor-will chants her vespers for half an hour. And when all is still at night, the owls take up the strain, like mourning women their ancient ululu. Their most dismal scream is truly Ben-Jonsonian. Wise midnight hags! It is no honest and blunt tu-whit to-who of the poets, but, without jesting, a most solemn graveyard ditty,—but the mutual consolations of suicide lovers remembering the pangs and the delights of supernal love in the infernal groves. And yet I love to hear their wailing, their doleful responses, trilled along the woodside, re-

[1]Nuttall says three.

minding me sometimes of music and singing birds, as if it were the dark and tearful side of music, the regrets and sighs, that would fain be sung. The spirits, the *low* spirits and melancholy forebodings, of fallen spirits who once in human shape night-walked the earth and did the deeds of darkness, now expiating with their wailing hymns, threnodiai, their sins in the very scenery of their transgressions. They give me a new sense of the vastness and mystery of that nature which is the common dwelling of us both. "Oh-o-o-o-o that I never had been bor-or-or-or-orn!" sighs one on this side of the pond, and circles in the restlessness of despair to some new perch in the gray oaks. Then, "That I never had been bor-or-or-or-orn!" echoes one on the further side, with a tremulous sincerity, and "Bor-or-or-or-orn" comes faintly from far in the Lincoln woods.

August 14, 1854 I hear the tremulous squealing scream of a screech owl in the Holden Woods, sounding somewhat like the neighing of a horse, not like the snipe.

May 7, 1855 A short distance beyond this and the hawk's-nest pine, I observed a middling-sized red oak standing a little aslant on the side-hill over the swamp, with a pretty large hole in one side about fifteen feet from the ground, where apparently a limb on which a felled tree lodged had been cut some years before and so broke out a cavity. I thought that such a hole was too good a one not to be improved by some inhabitant of the wood. Perhaps the gray squirrels I had just seen had their nest there. Or was not the entrance big enough to admit a screech owl? So I thought I would tap on it and put my ear to the trunk and see if I could hear anything stirring within it, but I heard nothing. Then I concluded to look into it. So I shinned up, and when I reached up one hand to the hole to pull myself up by it, the thought passed through my mind perhaps something may take hold my fingers, but nothing did. The first limb was nearly opposite to the hole, and, resting on this, I looked in, and, to my great surprise, there squatted, filling the hole, which was about six inches deep and five to six wide, a salmon-brown bird not so big as a partridge, seemingly asleep within three inches of the top and close to my face. It was a minute or two before I made it out to be an owl. It was a salmon-brown or fawn (?) above, the feathers shafted with small blackish-brown somewhat hastate (?) marks, *grayish* toward the ends of the wings and tail, as far as I could see. A large white circular space about or behind eye, banded in rear by a pretty broad (one third of an inch) and quite conspicuous perpendicular *dark*-brown stripe. Egret,[1] say one and a quarter inches long, sharp, triangular, reddish-brown without mainly. It lay crowded in that small space, with its tail somewhat bent up and one side of its head turned up with one egret, and its large dark eye open only by a long slit about a sixteenth of an inch wide; visible breathing. After a little while I put in one hand and stroked it repeatedly, whereupon it reclined its

[1][Wilson used the term "egret" for the "ears," or "horns," of the owls.]

head a little lower and closed its eye entirely. Though curious to know what was under it, I disturbed it no farther at that time.

In the meanwhile, the crows were making a great cawing amid and over the pine-tops beyond the swamp, and at intervals I heard the scream of a hawk, probably the surviving male hen-hawk, whom they were pestering (unless they had discovered the male screech owl), and a part of them came cawing about me. This was a very fit place for hawks and owls to dwell in,—the thick woods just over a white spruce[1] swamp, in which the glaucous kalmia grows; the gray squirrels, partridges, hawks, and owls, all together. It was probably these screech owls which I heard in moonlight nights hereabouts last fall.

★   ★   ★

Returning by owl's nest, about one hour before sunset, I climbed up and looked in again. The owl was gone, but there were four nearly round *dirty brownish white*[2] eggs, quite warm, on nothing but the bits of rotten wood which made the bottom of the hole. The eggs were very nearly as large at one end as the other, slightly oblong, 1⅜ inches by 1⅞, as nearly as I could measure. I took out

---

[1][Black spruce. See note, p. 203.]

[2]MacGillivray describes no eggs of this color,—only white,—and the same with Nuttall, except the great gray owl. [Screech owl's eggs, *when clean*, are always white and the same is true of all our owls, including the great gray owl.]

one. It would probably have hatched within a week, the young being considerably feathered and the bill remarkably developed. Perhaps she heard me coming, and so left the nest. My bird corresponds in color, as far as I saw it, with Wilson's *Strix asio*, but not his *nævia*, which Nuttall and others consider a young (?) bird,[1] though the egg was not pure white. I do not remember that my bird was barred or *mottled* at all.

May 12, 1855 As I approached the owl's nest, I saw her run past the hole up into that part of the hollow above it, and probably she was there when I thought she had flown on the 7th. I looked in, and at first did not know what I saw. One of the three remaining eggs was hatched, and a little downy *white* young one, two or three times as long as an egg, lay helpless between the two remaining eggs. Also a dead white-bellied mouse (*Mus leucopus*)[2] lay with them, its tail curled round one of the eggs.

May 25, 1855 Scared a screech owl out of an apple tree on a hill; flew swiftly off at first like a pigeon woodpecker and lit near

[1][The dichromatism of the screech owl gave our early ornithologists much trouble. The red phase was described as *Strix asio*, and the gray, or mottled, phase was given the name of *Strix nævia*. Wilson believed the two to be separate species, but Nuttall, in his first edition, called the red the young of the mottled owl (not the other way round, as Thoreau has it). In the edition of 1840, however, Nuttall makes two species of the screech owl, as Wilson had done before him, and it was left to later workers to discover that the two forms were only color phases of a single species, which is now known to science as *Otus asio*.]

[2][Now known as *Peromyscus leucopus noveboracensis*.]

by facing me; was instantly visited and spied at by a brown thrasher; then flew into a hole high in a hickory near by, the thrasher following close to the tree. It was reddish or ferruginous.

May 26, 1855 At the screech owl's nest I now find two young slumbering, almost uniformly gray above, about five inches long, with little dark-grayish tufts for incipient horns (?). Their heads about as broad as their bodies. I handle them without their stirring or opening their eyes. There are the feathers of a small bird and the leg of the *Mus leucopus* in the nest.

September 23, 1855 8 P.M.—I hear from my chamber a screech owl about Monroe's house this bright moonlight night,— a loud, piercing scream, much like the whinner of a colt perchance, a rapid trill, then subdued or smothered a note or two.

October 28, 1855 As I paddle under the Hemlock bank this cloudy afternoon, about 3 o'clock, I see a screech owl sitting on the edge of a hollow hemlock stump about three feet high, at the base of a large hemlock. It sits with its head drawn in, eying me, with its eyes partly open, about twenty feet off. When it hears me move, it turns its head toward me, perhaps one eye only open, with its great glaring golden iris. You see two whitish triangular lines above the eyes meeting at the bill, with a sharp reddish-brown triangle between and a narrow curved line of black under each eye. At this distance and in this light, you see only a black spot where the eye is, and the question is whether the eyes are open or not. It sits on the lee side of the tree this raw and windy day. You would say that this was a bird without a neck. Its short bill, which rests upon its breast, scarcely projects at all, but in a state of rest the whole upper part of the bird from the wings is rounded off smoothly, excepting the horns, which stand up conspicuously or are slanted back. After watching it ten minutes from the boat, I landed two rods above, and, stealing quietly up behind the hemlock, though from the windward, I looked carefully around it, and, to my surprise, saw the owl still sitting there. So I sprang round quickly, with my arm outstretched, and caught it in my hand. It was so surprised that it offered no resistance at first, only glared at me in mute astonishment with eyes as big as saucers. But ere long it began to snap its bill, making quite a noise, and, as I rolled it up in my handkerchief and put it in my pocket, it bit my finger slightly. I soon took it out of my pocket and, tying the handkerchief, left it on the bottom of the boat. So I carried it home and made a small cage in which to keep it, for a night. When I took it up, it clung so tightly to my hand as to sink its claws into my fingers and bring blood.

When alarmed or provoked most, it snaps its bill and hisses. It puffs up its feathers to nearly twice its usual size, stretches out its neck, and, with wide-open eyes, stares this way and that, moving its head slowly and undulatingly from side to side with a curious motion. While I write this evening, I see that there is ground for much superstition in it. It looks out on me from a dusky corner of its box with its great solemn eyes, so perfectly still itself. I was surprised to find that I could imitate its note as I remember it, by a *guttural* whinnering.

A remarkably squat figure, being very broad in proportion to its length, with a short tail, and very cat-like in the face with its horns and great eyes. Remarkably large feet and talons, legs thickly clothed with whitish down, down to the talons. It brought blood from my fingers by clinging to them. It would lower its head, stretch out its neck, and, bending it from side to side, peer at you with laughable circumspection; from side to side, as if to catch or absorb into its eyes every ray of light, strain at you with complacent yet earnest scrutiny. Raising and lowering its head and moving it from side to side in a slow and regular manner, at the same time snapping its bill smartly perhaps, and faintly hissing, and puffing itself up more and more,—cat-like, turtle-like, both in hissing and swelling. The slowness and gravity, not to say solemnity, of this motion are striking. There plainly is no jesting in this case.

★ ★ ★

General color of the owl a rather pale and perhaps slightly reddish brown, the feathers centred with black. Perches with two claws above and two below the perch. It is a slight body, covered with a mass of soft and light-lying feathers. Its head muffled in a great hood. It must be quite comfortable in winter. Dropped a pellet of fur and bones (?) in his cage. He sat, not really moping but trying to sleep, in a corner of his box all day, yet with one or both eyes slightly open all the while. I never once caught him with his eyes shut. Ordinarily stood rather than sat on his perch.

October 29, 1855 P.M.—Up Assabet.

Carried my owl to the hill again. Had to shake him out of the box, for he did not go of his own accord. (He had learned to alight on his perch, and it was surprising how lightly and noiselessly he would hop upon it.) There he stood on the grass, at first bewildered, with his horns pricked up and looking toward me. In this strong light the pupils of his eyes suddenly contracted and the iris expanded till they were two great brazen orbs with a centre spot merely. His attitude expressed astonishment more than anything. I was obliged to toss him up a little that he might feel his wings, and then he flapped away low and heavily to a hickory on the hillside twenty rods off. (I had let him out in the plain just east of the hill.) Thither I followed and tried to start him again. He was now on the *qui vive*, yet would not start. He erected his head, showing some neck, narrower than the round head above. His eyes were broad brazen rings around bullets of black. His horns stood quite an inch high, as not before. As I moved around him, he turned his head always toward me, till he looked *directly* behind himself as he sat crosswise on a bough. He behaved as if bewildered and dazzled, gathering all the light he could and ever straining his great eyes toward you to make out who you are, but not inclining to fly. I had to lift him again with a stick to make him fly, and then he only rose to a higher perch, where at last he seemed to seek the shelter of a thicker cluster of the sere leaves, partly crouching there. He never appeared so much alarmed as surprised and astonished.

When I first saw him yesterday, he sat on the edge of a hollow hemlock stump about three feet high, at the bottom of a large hemlock, amid the darkness of the evergreens that cloudy day. (It threatened to rain every moment.) At the bottom of the hollow, or eighteen inches beneath him, was a very soft bed of the fine green moss (hypnum) which grows on the bank close by, probably his own bed. It had been recently put there.

When I moved him in his cage he would cling to the perch, though it was in a perpendicular position, one foot above another, suggesting his habit of clinging to and climbing the inside of hollow trees. I do not remember any perpendicular line in his eyes, as in those of the cat.

July 10, 1856   As I was bathing under the swamp white oaks at 6 P.M., heard a suppressed sound often repeated, like, perhaps, the working of beer through a bung-hole, which I already suspected to be produced by owls. I was uncertain whether it was far or near. Proceeding a dozen rods up-stream on the south side, toward where a catbird was incessantly mewing, I found myself suddenly within a rod of a gray screech owl sitting on an alder bough with horns erect, turning its head from side to side and up and down, and peering at me in that same ludicrously solemn and complacent way that I had noticed in one in captivity. Another, more red, also horned, repeated the same warning sound, or apparently call to its young, about the same distance off, in another direction, on an alder. When they took to flight they made some noise with their wings. With their short tails and squat figures they looked very clumsy, all head and shoulders. Hearing a fluttering under the alders, I drew near and found a young owl, a third smaller than the old, all gray, without obvious horns, only four or five feet distant. It flitted along two rods, and I followed it. I saw at least two or more young. All this was close by that thick hemlock grove, and they perched on alders and an apple tree in the thicket there. These birds kept opening their eyes when I moved, as if to get clearer sight of me. The young were very quick to notice any motion of the old, and so betrayed their return by looking in that direction when they returned, though I had not heard it. Though they permitted me to come so near with so much noise, as if bereft of half their senses, they at [once] noticed the coming and going of the old birds, even when I did not. There were four or five owls in all. I have heard a somewhat similar note, further off and louder, in the night.

December 26, 1860 Melvin sent to me yesterday a perfect *Strix asio*, or red owl of Wilson,—not at all gray. This is now generally made the same with the *nævia*, but, while some consider the red the old, others consider the red the young. This is, as Wilson says, a bright "nut brown" like a hazelnut or dried hazel bur (not *hazel*). It is twenty-three inches in alar extent by about eleven long. Feet extend one inch beyond tail. Cabot makes the old bird red;

Audubon, the young. How well fitted these and other owls to withstand the winter! a mere core in the midst of such a muff of feathers! Then the feet of this are feathered finely to the claws, looking like the feet of a furry quadruped. Accordingly owls are common here in winter; hawks, scarce.

GREAT HORNED OWL (CAT OWL)[1]

November 18, 1851 Surveying these days the Ministerial Lot.

Now at sundown I hear the hooting of an owl,—*hoo hoo hoo, hoorer hoo*. It sounds like the hooting of an idiot or a maniac broke loose. This is faintly answered in a different strain, apparently from a greater distance, almost as if it were the echo, *i.e.* so far as the *succession* is concerned. This is my music each evening. I heard it last evening. The men who help me call it the "hooting owl" and think it is the cat owl. It is a sound admirably suited to the swamp and to the twilight woods, suggesting a vast undeveloped nature which men have not recognized nor satisfied. I rejoice that there are owls. They represent the stark, twilight, unsatisfied thoughts I have. Let owls do the idiotic and maniacal hooting for men. This

[1][From Thoreau's descriptions of the notes of his "hooting owls" it seems probable that they were all of this species. There appear to have been two pairs of these birds regularly settled in Concord in Thoreau's time,—one in the Walden woods and one in the Ministerial Swamp in the southwestern part of the town.]

sound faintly suggests the infinite roominess of nature, that there is a world in which owls live. Yet how few are seen, even by the hunters! The sun has shone for a day over this savage swamp, where the single spruce[1] stands covered with usnea moss, which a Concord merchant mortgaged once to the trustees of the ministerial fund and lost, but now for a different race of creatures a new day dawns over this wilderness, which one would have thought was sufficiently dismal before. Here hawks also circle by day, and chickadees are heard, and rabbits and partridges abound.

November 25, 1851 When surveying in the swamp on the 20th last, at sundown, I heard the owls. Hosmer[2] said: "If you ever minded it, it is about the surest sign of rain that there is. Don't you know that last Friday night you heard them and spoke of them, and the next day it rained?" This time there were other signs of rain in abundance. "But night before last," said I, "when you were not here, they hooted louder than ever, and we have had no rain yet." At any rate, it rained hard the 21st, and by that rain the water was raised much higher than it has been this fall.

February 3, 1852 My owl sounds *hōō hōō hōō, hōō.*[3]

---

[1][An old name for the white spruce. Thoreau afterwards learned that he had been mistaken as to the identification and that the Concord trees were *black* spruces.]

[2][Mr. Joseph Hosmer, an old citizen of Concord, who was helping Thoreau in his surveying.]

[3][This was at the cliffs of Fairhaven Hill near Walden Pond on a moonlight evening.]

May 1, 1852 When leaving the woods[1] I heard the hooting of an owl, which sounded very much like a clown calling to his team.

June 23, 1852 I hear my old Walden owl. Its first note is almost like a somewhat peevish scream or squeal of a child shrugging its shoulders, and then succeed two more moderate and musical ones.

July 5, 1852 I hear my hooting owl now just before sunset.[2] You can fancy it the most melancholy sound in Nature, as if Nature meant by this to stereotype and make permanent in her quire the dying moans of a human being, made more awful by a certain gurgling melodiousness. It reminds of ghouls and idiots and insane howlings. One answers from far woods in a strain made really sweet by distance. Some poor weak relic of mortality who has left hope behind, and howls like an animal, yet with human sobs, on entering the dark valley. I find myself beginning with the letters *gl* when I try to imitate it. Yet for the most part it is a sweet and melodious strain to me.

April 2, 1853 Heard the hooting owl in Ministerial Swamp. It sounded somewhat like the hounding or howling of some dogs, and as often as the whistle of the engine sounded I noticed a resemblance in the tone. A singular kind of squealing introduced into its note.

[1][Near Walden Pond.]
[2][At Ministerial Swamp.]

April 9, 1853 Beyond the desert,[1] hear the hooting owl, which, as formerly, I at first mistook for the hounding of a dog,— a squealing *eee* followed by *hoo hoo hoo* deliberately, and particularly sonorous and ringing. This at 2 P.M. Now mated. Pay their addresses by day, says Brooks.[2]

January 7, 1854 I went to these woods[3] partly to hear an owl, but did not; but, now that I have left them nearly a mile behind, I hear one distinctly, *hoorer hoo*. Strange that we should hear this sound so often, loud and far,—a voice which we call the owl,—and yet so rarely see the bird Oftenest at twilight. It has a singular prominence as a sound; is louder than the voice of a dear friend. Yet we see the friend perhaps daily and the owl but few times in our lives. It is a sound which the wood or the horizon makes. I see the cars almost as often as I hear the whistle.

December 9, 1856 From a little east of Wyman's I look over the pond[4] westward. The sun is near setting, away beyond Fair Haven. A bewitching stillness reigns through all the woodland and over the snow-clad landscape. Indeed, the winter day in the woods or fields has commonly the stillness of twilight. The pond is perfectly smooth and full of light. I hear only the strokes of a lingering woodchopper at a distance, and the melodious hooting of an owl,

[1] [Dugan Desert, near Ministerial Swamp.]
[2] [George Brooks, of Concord, doubtless.]
[3] [Ministerial Swamp.]
[4] [Walden Pond.]

which is as common and marked a sound as the axe or the locomotive whistle. Yet where does the ubiquitous hooter sit, and who
sees him? In whose wood-lot is he to be found? Few eyes have
rested on him hooting; few on him silent on his perch even. Yet cut
away the woods never so much year after year, though the chopper
has not seen him and only a grove or two is left, still his aboriginal
voice is heard indefinitely far and sweet, mingled oft, in strange
harmony, with the newly invented din of trade, like a sentence of
Allegri sounded in our streets,—hooting from invisible perch at his
foes the woodchoppers, who are invading his domains. As the
earth only a few inches beneath the surface is undisturbed and what
is was anciently, so are heard still some primeval sounds in the air.
Some of my townsmen I never see, and of a great proportion I do
not hear the voices in a year, though they live within my horizon;
but every week almost I hear the loud voice of the hooting owl,
though I do not see the bird more than once in ten years.

December 15, 1856 I still recall to mind that characteristic
winter eve of December 9th; the cold, dry, and wholesome diet my
mind and senses necessarily fed on,—oak leaves, bleached and
withered weeds that rose above the snow, the now dark green of
the pines, and perchance the faint metallic chip of a single tree sparrow; the hushed stillness of the wood at sundown, aye, all the winter day; the short boreal twilight; the smooth serenity and the reflections of the pond, still alone free from ice; the melodious
hooting of the owl, heard at the same time with the yet more dis-

tant whistle of a locomotive, more aboriginal, and perchance more enduring here than that, heard above the voices of all the wise men of Concord, as if they were not (how little he is Anglicized!); the last strokes of the woodchopper, who presently bends his steps homeward; the gilded bar of cloud across the apparent outlet of the pond, conducting my thoughts into the eternal west; the deepening horizon glow; and the hasty walk homeward to enjoy the long winter evening. The hooting of the owl! That is a sound which my red predecessors heard here more than a thousand years ago. It rings far and wide, occupying the spaces rightfully,—grand, primeval, aboriginal sound. There is no whisper in it of the Buckleys, the Flints, the Hosmers who recently squatted here, nor of the first parish, nor of Concord Fight, nor of the last town meeting.

December 19, 1856   As I stand here, I hear the hooting of my old acquaintance the owl in Wheeler's Wood.[1] Do I not oftenest hear it just before sundown? This sound, heard near at hand, is more simply animal and guttural, without resonance or reverberation, but, heard here from out the depths of the wood, it sounds peculiarly hollow and drum-like, as if it struck on a tense skin drawn around, the tympanum of the wood, through which all we denizens of nature hear. Thus it comes to us an accredited and universal or melodious sound; is more than the voice of the owl, the voice of the wood as well. The owl only touches the stops, or rather wakes

[1][Near Walden Pond.]

the reverberations. For all Nature is a musical instrument on which her creatures play, celebrating their joy or grief unconsciously often. It sounds now, *hoo | hoo hoo* (very fast) | *hoo-rer* | *hoo*.

May 20, 1858   Saw in the street a young cat owl, one of two which Skinner killed in Walden Woods yesterday. It was almost ready to fly, at least two and a half feet in alar extent; tawny with many black bars, and darker on wings. Holmes, in Patent Office Report,[1] says they "pair early in February." So I visited the nest. It was in a large white pine close on the north side of the path, some ten rods west of the old Stratton cellar in the woods. This is the largest pine thereabouts, and the nest is some thirty-five feet high on two limbs close to the main stem, and, according to Skinner, was not much more than a foot across, made of small sticks, nearly flat, "without fine stuff!" There were but two young. This is a path which somebody travels every half-day, at least, and only a stone's throw from the great road. There were many white droppings about and large rejected pellets containing the vertebræ and hair of a skunk. As I stood there, I heard the crows making a great noise some thirty or forty rods off, and immediately suspected that they were pestering one of the old owls, which Skinner had not seen. It proved so, for, as I approached, the owl sailed away from amidst a white pine top, with the crows in full pursuit, and he looked very

---

[1][1856, p. 122, in paper on "Birds Injurious to Agriculture," by Ezekiel Holmes, M.D., of Winthrop, Maine, pp. 110–160.]

large, stately, and heavy, like a seventy-four among schooners. I soon knew by the loud cawing of the crows that he had alighted again some forty rods off, and there again I found him perched high on a white pine, the large tawny fellow with black dashes and large erect horns. Away he goes again, and the crows after him.

June 18, 1858 A boy climbs to the cat owl's nest and casts down what is left of it,—a few short sticks and some earthy almost turfy foundation, as if it were the accumulation of years. Beside much black and white skunk-hair, there are many fishes' scales (!) intimately mixed with its substance, and some skunk's bones.

January 30, 1859 How peculiar the hooting of an owl! It is not shrill and sharp like the scream of a hawk, but full, round, and sonorous, waking the echoes of the wood.

CUCKOOS

KINGFISHERS

WOODPECKERS

BLACK-BILLED CUCKOO
(ST. DOMINGO CUCKOO)[1]

June 18, 1853 Found the nest of a cuckoo,—a long, slender, handsome bird, probably St. Domingo cuckoo,—at the edge of the meadow on a bent sallow, not in a crotch, covered by the broad, shining leaves of a swamp white oak, whose boughs stretched over it, two feet or more from the ground. The nest was made of dry twigs and was small for the size of the bird and very shallow, but handsomely lined with an abundance of what looked like the dry yellowish-brown (?) catkins of the hickory, which

---

[1][The black-billed, or, as Thoreau called it, after Nuttall, the St. Domingo, cuckoo being much the commoner of the two Northern species in the Concord region, it is probably that most if not all of his cuckoos were of this species.]

made a pleasing contrast with the surrounding grayish twigs. There were some worm-eaten green leaves inwoven. It contained a single greenish-white elliptical egg, an inch or more long. The bird flew off a little way and *clow-clow-clowed*.

June 27, 1853 The cuckoo's nest is robbed, or perhaps she broke her egg because I found it. Thus three out of half a dozen nests which I have revisited have been broken up. It is a very shallow nest, six or seven inches in diameter by two and a half or three deep, on a low bending willow, hardly half an inch deep within; concealed by overlying leaves of a swamp white oak on the edge of the river meadow, two to three feet from ground, made of slender twigs which are prettily ornamented with much ramalina lichen, lined with hickory catkins and pitch pine needles.

May 14, 1854 A St. Domingo cuckoo, black-billed with red round eye, a silent, long, slender, graceful bird, dark cinnamon (?) above, pure white beneath. It is in a leisurely manner picking the young caterpillars out of a nest (now about a third of an inch long) with its long, curved bill. Not timid.

July 17, 1854 The cuckoo is a very neat, slender, and graceful bird. It belongs to the nobility of birds. It is elegant.

June 5, 1856 A cuckoo's nest with three light bluish-green eggs partly developed, short with rounded ends, nearly of a size; in the thicket up railroad this side high wood, in a black cherry that had been lopped three feet from ground, amid the thick sprouts; a nest of nearly average depth (?), of twigs lined with *green* leaves, pine-needles, etc., and edged with some dry, branchy weeds. The bird stole off silently at first.

August 20, 1857   As I stand there, I hear a peculiar sound which I mistake for a woodpecker's tapping, but I soon see a cuckoo hopping near suspiciously or inquisitively, at length within twelve feet, from time to time uttering a hard, dry note, very much like a woodpecker tapping a dead dry tree rapidly, its *full* clear white throat and breast toward me, and slowly lifting its tail from time to time. Though somewhat allied to that throttled note it makes by night, it was quite different from that.

BELTED KINGFISHER

April 24, 1854   The kingfisher flies with a *crack cr-r-r-ack* and a limping or flitting flight from tree to tree before us, and finally, after a third of a mile, circles round to our rear. He sits rather low over the water. Now that he has come I suppose that the fishes on which he preys rise within reach.

April 15, 1855   Saw and heard a kingfisher—do they not come with the smooth waters of April?—hurrying over the meadow as if on urgent business.

April 22, 1855   The bluish band on the breast of the kingfisher leaves the pure white beneath in the form of a heart.

April 11, 1856   Saw a kingfisher on a tree over the water. Does not its arrival mark some new movement in its finny prey? He is the bright buoy that betrays it!

July 28, 1858 Heard a kingfisher, which had been hovering over the river, plunge forty rods off.

August 6, 1858 The kingfisher is seen hovering steadily over one spot, or hurrying away with a small fish in his mouth, sounding his alarum nevertheless.

HAIRY WOODPECKER

April 9, 1855 Heard a loud, long, dry, tremulous shriek which reminded me of a kingfisher, but which I found proceeded from a woodpecker which had just alighted on an elm; also its clear whistle or *chink* afterward. It is probably the hairy woodpecker and I am not so certain I have seen it earlier this year.[1]

June 5, 1857 In that first apple tree at Wyman's an apparent hairy woodpecker's nest (from the size of the bird), about ten feet from ground. The bird darts away with a shrill, loud chirping of alarm, incessantly repeated, long before I get there, and keeps it up as long as I stay in the neighborhood. The young keep up an incessant fine, breathing peep which can be heard across the road and is much increased when they hear you approach the hole, they evidently expecting the old bird. I perceive no offensive odor. I saw the bird fly out of this hole, May 1st, and probably the eggs were laid about that time.

[1] [The kingfisher-like rattle is diagnostic of the hairy woodpecker.]

October 16, 1859 See a hairy woodpecker on a burnt pitch pine. He distinctly rests on his tail constantly. With what vigor he taps and bores the bark, making it fly far and wide, and then darts off with a sharp whistle!

May 18, 1860 A hairy woodpecker betrays its hole in an apple tree by its anxiety. The ground is strewn with the chips it has made, over a large space. The hole, so far as I can see, is exactly like that of the downy woodpecker,—the entrance (though not so round) and the conical form within above,—only larger. The bird scolds at me from a dozen rods off.

DOWNY WOODPECKER

March 24, 1853 The downy (?) woodpeckers are quite numerous this morning, the skirts of their coats barred with white and a large, long white spot on their backs. They have a smart, shrill peep or whistle, somewhat like a robin, but more metallic.

January 8, 1854 Stood within a rod of a downy woodpecker on an apple tree. How curious and exciting the blood-red spot on its hindhead! I ask why it is there, but no answer is rendered by these snow-clad fields. It is so close to the bark I do not see its feet. It looks behind as if it had on a black cassock open behind and showing a white undergarment between the shoulders and down the back. It is briskly and incessantly tapping all round the dead limbs, but rarely twice in a place, as if to sound the tree and so see if it has any worm in it, or perchance to start them. How much he deals with the bark of trees, all his life long tapping and inspecting it! He it is that scatters those fragments of bark and lichens about on the snow at the base of trees. What a lichenist he must be! Or rather, perhaps it is fungi makes his favorite study, for he deals most with dead limbs. How briskly he glides up or drops himself down a limb, creeping round and round, and hopping from limb to limb, and now flitting with a rippling sound of his wings to another tree!

April 4, 1855 The rows of white spots near the end of the wings of the downy [woodpecker] remind me of the lacings on the skirts of a soldier's coat.

December 14, 1855 A little further I heard the sound of a downy woodpecker tapping a pitch pine in a little grove, and saw him inclining to dodge behind the stem. He flitted from pine to pine before me. Frequently, when I pause to listen, I hear this sound in the orchards or streets. This was in one of these dense groves of young pitch pines.

June 20, 1856 Walking under an apple tree in the little Baker Farm peach orchard, heard an incessant shrill musical twitter or peeping, as from young birds, over my head, and, looking up, saw a hole in an upright dead bough, some fifteen feet from ground. Climbed up and, finding that the shrill twitter came from it, guessed it to be the nest of a downy woodpecker, which proved to be the case,—for it reminded me of the hissing squeak or squeaking hiss of young pigeon woodpeckers, but this was more musical or bird-like. The bough was about four and a half inches in diameter, and the hole perfectly circular, about an inch and a quarter in diameter. Apparently nests had been in holes above, now broken out, higher up. When I put my fingers in it, the young breathed their shrill twitter louder than ever. Anon the old appeared, and came quite near, while I stood in the tree, keeping up an incessant loud and shrill scolding note, and also after I descended; not to be relieved.

July 19, 1856   The downy woodpecker's nest which I got July 8th was in a dead and partly rotten upright apple bough four and three quarters inches in diameter. Hole *perfectly* elliptical (or oval) one and two sixteenths by one and five sixteenths inches; whole depth below it eight inches. It is excavated directly inward about three and a half inches, with a conical roof, also arching at back, with a recess in one side on level with the hole, where the bird turns. Judging from an old hole in the same bough, directly above, it enlarges directly to a diameter of two and one fourth to two and one half inches, not in this case descending exactly in the middle of the bough, but leaving one side not a quarter of an inch thick. At the hole it is left one inch thick. At the nest it is about two and three eighths inches in diameter. I find nothing in the first but bits of rotten wood, remains of insects, etc., when I tip it up,—for I cannot see the bottom,—yet in the old one there is also quite a nest of fine stubble (?), bark shred (?), etc., mixed with the bits of rotten wood.

ARCTIC THREE-TOED
WOODPECKER

October 8, 1860 Standing by a pigeon-place on the north edge of Damon's lot, I saw on the dead top of a white pine four or five rods off—which had been stripped for fifteen feet downward that it might die and afford with its branches a perch for the pigeons about the place, like the more artificial ones that were set up—two woodpeckers that were new to me. They uttered a peculiar sharp *kek kek* on alighting (not so sharp as that of the hairy or downy woodpecker) and appeared to be about the size of the hairy woodpecker, or between that and the golden-winged. I had a good view of them with my glass as long as I desired. With the back to me, they were clear black all above, as well as their feet and bills, and each had a yellow or orange (or possibly orange-scarlet?) front (the anterior part of the head at the base of the upper mandible). A long white line along the side of the head to the neck, with a black one below it. The breast, as near as I could see, was gray specked with white, and the under side of the wing expanded was also gray, with small white spots. The throat white and vent also white or whitish. Is this the arctic three-toed?[1] Probably many trees dying on this large burnt tract will attract many woodpeckers to it.

[1][The birds must have been arctic three-toed woodpeckers, though Thoreau misplaces the yellow crown-patch. This species, usually very rare in Massachusetts, visited the State in considerable numbers in this winter of 1860–1861.]

PILEATED WOODPECKER

July 25, 1857   Our path up the bank here[1] led by a large dead white pine, in whose trunk near the ground were great square-cornered holes made by the woodpeckers, probably the red-headed. They were seven or eight inches long by four wide and reached to the heart of the tree through an inch or more of sound wood, and looked like great mortise-holes whose corners had been somewhat worn and rounded by a loose tenon. The tree for some distance was quite honeycombed by them. It suggested woodpeckers on a larger scale than ours, as were the trees and the forest.[2]

FLICKER
(PIGEON WOODPECKER)

April 3, 1842   I have just heard the flicker among the oaks on the hillside ushering in a new dynasty. It is the age and youth of time. Why did Nature set this lure for sickly mortals? Eternity could not begin with more security and momentousness than the spring. The summer's eternity is reëstablished by this

[1][On the West Branch of the Penobscot, Maine.]
[2][These mortise-shaped holes, found abundantly in the forests of northern New England, are the work of the pileated woodpecker, which Thoreau saw and heard in the Maine woods, but somewhat hastily denominated the red-headed woodpecker from the conspicuous red crest.]

note. All sights and sounds are seen and heard both in time and eternity. And when the eternity of any sight or sound strikes the eye or ear, they are intoxicated with delight.

April 23, 1852 Heard the pigeon woodpecker to-day, that long-continued unmusical note,—somewhat like a robin's, heard afar,—yet pleasant to hear because associated with a more advanced stage of the season.

April 6, 1853 Returning by Harrington's, saw a pigeon woodpecker flash away, showing the rich golden under side of its glancing wings and the large whitish spot on its back, and presently I heard its familiar long-repeated loud note, almost familiar as that of a barn-door fowl, which it somewhat resembles.

June 21, 1853 Where the other day I saw a pigeon woodpecker tapping and enlarging a hole in the dead limb of an apple tree, when as yet probably no egg was laid, to-day I see two well-grown young woodpeckers about as big as the old, looking out at the hole, showing their handsome spotted breasts and calling lustily for something to eat, or, it may be, suffering from the heat. Young birds in some situations must suffer greatly from heat these days, so closely packed in their nests and perhaps insufficiently shaded. It is a wonder they remain so long there patiently. I saw a yellowbird's[1] nest in the willows on the causeway this afternoon

---

[1] [The summer yellowbird, or yellow warbler.]

and three young birds, nearly ready to fly, overflowing the nest, all holding up their open bills and keeping them steadily open for a minute or more, on noise of my approach.

August 10, 1854 That is a peculiar and distinct hollow sound made by the pigeon woodpecker's wings, as it flies past near you.

April 23, 1855 Saw two pigeon woodpeckers approach and, I think, but their bills together and utter that *o-week, o-week.*

April 14, 1856 Hear the flicker's cackle on the old aspen, and his tapping sounds afar over the water. Their tapping resounds thus far, with this peculiar ring and distinctness, because it is a hollow tree they select to play on, as a drum or tambour. It is a hollow sound which rings distinct to a great distance, especially over water.

April 22, 1856 Going through Hubbard's root-fence field, see a pigeon woodpecker on a fence-post. He shows his lighter back between his wings cassock-like and like the smaller woodpeckers. Joins his mate on a tree and utters the wooing note *o-week o-week*, etc.

April 27, 1856 The tapping of a woodpecker is made a more remarkable and emphatic sound by the hollowness of the trunk, the expanse of water which conducts the sound, and the morning hour at which I commonly hear it. I think that the pigeon woodpeckers must be building, they frequent the old aspen now so much.

April 29, 1856   A pigeon woodpecker alights on a dead cedar top near me. Its cackle, thus near, sounds like *eh eh eh eh eh*, etc., rapidly and emphatically repeated.

June 10, 1856   In a hollow apple tree, hole eighteen inches deep, young pigeon woodpeckers, large and well feathered. They utter their squeaking hiss whenever I cover the hole with my hand, apparently taking it for the approach of the mother. A strong, rank fetic smell issues from the hole.

March 17, 1858   Ah! there is the note of the first flicker, a prolonged, monotonous *wick-wick-wick-wick-wick-wick*, etc., or, if you please, *quick-quick*, heard far over and through the dry leaves. But how that single sound peoples and enriches all the woods and fields! They are no longer the same woods and fields that they were. This note really *quickens* what was dead. It seems to put a life into withered grass and leaves and bare twigs, and henceforth the days shall not be as they have been. It is as when a family, your neighbors, return to an empty house after a long absence, and you hear the cheerful hum of voices and the laughter of children, and see the smoke from the kitchen fire. The doors are thrown open, and children go screaming through the hall. So the flicker dashes through the aisles of the grove, throws up a window here and cackles out it, and then there, airing the house. It makes its voice ring up–stairs and down–stairs, and so, as it were, fits it for its habitation and ours, and takes possession. It is as good as a housewarming to all nature. Now I hear and see him louder and nearer on the top of the long-armed white oak, sitting very upright, as is their wont, as it were calling for some of his kind that may also have arrived.

April 15, 1858 See a pair of woodpeckers on a rail and on the ground a-courting. One keeps hopping near the other, and the latter hops away a few feet, and so they accompany one another a long distance, uttering sometimes a faint or short *a-week*.

March 23, 1859 The loud *peop* (?) of a pigeon woodpecker is heard . . . and anon the prolonged loud and shrill *cackle*, calling the thin-wooded hillsides and pastures to life. It is like the note of an alarm-clock set last fall so as to wake Nature up at exactly this date. *Up up up up up up up up up!* What a rustling it seems to make among the dry leaves!

May 4, 1860 As I stood there I heard a thumping sound, which I referred to Peter's, three quarters of a mile off over the meadow, but it was a pigeon woodpecker excavating its nest within a maple within a rod of me. Though I had just landed and made a noise with my boat, he was too busy to hear me, but now he hears my tread, and I see him put out his head then withdraw it warily and keep still, while I stay there.

WOODPECKERS
(SPECIES UNNAMED)

January 26, 1852 The woodpeckers work in Emerson's wood on the Cliff-top, the trees being partly killed by the top, and the grubs having hatched under the bark. The woodpeckers have stripped a whole side of some trees, and in a sound red oak they have dug out a mortise-hole with squarish shoulders, as if with a chisel. I have often seen these holes.

March 22, 1853   The tapping of the woodpecker, *rat-tat-tat*, knocking at the door of some sluggish grub to tell him that the spring has arrived, and his fate, this is one of the season sounds, calling the roll of birds and insects, the reveille.

May 10, 1853   How far the woodpecker's tapping is heard! And no wonder, for he taps very hard as well as fast, to make a hole, and the dead, dry wood, is very resounding withal. Now he taps on one part of the tree, and it yields one note; then on that side, a few inches distant, and it yields another key; propped on its tail the while.

January 6, 1855   I see where a woodpecker has drilled a hole about two inches over in a decayed white maple; quite recently, for the chippings are strewn over the ice beneath and were the first sign that betrayed it. The tree was hollow. Is it for a nest next season?[1] There was an old hole higher up.

March 8, 1859   I see there a dead white pine, some twenty-five feet high, which has been almost entirely stripped of its bark by the woodpeckers. Where any bark is left, the space between it and the wood is commonly closely packed with the gnawings of worms, which appear to have consumed the inner bark. But where

---

[1][Probably for winter quarters.]

the bark is gone, the wood also is eaten to some depth, and there are numerous holes penetrating deep into the wood. Over all this portion, which is almost all the tree, the woodpeckers have knocked off the bark and enlarged the holes in pursuit of the worms.

March 11, 1859 But methinks the sound of the woodpecker tapping is as much a spring note as any these mornings; it echoes peculiarly in the air of a spring morning.

GOATSUCKERS

SWIFTS

HUMMINGBIRDS

WHIP-POOR-WILL

June 11, 1851 The whip-poor-will suggests how wide asunder are the woods and the town. Its note is very rarely heard by those who live on the street, and then it is thought to be of ill omen. Only the dwellers on the outskirts of the village hear it occasionally. It sometimes comes into their yards. But go into the woods in a warm night at this season, and it is the prevailing sound. I hear now five or six at once. It is no more of ill omen therefore here than the night and the moonlight are. It is a bird not only of the woods, but of the night side of the woods.

New beings have usurped the air we breathe, rounding Nature, filling her crevices with sound. To sleep where you may hear the whip-poor-will in your dreams!

★   ★   ★

I hear some whip-poor-wills on hills, others in thick wooded vales, which ring hollow and cavernous, like an apartment or cellar, with their note. As when I hear the working of some artisan from within an apartment.

June 13, 1851 It is not nightfall till the whip-poor-wills begin to sing.

June 14, 1851 From Conant's summit I hear as many as fifteen whip-poor-wills—or whip-or-I-wills—at once, the succeeding cluck sounding strangely foreign, like a hewer at work elsewhere.

August 12, 1851 There was a whip-poor-will in the road just beyond Goodwin's, which flew up and lighted on the fence and kept alighting on the fence within a rod of me and circling round me with a slight squeak as if inquisitive about me.

September 9, 1851 The whip-poor-wills now begin to sing in earnest about half an hour before sunrise, as if making haste to improve the short time that is left them. As far as my observation goes, they sing for several hours in the early part of the night, are silent commonly at midnight,—though you may meet them then sitting on a rock or flitting silently about,—then sing again just before sunrise.

NIGHTHAWK

June 11, 1851 I hear the nighthawks uttering their squeaking notes high in the air now at nine o'clock P.M., and occasionally—what I do not remember to have heard so late—their booming note. It sounds more as if under a cope than by day. The sound is not so fugacious, going off to be lost amid the spheres, but is echoed hollowly to earth, making the low roof of heaven vibrate. Such a sound is more confused and dissipated by day.

June 23, 1851 It is a pleasant sound to me, the squeaking and the booming of nighthawks flying over high open fields in the woods. They fly like butterflies, not to avoid birds of prey but, apparently, to secure their own insect prey. There is a particular part of the railroad just below the shanty where they may be heard and seen in greatest numbers. But often you must look a long while before you can detect the mote in the sky from which the note proceeds.

June 1, 1853 Walking up this side-hill, I disturbed a night-hawk eight or ten feet from me, which went, half fluttering, half hopping, the mottled creature, like a winged toad, as Nuttall says the French of Louisiana (?) call them,[1] down the hill as far as I could see. Without moving, I looked about and saw its two eggs on the bare ground, on a slight shelf of the hill, on the dead pine-needles and sand, without any cavity or nest whatever, very obvious when once you had detected them, but not easily detected from their color, a coarse gray formed of white spotted with a bluish or slaty brown or umber,—a stone—granite—color, like the places it selects. I advanced and put my hand on them, and while I stooped, seeing a shadow on the ground, looked up and saw the bird, which had fluttered down the hill so blind and helpless, circling low and swiftly past over my head, showing the white spot on each wing in true nighthawk fashion. When I had gone a dozen rods, it appeared again higher in the air, with its peculiar flitting, limping kind of flight, all the while noiseless, and suddenly descending, it dashed at

[1][Nuttall speaks of "the metaphorical French name of '*Crapaud volans*,' or Flying Toad."]

me within ten feet of my head, like an imp of darkness, then swept away high over the pond, dashing now to this side now to that, on different tacks, as if, in pursuit of its prey, it had already forgotten its eggs on the earth. I can see how it might easily come to be regarded with superstitious awe.

June 7, 1853 Visited my nighthawk on her nest. Could hardly believe my eyes when I stood within seven feet and beheld her sitting on her eggs, her head to me. She looked so Saturnian, so one with the earth, so sphinx-like, a relic of the reign of Saturn which Jupiter did not destroy, a riddle that might well cause a man to go dash his head against a stone. It was not an actual living creature, far less a winged creature of the air, but a figure in stone or bronze, a fanciful production of art, like the gryphon or phœnix. In fact, with its breast toward me, and owing to its color or size no bill perceptible, it looked like the end of a brand, such as are common in a clearing, its breast mottled or alternately waved with dark brown and gray, its flat, grayish, weather-beaten crown, its eyes nearly closed, purposely, lest those bright beads should betray it, with the stony cunning of the Sphinx. A fanciful work in bronze to ornament a mantel. It was enough to fill one with awe. The sight of this creature sitting on its eggs impressed me with the venerableness of the globe. There was nothing novel about it. All the while, this seemingly sleeping bronze sphinx, as motionless as the earth, was watching me with intense anxiety through those narrow slits in its eyelids. Another step, and it fluttered down the hill close to the ground, with a wabbling motion, as if touching the ground now with the tip of one wing, now with the other, so ten rods to the water, which it skimmed close over a few rods, then rose and soared in the air above me. Wonderful creature, which sits motion-less on its eggs on the barest, most exposed hills, through pelting storms of rain or hail, as if it were a rock or a part of the earth itself, the outside of the globe, with its eyes shut and its wings folded, and, after the two days' storm, when you think it has become a fit symbol of the rheumatism, it suddenly rises into the air a bird, one of the most aerial, supple, and graceful of creatures, without stiff-ness in its wings or joints! It was a fit prelude to meeting Prome-theus bound to his rock on Caucasus.

June 17, 1853 One of the nighthawk's eggs is hatched. The young is unlike any that I have seen, exactly like a pinch of rabbit's fur or down of that color dropped on the ground, not two inches long, with a dimpling or geometrical or somewhat regular ar-rangement of minute feathers in the middle, destined to become the wings and tail. Yet even it half opened its eye, and peeped if I mistake not. Was ever bird more completely protected, both by the color of its eggs and of its own body that sits on them, and of the young bird just hatched? Accordingly the eggs and young are rarely discovered. There was one egg still, and by the side of it this little pinch of down, flattened out and not observed at first, and a foot down the hill had rolled a half of the egg it came out of. There was no callowness, as in the young of most birds. It seemed a sin-

gular place for a bird to begin its life,—to come out of its egg,—
this little pinch of down,—and lie still on the exact spot where the
egg lay, on a flat exposed shelf on the side of a bare hill, with nothing but the whole heavens, the broad universe above, to brood it
when its mother was away.

June 5, 1854 Now, just before sundown, a nighthawk is circling, imp-like, with undulating, irregular flight over the sprout-
land on the Cliff Hill, with an occasional squeak and showing the
spots on his wings. He does not circle away from this place, and I
associate him with two gray eggs somewhere on the ground beneath and a mate there sitting. This squeak and occasional booming
is heard in the evening air, while the stillness on the side of the village makes more distinct the increased hum of insects.

May 31, 1856 As I return in the dusk, *many* nighthawks,
with their great spotted wings, are circling low over the river, as
the swallows were when I went out. They skim within a rod of me.
After dusk these greater swallows come forth, and circle and play
about over the water like those lesser ones, or perhaps making a
larger circuit, also uttering a louder note. It would not be safe for
such great birds to fly so near and familiarly by day.

May 26, 1857 As I am going down the footpath from Britton's camp to the spring, I start a pair of nighthawks (they had the
white on the wing) from amid the dry leaves at the base of a bush,
a bunch of sprouts, and away they flitted in zigzag noiseless flight
a few rods through the sprout-land, dexterously avoiding the

twigs, uttering a faint hollow *what*, as if made by merely closing the bill, and one alighted flat on a stump.

June 2, 1858[1] The chewink sang before night, and this, as I have before observed, is a very common bird on mountain-tops.[2] It seems to love a cool atmosphere, and sometimes lingers quite late with us. And the wood thrush,[3] indefinitely far or near, a little more distant and unseen, as great poets are. Early in the evening the nighthawks were heard to spark[4] and boom over these bare gray rocks, and such was our serenade at first as we lay on our spruce bed. We were left alone with the nighthawks. These withdrawn bare rocks must be a very suitable place for them to lay their eggs, and their dry and unmusical, yet supramundane and spirit-like, voices and sounds gave fit expression to this rocky mountain solitude. It struck the very key-note of the stern, gray, barren solitude. It was a thrumming of the mountain's rocky chords; strains from the music of Chaos, such as were heard when the earth was rent and these rocks heaved up. Thus they went sparking and booming, while we were courting the first access of sleep, and I could imag-

[1][In camp near the summit of Mt. Monadnock.]

[2][This is true only of the lower summits in the latitude of New England. In "A Walk to Wachusett" he speaks of hearing the bird on or near the top of that mountain.]

[3][Probably either the hermit thrush or the olive-backed thrush. See note in Chapter 21.]

[4][Thoreau's word for the nighthawk's note, which to most persons sounds like *speak* or *peent*.]

ine their dainty limping flight, circling over the kindred rock, with a spot of white quartz in their wings. No sound could be more in harmony with that scenery. Though common below, it seemed peculiarly proper here.

June 3, 1858 Lying up there at this season, when the nighthawk is most musical, reminded me of what I had noticed before, that this bird is crepuscular in its habits. It was heard by night only up to nine or ten o'clock and again just before dawn, and marked those periods or seasons like a clock. Its note very conveniently indicated the time of night. It was sufficient to hear the nighthawk booming when you awoke to know how the night got on, though you had no other evidence of the hour.

July 17, 1860 The nighthawk's ripping sound, heard overhead these days, reminds us that the sky is, as it were, a roof, and that our world is limited on that side, it being reflected as from a roof back to earth. It does not suggest an infinite depth in the sky, but a nearness to the earth, as of a low roof echoing back its sounds.

August 9, 1860 But, above all, this[1] was an excellent place to observe the habits of the nighthawks. They were heard and seen regularly at sunset,—one night it was at 7.10, or exactly at sunset,—coming upward from the lower and more shaded portion of the rocky surface below our camp, with their *spark spark*, soon answered by a companion, for they seemed always to hunt in pairs,—

[1][Mt. Monadnock again.]

yet both would dive and boom and, according to Wilson, only the male utters this sound. They pursued their game thus a short distance apart and some sixty or one hundred feet above the gray rocky surface, in the twilight, and the constant *spark spark* seemed to be a sort of call-note to advertise each other of their neighborhood. Suddenly one would hover and flutter more stationarily for a moment, somewhat like a kingfisher, and then dive almost perpendicularly downward with a rush, for fifty feet, frequently within three or four rods of us, and the loud booming sound or rip was made just at the curve, as it ceased to fall, but whether voluntarily or involuntarily I know not. They appeared to be diving for their insect prey. What eyes they must have to be able to discern it *beneath* them against the rocks in the twilight! As I was walking about the camp, one flew low, within two feet of the surface, about me, and lit on the rock within three rods of me, and uttered a harsh note like *c-o-w, c-o-w*,—hard and gritty and allied to their common notes,—which I thought expressive of anxiety, or to alarm me, or for its mate.

I suspect that their booming on a distant part of the mountain was the sound which I heard the first night which was like very distant thunder, or the fall of a pile of lumber.

They did not fly or boom when there was a cloud or fog, and ceased pretty early in the night. They came up from the same quarter—the shaded rocks below—each night, two of them, and left off booming about 8 o'clock. Whether they then ceased hunting or withdrew to another part of the mountain, I know not. Yet I heard one the first night at 11.30 P.M., but, as it had been a rainy day and did not clear up here till some time late in the night, it may have been compelled to do its hunting then. They began to boom again at 4 A.M. (other birds about 4.30) and ceased about 4.20. By their color they are related to the gray rocks over which they flit and circle.

CHIMNEY SWIFT
(CHIMNEY SWALLOW)

July 29, 1856 Pratt gave me a chimney swallow's nest, which he says fell down Wesson's chimney with young in it two or three days ago. As it comes to me, it is in the form of the segment of the circumference of a sphere whose diameter is three and a half inches, the segment being two plus wide, one side, of course, longer than the other. It bears a little soot on the inner side. It may have been placed against a slanting part of the chimney, or perhaps some of the outer edge is broken off. It is composed wholly of stout twigs, one to two inches long, one sixteenth to one eighth inch in diameter, held quasi cob-fashion, so as to form a sort of basketwork one third to one half inch thick, without any lining, at least in this, but very open to the air. These twigs, which are quite knubby, seem to be of the apple, elm, and the like, and are firmly fastened together by a very conspicuous whitish semi-transparent glue, which is laid on pretty copiously, sometimes extending continuously one inch. It reminds me of the edible nests of the Chinese swallow. Who knows but their edibleness is due to a similar glue secreted by the bird and used still more profusely in building its nests? The chimney swallow is said to break off the twigs as it flies.

August 23, 1856 J. Farmer says that he found that the gummed twig of a chimney swallow's nest, though it burned when held in a flame, went out immediately when taken out of it, and he thinks it owing to a peculiarity in the gum, rendering the twig partly fire-proof, so that they cannot be ignited by the sparks in a chimney. I suggested that these swallows had originally built in hollow trees, but it would be interesting to ascertain whether they constructed their nests in the same way and of the same material then.

RUBY-THROATED HUMMINGBIRD

May 17, 1856 Meanwhile I hear a loud hum and see a splendid male hummingbird coming zigzag in long tacks, like a bee, but far swifter, along the edge of the swamp, in hot haste. He turns aside to taste the honey of the *Andromeda calyculata*[1] (already visited by bees) within a rod of me. This golden-green gem. Its burnished back looks as if covered with green scales dusted with

---

[1][The cassandra, or leather-leaf, now known to botanists as *Chamœdaphne calyculata*.]

gold. It hovers, as it were stationary in the air, with an intense humming before each little flower-bell of the humble *Andromeda calyculata*, and inserts its long tongue in each, turning toward me that splendid ruby on its breast, that glowing ruby. Even this is coal-black in some lights! There, along with me in the deep, wild swamp, above the andromeda, amid the spruce. Its hum was heard afar at first, like that of a large bee, bringing a larger summer. This sight and sound would make me think I was in the tropics,—in Demerara or Maracaibo.

May 29, 1857   Soon I hear the low all-pervading hum of an approaching hummingbird circling above the rock, which afterward I mistake several times for the gruff voices of men approaching, unlike as these sounds are in some respects, and I perceive the resemblance even when I know better. Now I am sure it is a hummingbird, and now that it is two farmers approaching. But presently the hum becomes more sharp and thrilling, and the little fellow suddenly perches on an ash twig within a rod of me, and plumes himself while the rain is fairly beginning. He is quite out of proportion to the size of his perch. It does not acknowledge his weight.

May 16, 1858   A hummingbird yesterday came into the next house and was caught. Flew about our parlor to-day and tasted Sophia's flowers. In some lights you saw none of the colors of its throat. In others, in the shade the throat was a clear bright scarlet, but in the sun it glowed with splendid metallic, *fiery* reflections about the neck and throat. It uttered from time to time, as it flew, a faint squeaking chirp or chirrup. The hum sounded more hollow when it approached a flower. Its wings fanned the air so forcibly that you felt the cool wind they raised a foot off, and nearer it was very remarkable. Does not this very motion of the wings keep a bird cool in hot weather?

May 17, 1858   When the hummingbird flew about the room yesterday, his body and tail hung in a singular manner between the wings, swinging back and forth with a sort of oscillating motion, not hanging directly down, but yet pulsating or teetering up and down.

July 9, 1860   There is a smart shower at 5 P.M., and in the midst of it a hummingbird is busy about the flowers in the garden, unmindful of it, though you would think that each big drop that struck him would be a serious accident.

Twelve

FLYCATCHERS

KINGBIRD

July 16, 1851 I hear the kingbird twittering or chattering like a stout-chested swallow.

May 29, 1853 How still the hot noon! People have retired behind blinds. Yet the kingbird—lively bird, with white belly and tail edged with white, and with its lively twittering—stirs and keeps the air brisk.

June 2, 1854 Are these not kingbird days, when, in clearer first June days full of light, this aerial, twittering bird flutters from willow to willow and swings on the twigs, showing his white-edged tail?

June 5, 1854 I see at a distance a kingbird or blackbird pursuing a crow lower down the hill, like a satellite revolving about a black planet.

June 14, 1855 A kingbird's nest with four eggs on a large horizontal stem or trunk of a black willow, four feet high, over the edge of the river, amid small shoots from the willow; outside of mikania, roots, and knotty sedge, well lined with root-fibres and wiry weeds.

January 20, 1856 A probable kingbird's nest, on a small horizontal branch of a young swamp white oak, amid the twigs, about ten feet from ground. This tree is very scraggy; has numerous short twigs at various angles with the branches, making it unpleasant to climb and affording support to birds' nests. The nest is round, running to rather a sharp point on one side beneath. Extreme diameter outside, four and a half to five inches; within, three inches; depth within, two inches; without, four or more. The principal materials are ten, in the order of their abundance thus:—

1. Reddish and gray twigs, some a foot and more in length, which are cranberry vines, with now and then a leaf on, probably such as were torn up by the rakers. Some are as big round as a knitting-needle, and would be taken for a larger bush. These make the stiff mass of the outside above and rim.

2. Woody roots, rather coarser, intermixed from waterside shrubs. Probably some are from cranberry vines. These are mixed with the last and with the bottom.

3. Softer and rather smaller roots and root-fibres of herbaceous plants, mixed with the last and a little further inward, for the harshest arc always most external.

4. (Still to confine myself to the order of abundance) with-

ered flowers and short bits of the gray downy stems of the fragrant everlasting; these more or less compacted and apparently agglutinated from the mass of the solid bottom, and more loose, with the stems run down to a point on one side the bottom.

5. What I think is the fibrous growth of a willow, moss-like with a wiry dark-colored hair-like stem (possibly it is a moss).

This, with or without the tuft, is the lining, and lies contiguous in the sides and bottom.

6. What looks like brown decayed leaves and confervæ from the dried bottom of the riverside, mixed with the everlasting-tops internally in the solid bottom.

7. Some finer brown root-fibres, chiefly between the lining of No. 6 and hair and the coarser fibres of No. 3.

8. A dozen whitish cocoons, mixed with the everlasting-tops and dangling about the bottom peak externally; a few within the solid bottom. Also eight or ten very minute cocoons mixed with these, attached in a cluster to the top of an everlasting.

9. A few black much branched roots (?) (perhaps some utricularia from the dried bottom of river), mixed with Nos. 2 and 3.

10. Some horsehair, white and black, together with No. 5 forming the lining.

There are also, with the cocoons and everlasting-tops externally, one or two cotton-grass heads, one small white feather, and a little greenish-fuscous moss from the button-bush, and, in the bottom, a small shred of grape-vine bark.

August 5, 1858   [The black willows on the river-banks] resound still with the sprightly twitter of the kingbird, that aerial and spirited bird hovering over them, swallow-like, which loves best, methinks, to fly where the sky is reflected beneath him. Also now from time to time you hear the chattering of young blackbirds or the *link* of bobolinks there, or see the great bittern flap slowly away. The kingbird, by his activity and lively note and his white breast, keeps the air sweet. He sits now on a dead willow twig, akin to the flecks of mackerel sky, or its reflection in the water, or the white clamshell, wrong side out, opened by a musquash, or the fine particles of white quartz that may be found in the muddy river's sand. He is here to give a voice to all these. The willow's dead twig is aerial perch enough for him. Even the swallows deign to perch on it.

August 6, 1858   If our sluggish river, choked with potamogeton, might seem to have the slow-flying bittern for its peculiar genius, it has also the sprightly and aerial kingbird to twitter over and lift our thoughts to clouds as white as its own breast.

August 7, 1858   The sprightly kingbird glances and twitters above the glossy leaves of the swamp white oak. Perchance this tree, with its leaves glossy above and whitish beneath, best expresses the life of the kingbird and is its own tree.

PHŒBE
(PEWEE)

April 2, 1852 What ails the pewee's tail? It is loosely hung, pulsating with life. What mean these wag-tail birds? Cats and dogs, too, express some of their life through their tails.

★   ★   ★

For a long distance, as we paddle up the river, we hear the two-stanza'd lay of the pewee on the shore,—*pee-wet, pee-wee,* etc. Those are the two obvious facts to eye and ear, the river and the pewee.

April 11, 1852 As I go over the railroad bridge, I hear the pewee singing *pewet pewee, pee-wet pee-wee.* The last time rising on the last syllable, sometimes repeating it thus many times, *pe-wee.*

April 6, 1856 Just beyond Wood's Bridge, I hear the pewee. With what confidence after the lapse of many months, I come out to this waterside, some warm and pleasant spring morning, and, listening, hear, from farther or nearer, through the still concave of the air, the note of the first pewee! If there is one within half a mile, it will be here, and I shall be sure to hear its simple notes from those trees, borne over the water. It is remarkable how large a mansion of the air you can explore with your ears in the still morning by the waterside.

April 1, 1859 At the Pokelogan[1] up the Assabet, I see my first phœbe, the mild bird. It flirts its tail and sings *pre vit, pre vit, pre vit, pre vit* incessantly, as it sits over the water, and then at last, rising on the last syllable, says *pre*-VEE, as if insisting on that with peculiar emphasis.

May 5, 1860 See at Lee's a pewee (phœbe) building. She has just woven in, or laid on the edge, a fresh sprig of saxifrage in flower. I notice that phœbes will build in the same recess in a cliff year after year. It is a constant thing here, though they are often disturbed. Think how many pewees must have built under the eaves of this cliff since pewees were created and this cliff itself built! You can possibly find the crumbling relics of how many, if you should look carefully enough! It takes us many years to find out that Nature repeats herself annually. But how perfectly regular and calculable all her phenomena must appear to a mind that has observed her for a thousand years!

[1][A term evidently imported by Thoreau from Maine, where he learned it from the loggers and Indians. It is used to signify a little bay in the river-shore which leads nowhere and is perhaps derived from "poke" (= pouch or pocket) and "logan," a bay-like inlet to the river. "Logan" is supposed to be a corruption of the word "lagoon." Thoreau supposed "pokelogan" to be an Indian word, but his Indian guide told him there was "no Indian in 'em."]

OLIVE-SIDED FLYCATCHER
(PE-PE)

June 6, 1857   As I sit on Lee's Cliff, I see a pe-pe[1] on the topmost dead branch of a hickory eight or ten rods off. Regularly, at short intervals, it utters its monotonous note like *till-till-till,* or *pe-pe-pe.* Looking round for its prey and occasionally changing its perch, it every now and then darts off (phœbe-like), even five or six rods, toward the earth to catch an insect, and then returns to its favorite perch. If I lose it for a moment, I soon see it settling on the dead twigs again and hear its *till, till, till.* It appears through the glass mouse-colored above and head (which is perhaps darker), white throat, and narrow white beneath, with no white on tail.

WOOD PEWEE

May 22, 1854   I hear also *pe-a-wee pe-a-wee,* and then occasionally *pee-yu,* the first syllable in a different and higher key, emphasized,—all very sweet and naïve and innocent.

May 23, 1854   The wood pewee sings now in the woods behind the spring in the heat of the day (2 P.M.), sitting on a low limb near me, *pe-a-wee, pe-a-wee,* etc., five or six times at short and reg-

---

[1] [This is one of Nuttall's names for the olive-sided flycatcher. He indicated the pronunciation thus: pĕ-pe. Thoreau had met with the bird in the spring migrations of the two preceding years.]

ular intervals, looking about all the while, and then, naïvely, *pee-a-oo*, emphasizing the first syllable, and begins again. The last is, in emphasis, like the scream of a hen-hawk. It flies off occasionally a few feet, and catches an insect and returns to its perch between the bars, not allowing this to interrupt their order.

June 27, 1858 Find two wood pewees' nests, made like the one I have. One on a dead horizontal limb of a small oak, fourteen feet from ground, just on a horizontal fork and looking as old as the limb, color of the branch, three eggs far advanced. The other, with two eggs, was in a similar position exactly over a fork, but on a living branch of a slender white oak, eighteen feet from ground; lichens without, then pine-needles, lined with usnea, willow down. Both nests three to five feet from main stem.

August 13, 1858 I come to get the now empty nests of the wood pewees found June 27th. In each case, on approaching the spot, I hear the sweet note of a pewee lingering about, and this alone would have guided me within four or five rods. I do not know why they should linger near the empty nest, but perhaps they have built again near there or intend to use the same nest again (?). Their full strain is *pe-ah-ee'* (perhaps repeated), rising on the last syllable and emphasizing that, then *pe'-ee*, emphasizing the first and falling on the last, all very sweet and rather plaintive, suggesting innocence and confidence in you. In this case the bird uttered only its last strain, regularly at intervals.

These two pewee nests are remarkably alike in their position and composition and form, though half a mile apart. They are both placed on a horizontal branch of a young oak (one about fourteen, the other about eighteen, feet from ground) and three to five feet from main trunk, in a young oak wood. Both rest directly on a horizontal fork, and such is their form and composition that they have almost precisely the same color and aspect from below and from above.

The first is on a dead limb, very much exposed, is three inches in diameter outside to outside, and two inches in diameter within, the rim being about a quarter of an inch thick, and it is now one inch deep within. Its framework is white pine needles, especially in the rim, and a very little fine grass stem, covered on the rim and all without closely with small bits of lichen (cetraria?), slate-colored without and blackish beneath, and some brown caterpillar (?) or cocoon (?) silk with small seed-vessels in it. They are both now thin and partially open at the bottom, so that I am not sure they contain all the original lining. This one has no distinct lining, unless it is a very little green usnea amid the loose pine needles. The lichens of the nest would readily be confounded with the lichens of the limb. Looking down on it, it is a remarkably round and neat nest.

The second nest is rather more shallow now and half an inch wider without, is lined with much more usnea (the willow down which I saw in it June 27 is gone; perhaps they cast it out in warm weather!), and shows a little of some slender brown catkin (oak?) beneath, without.

These nests remind me of what I suppose to be the yellow-throat vireo's and hummingbird's. The lining of a nest is not in good condition—perhaps is partly gone—when the birds have done with it.

August 14, 1858 The more characteristic notes [of late] would appear to be the wood pewee's and the goldfinch's, with the squeal of young hawks. These might be called the pewee-days.

August 18, 1858 I sit under the oaks at the east end of Hubbard's Grove, and hear two wood pewees singing close by. They are perched on dead oak twigs four or five rods apart, and their notes are so exactly alike that at first I thought there was but one. One appeared to answer the other, and sometimes they both sung together,—even as if the old were teaching her young. It was not the usual spring note of this bird, but a simple, clear *pe-e-eet*, rising steadily with one impulse to the end. They were undistinguishable in tone and rhythm, though one which I thought might be the young was feebler. In the meanwhile, as it was perched on the twig, it was incessantly turning its head about, looking for insects, and suddenly would dart aside or downward a rod or two, and I could hear its bill snap as it caught one. Then it returned to the same or another perch.

Thirteen

LARKS

CROWS

JAYS

SHORE LARK

March 24, 1858 Returning about 5 P.M. across the Depot Field, I scare up from the ground a flock of about twenty birds, which fly low, making a short circuit to another part of the field. At first they remind me of bay-wings, except that they are in a flock, show no white in tail, are, I see, a little larger, and utter a faint *sveet sveet* merely, a sort of sibilant *chip*. Starting them again, I see that they have black tails, very conspicuous when they pass near. They fly in a flock somewhat like snow buntings, occasionally one surging upward a few feet in pursuit of another, and they alight about where they first were. It is almost impossible to discover them on the ground, they squat so flat and so much resemble it, running amid the stubble. But at length I stand within two rods of one and get a good view of its markings with my glass. They

are the *Alauda alpestris*,[1] or shore lark, quite a sizable and handsome bird.

October 4, 1859 Going over the large hillside stubble-field west of Holden Wood, I start up a large flock of shore larks; hear their *sveet sveet* and *sveet sveet sveet*, and see their tails dark beneath. They are very wary, and run in the stubble for the most part invisible, while one or two appear to act the sentinel on rock, peeping out behind it perhaps, and give their note of alarm, when away goes the whole flock. Such a flock circled back and forth several times over my head, just like ducks reconnoitring before they alight. If you look with a glass you are surprised to see how alert these spies are. When they alight in some stubbly hollow they set a watch or two on the rocks to look out for foes. They have dusky bills and legs.

BLUE JAY

1846–47[2] The blue jays suffered few chestnuts to reach the ground, resorting to your single tree in flocks in the early morning, and picking them out of the burs at a great advantage.

November 16, 1850 I hear deep amid the birches some row among the birds or the squirrels, where evidently some mystery is being developed to them. The jay is on the alert, mimicking every

---

[1] [Now called *Otocoris alpestris*.]
[2] [Undated entry in journal of this period.]

woodland note. What *has* happened? Who's dead? The twitter retreats before you, and you are never let into the secret. Some tragedy surely is being enacted, but murder will out. How many little dramas are enacted in the depth of the woods at which man is not present!

December 31, 1850   The blue jays evidently notify each other of the presence of an intruder, and will sometimes make a great chattering about it, and so communicate the alarm to other birds and to beasts.

July 8, 1852   The jay's note, resounding along a raw woodside, suggests a singular wildness.

February 2, 1854   The scream of the jay is a true winter sound. It is wholly without sentiment, and in harmony with winter. I stole up within five or six feet of a pitch pine behind which a downy woodpecker was pecking. From time to time he hopped round to the side and observed me without fear. They are very confident birds, not easily scared, but incline to keep the other side of the bough to you, perhaps.

February 12, 1854   You hear the lisping tinkle of chickadees from time to time and the unrelenting steel-cold scream of a jay, unmelted, that never flows into a song, a sort of wintry trumpet, screaming cold; hard, tense, frozen music, like the winter sky itself; in the blue livery of winter's band. It is like a flourish of trumpets to the winter sky. There is no hint of incubation in the jay's scream. Like the creak of a cart-wheel.

March 12, 1854 I hear a jay loudly screaming *phe-phay phe-phay*,—a loud, shrill chickadee's *phebe*.

March 10, 1856 The pinched crows are feeding in the road to-day in front of the house and alighting on the elms, and blue jays also, as in the middle of the hardest winter, for such is this weather. The blue jays hop about in yards.[1]

June 5, 1856 A blue jay's nest on a white pine, eight feet from ground, next to the stem, of twigs lined with root-fibres; three fresh eggs, dark dull greenish, with dusky spots equally distributed all over, in Hosmer (?) pines twenty-seven paces east of wall and fifty-seven from factory road by wall. Jay screams as usual. Sat till I got within ten feet at first.

October 11, 1856 In the woods I hear the note of the jay, a metallic, *clanging* sound, sometimes a mew. Refer any strange note to him.

October 5, 1857 There is not that profusion and consequent confusion of events which belongs to a summer's walk. There are few flowers, birds, insects, or fruits now, and hence what does occur affects us as more simple and significant. The cawing of a crow, the screams of a jay. The latter seems to scream more fitly and with more freedom now that some fallen maple leaves have made way

---

[1] [The jay is not so terrestrial in its habits as the crow and therefore, unlike its relative, is a hopper, not a walker.]

for his voice. The jay's voice resounds through the vacancies occasioned by fallen maple leaves.

November 3, 1858   The jay is the bird of October. I have seen it repeatedly flitting amid the bright leaves, of a different color from them all and equally bright, and taking its flight from grove to grove. It, too, with its bright color, stands for some ripeness in the bird harvest. And its scream! it is as if it blowed on the edge of an October leaf. It is never more in its element and at home than when flitting amid these brilliant colors. No doubt it delights in bright color, and so has begged for itself a brilliant coat. It is not gathering seeds from the sod, too busy to look around, while fleeing the country. It is wide awake to what is going on, on the *qui vive*. It flies to some bright tree and bruits its splendors abroad.

November 10, 1858   Hearing in the oak and near by a sound as if some one had broken a twig, I looked up and saw a jay pecking at an acorn. There were several jays busily gathering acorns on a scarlet oak. I could hear them break them off. They then flew to a suitable limb and, placing the acorn under one foot, hammered away at it busily, looking round from time to time to see if any foe was approaching, and soon reached the meat and nibbled at it, holding up their heads to swallow, while they held it very firmly with their claws. (Their hammering made a sound like the woodpecker's.) Nevertheless it sometimes dropped to the ground before they had done with it.

November 13, 1858 I saw some feathers of a blue jay scattered along a wood-path, and at length come to the body of the bird. What a neat and delicately ornamented creature, finer than any work of art in a lady's boudoir, with its soft light purplish-blue crest and its dark-blue or purplish secondaries (the narrow half) finely barred with dusky. It is the more glorious to live in Concord because the jay is so splendidly painted.

June 10, 1859 Surveying for D. B. Clark on "College Road," so called in Peter Temple's deed in 1811, Clark thought from a house so called once standing on it. Cut a line, and after measured it, in a thick wood, which passed within two feet of a blue jay's nest which was about four feet up a birch, beneath the leafy branches and quite exposed. The bird sat perfectly still with its head up and bill open upon its pretty large young, not moving in the least, while we drove a stake close by, within three feet, and cut and measured, being about there twenty minutes at least.

October 27, 1860 As I am coming out of this,[1] looking for seedling oaks, I see a jay, which was screaming at me, fly to a white oak eight or ten rods from the wood in the pasture and directly alight on the ground, pick up an acorn, and fly back into the woods with it. This was one, perhaps the most effectual, way in which this wood was stocked with the numerous little oaks which I saw under

[1][A white pine wood.]

that dense white pine grove. Where will you look for a jay sooner than in a dense pine thicket? It is there they commonly live, and build.

*   *   *

What if the oaks are far off? Think how quickly a jay can come and go, and how many times in a day!

October 29, 1860   Again, as day before yesterday, sitting on the edge of a pine wood, I see a jay fly to a white oak half a dozen rods off in the pasture, and, gathering an acorn from the ground, hammer away at it under its foot on a limb of the oak, with an awkward and rapid seesaw or teetering motion, it has to lift its head so high to acquire the requisite momentum. The jays scold about almost every white oak tree, since we hinder their coming to it.

AMERICAN CROW

September 17, 1852   The crows congregate and pursue me through the half-covered woodland path, cawing loud and angrily above me, and when they cease, I hear the winnowing sound of their wings. What ragged ones!

November 1, 1853   As I return, I notice crows flying southwesterly in a very long straggling flock, of which I see probably neither end. A small flock of red-wings singing as in spring.

January 8, 1855   I hear a few chickadees near at hand, and hear and see jays further off, and, as yesterday, a crow sitting sentinel on an apple tree. Soon he gives the alarm, and several more take their places near him. Then off they flap with their *caw* of various hoarseness.

January 12, 1855 Perhaps what most moves us in winter is some reminiscence of far-off summer. How we leap by the side of the open brooks! What beauty in the running brooks! What life! What society! The cold is merely superficial; it is summer still at the core, far, far within. It is in the cawing of the crow, the crowing of the cock, the warmth of the sun on our backs. I hear faintly the cawing of a crow far, far away, echoing from some unseen wood-side, as if deadened by the springlike vapor which the sun is draw-ing from the ground. It mingles with the slight murmur of the vil-lage, the sound of children at play, as one stream empties gently into another, and the wild and tame are one. What a delicious sound! It is not merely crow calling to crow, for it speaks to me too. I am part of one great creature with him; if he has voice, I have ears. I can hear when he calls, and have engaged not to shoot nor stone him if he will caw to me each spring. On the one hand, it may be, is the sound of children at school saying their a, b, ab's, on the other, far in the wood-fringed horizon, the cawing of crows from their blessed eternal vacation, out at their long recess, children who have got dismissed! While the vaporous incense goes up from all the fields of the spring—if it were spring. Ah, bless the Lord, O my soul! bless him for wildness, for crows that will not alight within gunshot! and bless him for hens, too, that croak and cackle in the yard!

May 5, 1855   Looking over my book, I found I had done my errands, and said to myself I would find a crow's nest. (I had heard a crow scold at a passing hawk a quarter of an hour before.) I had hardly taken this resolution when, looking up, I saw a crow wending his way across an interval in the woods towards the highest pines in the swamp, on which he alighted. I directed my steps to them and was soon greeted with an angry *caw*, and, within five minutes from my resolve, I detected a new nest close to the top of the tallest white pine in the swamp. A crow circled cawing about it within gunshot, then over me surveying, and, perching on an oak directly over my head within thirty-five feet, cawed angrily. But suddenly, as if having taken a new resolution, it flitted away, and was joined by its mate and two more, and they went off silently a quarter of a mile or more and lit in a pasture, as if they had nothing to concern them in the wood.

May 7, 1855   Climbed to two crows' nests,—or maybe one of them a squirrel's,—in Hubbard's Grove. Do they not sometimes use a squirrel's nest for a foundation? A ruby-crested wren is apparently attracted and eyes me. It is wrenching and fatiguing, as well as dirty, work to climb a tall pine with nothing, or maybe only dead twigs and stubs, to hold by. You must proceed with great deliberation and see well where you put your hands and your feet.

May 11, 1855 You can hardly walk in a thick pine wood now, especially a swamp, but presently you will have a crow or two over your head, either silently flitting over, to spy what you would be at and if its nest is in danger, or angrily cawing. It is most impressive when, looking for their nests, you first detect the presence of the bird by its shadow.

December 15, 1855 How like a bird of ill omen the crow behaves! Still holding its ground in our midst like a powwow that is not to be exterminated! Sometimes when I am going through the Deep Cut, I look up and see half a dozen black crows flitting silently across in front and ominously eying down; passing from one wood to another, yet as if their passage had reference to me.

January 22, 1856 Somebody has been fishing in the pond this morning, and the water in the holes is beginning to freeze. I see the track of a crow, the toes as usual less spread and the middle one making a more curved furrow in the snow than the partridge, as if they moved more unstably, recovering their balance,—feeble on their feet. The inner toe a little the nearest to the middle one. This track goes to every hole but one or two out of a dozen,—directly from hole to hole, sometimes flying a little,—and also to an apple-core on the snow. I am pretty sure that this bird was

after the bait which is usually dropped on the ice or in the hole. E. Garfield says they come regularly to his holes for bait as soon as he has left. So, if the pickerel are not fed, it is. It had even visited, on the wing, a hole, now frozen and snowed up, which I made far from this in the middle of the pond several days since, as I discovered by its droppings, the same kind that it had left about the first holes.

★ ★ ★

I brought home and examined some of the droppings[1] of the crow mentioned [above]. They were brown and dry, though partly frozen. After long study with a microscope, I discovered that they consisted of the seeds and skins and other indigestible parts of red cedar berries and some barberries (I detected the imbricated scale-like leaves of a berry stem and then the seeds and the now black skins of the cedar berries, but easily the large seeds of the barberries) and perhaps something more, and I knew whence it had probably come, *i.e.* from the cedar woods and barberry bushes by Flint's Pond. These, then, make part of the food of crows in severe weather when the snow is deep, as at present.

January 24, 1856 I knew that a crow had that day plucked the cedar berries and barberries by Flint's Pond and then flapped si-

---

[1][Evidently the pellets of indigestible matter which the crow, in common with hawks, owls, gulls, and some other birds, disgorges from time to time.]

lently through the trackless air to Walden, where it dined on fisherman's bait, though there was no living creature to tell me.

★   ★   ★

Here are the tracks of a crow, like those of the 22d, with a *long
hind toe*, nearly two inches. The two feet are also nearly two inches
apart. I see where the bird alighted, descending with an impetus
and breaking through the slight crust, planting its feet side by side.

How different this partridge-track, with its slight hind toe,
open and wide-spread toes on each side, both feet forming one
straight line, exactly thus:—

(Five inches from centre to centre.) The middle toe alternately
curved to the right and to the left, and what is apparently the outer
toe in each case shorter than the inner one.

January 31, 1856   But what track is this, just under the bank?

It must be a bird, which at last struck the snow with its wings and
took to flight. There were but four hops in all, and then it ended as

above, though there was nothing near enough for it to hop upon from the snow. The form of the foot was somewhat like that of a squirrel, though only the outline was distinguished. The foot was about two inches long, and it was about two inches from outside of one foot to outside of the other. Sixteen inches from hop to hop, the rest in proportion. Looking narrowly, I saw where one wing struck the bank ten feet ahead, thus:

as it passed. A quarter of a mile down-stream it occurred again, thus:

and near by still less of a track, but marks as if it had pecked in the snow. Could it be the track of a crow with its toes unusually close together? Or was it an owl?[1]

[1]Probably a crow. *Vide* Feb. 1st. Hardly a doubt of it. [The crow, though habitually a walker, sometimes hops when in a particular hurry.]

February 1, 1856 Nut Meadow Brook open for some distance in the meadow. . . . I see where a crow has walked along its side. In one place it hopped, and its feet were side by side, as in the track of yesterday, though a little more spread, the toes. I have but little doubt that yesterday's track was a crow's. The two inner toes are near together; the middle, more or less curved often.

February 6, 1856 Goodwin says that he has caught two crows this winter in his traps set *in water* for mink, and baited with fish. The crows, probably put to it for food and looking along the very few open brooks, attracted by this bait, got their feet into the traps.

February 27, 1857 I see many crows on the hillside, with their sentinel on a tree. They are picking the cow-dung scattered about, apparently for the worms, etc., it contains. They have done this in so many places that it looks as if the farmer had been at work with his maul. They must save him some trouble thus.[1]

September 30, 1857 I was telling him[2] how some crows two or three weeks ago came flying with a scolding caw toward me as

[1]Notice the like extensively early in March, 1860.
[2][George Minott.]

I stood on "Cornel Rock," and alighted within fifty feet on a dead tree above my head, unusually bold. Then away go all but one, perchance, to a tall pine in the swamp, twenty rods off; anon he follows. Again they go quite out of sight amid the tree-tops, leaving one behind. This one, at last, quite at his leisure, flaps away cawing, knowing well where to find his mates, though you might think he must winter alone.

Minott said that as he was going over to Lincoln one day thirty or forty years ago, taking his way through Ebby Hubbard's woods, he heard a great flock of crows cawing over his head, and one alighted just within gunshot. He raised his little gun marked London, which he knew would fetch down anything that was within gunshot, and down came the crow; but he was not killed, only so filled with shot that he could not fly. As he was going by John Wyman's at the pond, with the live crow in his hand, Wyman asked him what he was going to do with that crow, to which he answered, "Nothing in particular,"—he happened to alight within gunshot, and so he shot him. Wyman said that he'd like to have him. "What do you want to do with him?" asked M. "If you'll give him to me, I'll tell you," said the other. To which Minott said, "You may have him and welcome." Wyman then proceeded to inform him that the crows had eaten a great space in Josh Jones the blacksmith's corn-field, which Minott had passed just below the almshouse, and that Jones had told him that if he could kill a crow in his corn-field he would give him half a bushel of rye. He could guess what he wanted the crow for. So Wyman took the crow and the next time he went into town he tossed him over the wall into the corn-field and then shot him, and, carrying the dead crow to Jones, he got his half-bushel of rye.

October 29, 1857 A flock of about eighty crows flies ramblingly over toward the sowing, cawing and loitering and making a great ado, apparently about nothing.

November 18, 1857 Crows will often come flying much out of their way to caw at me.

January 18, 1859 P.M.—Up Assabet to bridge.

Two or more inches of snow fell last night. In the expanse this side Mantatuket Rock I see the tracks of a crow or crows in and about the button-bushes and willows. They have trampled and pecked much in some spots under the button-bushes where these seeds are still left and dibbled into the snow by them. It would seem, then, that they eat them. The only other seeds there can be there are those of the mikania, for I look for them. You will see a crow's track beginning in the middle of the river, where one alighted. I notice such a track as this, where one alighted, and ap-

parently struck its spread tail into the snow at the same time with its feet. I see afterward where a wing's quills have marked the snow much like a partridge's. The snow is very light, so that the tracks are rarely distinct, and as they often advance by hops some might mistake it for a squirrel's or mink's track. I suspect that they came here yesterday after minnows when the fishermen were gone, and that has brought them here to-day in spite of the snow. They evidently look out sharp for a morsel of fish. I see where, by the red maple above Pinxter Swamp, they have picked over the fine dark-greenish moss from button-bush, and the leaves which had formed a squirrel's nest, knocking it down on to the river and there treading about and pecking a small piece, apparently for some worms or insects that were in it, as if they were hard pushed.

January 19, 1859 By the swamp between the Hollow and Peter's I see the tracks of a crow or crows, chiefly in the snow, two or more inches deep, on a broad frozen ditch where mud has been taken out. The perpendicular sides of the ditch expose a foot or two of dark, sooty mud which had attracted the crows, and I see where they have walked along beneath it and pecked it. Even here also they have alighted on any bare spot where a foot of stubble was visible, or even a rock. Where one walked yesterday, I see, notwithstanding the effect of the sun on it, not only the foot-tracks, but the distinct impression of its tail where it alighted, counting distinctly eleven (of probably twelve) feathers,—about four inches of each, —the whole mark being some ten inches wide and six deep, or more like a semicircle than that of yesterday. The same crow, or one of the same, has come again to-day, and, the snow being sticky this warm weather, has left a very distinct track. The width of the whole track is about two and three quarters inches, length of pace about seven inches, length of true track some two inches (not including the nails), but the mark made in setting down the foot and withdrawing it is in each case some fifteen or eighteen inches long, for its hind toe makes a sharp scratch four or five inches long before it settles, and when it lifts its foot again, it makes two other fine scratches with its middle and outer toe on each side, the first some nine inches long, the second six. The inner toe is commonly close to the middle one. It makes a peculiar curving track (or succession of curves), stepping round the planted foot each time with a sweep, thus:—

You would say that it toed in decidedly and walked feebly. It must be that they require but little and glean that very assiduously.

March 4, 1859   What a perfectly New England sound is this voice of the crow! If you stand perfectly still anywhere in the outskirts of the town and listen, stilling the almost incessant hum of your own personal factory, this is perhaps the sound which you will be most sure to hear rising above all sounds of human industry and leading your thoughts to some far bay in the woods where the crow is venting his disgust. This bird sees the white man come and the Indian withdraw, but it withdraws not. Its untamed voice is still heard above the tinkling of the forge. It sees a race pass away, but it passes not away. It remains to remind us of aboriginal nature.

March 5, 1859   I see crows walking about on the ice half covered with snow in the middle of the meadows, where there is no grass, apparently to pick up the worms and other insects left there since the midwinter freshet.

December 31, 1859   Crows yesterday flitted silently, if not ominously, over the street, just after the snow had fallen, as if men, being further within, were just as far off as usual. This is a phenomenon of both cold weather and snowy. You hear nothing; you merely see these black apparitions, though they come near enough to look down your chimney and scent the boiling pot, and pass between the house and barn.

January 30, 1860   There are certain sounds invariably heard in warm and thawing days in winter, such as the crowing of cocks, the cawing of crows, and sometimes the gobbling of turkeys. The crow, flying high, touches the tympanum of the sky for us, and reveals the tone of it. What does it avail to look at a thermometer or barometer compared with listening to his note? He informs me that Nature is in the tenderest mood possible, and I hear the very flutterings of her heart.

Crows have singular wild and suspicious ways. You will see a couple flying high, as if about their business, but lo, they turn and circle and caw over your head again and again for a mile; and this is their business,—as if a mile and an afternoon were nothing for them to throw away. This even in winter, when they have no nests to be anxious about. But it is affecting to hear them cawing about their ancient seat (as at F. Wheeler's wood) which the choppers are laying low.

March 2, 1860 See thirty or more crows come flying in the usual irregular zigzag manner in the strong wind, from over M. Miles's, going northeast,—the first migration of them,—without cawing.

May 13, 1860 See two crows pursuing and diving at a hen-hawk very high in the air over the river. He is steadily circling and rising. While they, getting above, dive down toward him, passing within a foot or two, making a feint, he merely winks, as it were, bends or jerks his wings slightly as if a little startled, but never ceases soaring, nor once turns to pursue or shake them off. It seemed as if he was getting uncomfortably high for them.

October 6, 1860 As I go over the hill, I see a large flock of crows on the dead white oak and on the ground under the living one. I find the ground strewn with white oak acorns, and many of these have just been broken in two, and their broken shells are strewn about, so that I suppose the crows have been eating them. Some are merely scratched, as if they had been pecked at without being pierced; also there are two of the large swamp white oak acorn-cups joined together dropped under this oak, perhaps by a crow, maybe a quarter of a mile from its tree, and that probably across the river. Probably a crow had transported one or more swamp white oak acorns this distance. They must have been too heavy for a jay.

The crow, methinks, is our only large bird that hovers and circles about in flocks in an irregular and straggling manner, filling the air over your head and sporting in it as if at home here. They often burst up above the woods where they were perching, like the black fragments of a powder-mill just exploded.

One crow lingers on a limb of the dead oak till I am within a dozen rods. There is strong and blustering northwest wind, and when it launches off to follow its comrades it is blown up and backward still nearer to me, and it is obliged to tack four or five times just like a vessel, a dozen rods or more each way, very deliberately, first to the right, then to the left, before it can get off; for as often as it tries to fly directly forward against the wind, it is blown upward and backward within gunshot, and it only advances directly forward at last by stooping very low within a few feet of the ground where the trees keep off the wind. Yet the wind is not remarkably strong.

December 30, 1860 I saw the crows a week ago perched on the swamp white oaks over the road just beyond Wood's Bridge, and many acorns and bits of bark and moss, evidently dropped or knocked off by them, lay on the snow beneath. One sat within twenty feet over my head with what looked like a piece of acorn in his bill. To-day I see that they have carried these same white oak acorns, cups and all, to the ash tree by the riverside, some thirty rods southeast, and dropped them there. Perhaps they find some grubs in the acorns, when they do not find meat. The crows now and of late frequent thus the large trees by the river, especially swamp white oak, and the snow beneath is strewn with bits of bark and moss and with acorns (commonly worthless). They are foraging. Under the first swamp white oak in Hubbard's great meadow (Cyanean) I see a little snap-turtle (shell some one and a quarter inches in diameter—on his second year, then) on its back on the ice—shell, legs, and tail perfect, but head pulled off, and most of the inwards with it by the same hole (where the neck was). What is left smells quite fresh, and this head must have been torn off to-day—or within a day or two. I see two crows on the next swamp white oak westward, and I can scarcely doubt that they did it. Probably one found the young turtle at an open and springy place in the meadow, or by the river, where they are constantly preying, and flew with it to this tree. Yet it is possible (?) that it was frozen to death when they found it.

January 11, 1861 Horace Mann brings me the contents of a crow's stomach in alcohol. It was killed in the village within a day or two. It is quite a mass of frozen-thawed apple,—pulp and skin,—with a good many pieces of skunk-cabbage berries one fourth inch or less in diameter, and commonly showing the pale-brown or blackish outside, interspersed, looking like bits of acorns,—never a whole or even half a berry,—and two little bones as of frogs (?) or mice (?) or *tadpoles*; also a street pebble a quarter of an inch in diameter, hard to be distinguished in appearance from the cabbage seeds.

Fourteen

BLACKBIRDS

ORIOLES

ETC.

BOBOLINK

June 29, 1851   At a distance in the meadow I hear still, at long intervals, the hurried commencement of the bobolink's strain, the bird just dashing into song, which is as suddenly checked, as it were, by the warder of the seasons, and the strain is left incomplete forever. Like human beings they are inspired to sing only for a short season.[1]

May 16, 1852   The bobolink sits on a hardhack, swaying to and fro, uncertain whether to begin his strain, dropping a few bubbling notes by way of prelude,—with which he overflows.

August 15, 1852   Some birds fly in flocks. I see a dense, compact flock of bobolinks going off in the air over a field. They cover

---

[1] I have since heard some complete strains.

the rails and alders, and go rustling off with a brassy, tinkling note like a ripe crop as I approach, revealing their yellow breasts and bellies. This is an autumnal sight, that small flock of grown birds in the afternoon sky.

May 10, 1853 When I heard the first bobolink strain this morning I could not at first collect myself enough to tell what it was I heard,—a reminiscence of last May in all its prime occurring in the midst of the experience of this in its unripe state. Suddenly, the season being sufficiently advanced, the atmosphere in the right condition, these flashing, scintillating notes are struck out from it where that dark mote disappears through it, as sparks by a flint, with a tinkling sound. This flashing, tinkling meteor bursts through the expectant meadow air, leaving a train of tinkling notes behind. Succcesive regiments of birds arrive and are disbanded in our fields, like soldiers still wearing their regimentals. I doubted at first if it were not a strain brought on a few days in advance by an imitative catbird or thrush (?) from where he had been staying.

May 12, 1853 This, too, is the era of the bobolink, now, when apple trees are ready to burst into bloom.

May 17, 1853 The bobolink skims by before the wind how far without motion of his wings! sometimes borne sidewise as he turns his head—for thus he can fly—and tinkling, *linking*, incessantly all the way.

May 25, 1857   It is interesting to hear the bobolinks from the meadow sprinkle their lively strain along amid the tree-tops as they fly over the wood above our heads. It resounds in a novel manner through the aisles of the wood, and at the end that fine buzzing, wiry note.

June 1, 1857   I hear the note of a bobolink concealed in the top of an apple tree behind me. Though this bird's full strain is ordinarily somewhat trivial, this one appears to be meditating a strain as yet unheard in meadow or orchard. *Paulo majora canamus*. He is just touching the strings of his theorbo, his glassichord, his water organ, and one or two notes globe themselves and fall in liquid bubbles from his teeming throat. It is as if he touched his harp within a vase of liquid melody, and when he lifted it out, the notes fell like bubbles from the trembling strings. Methinks they are the most *liquidly* sweet and melodious sounds I ever heard. They are refreshing to my ear as the first distant tinkling and gurgling of a rill to a thirsty man. Oh, never advance farther in your art, never let us hear your full strain, sir. But away he launches, and the meadow is all bespattered with melody. His notes fall with the apple blossoms, in the orchard. The very divinest part of his strain dropping from his overflowing breast *singultim*, in globes of melody. It is the foretaste of such strains as never fell on mortal ears, to hear which we should rush to our doors and contribute all that we possess and are. Or it seemed as if in that vase full of melody some notes sphered themselves, and from time to time bubbled up to the surface and were with difficulty repressed.

June 2, 1857　That bobolink's song affected me as if one were endeavoring to keep down globes of melody within a vase full of liquid, but some bubbled up irrepressible,—kept thrusting them down with a stick, but they slipped and came up one side.

June 26, 1857　I must be near bobolinks' nests many times these days,—in E. Hosmer's meadow by the garlic and here in Charles Hubbard's,—but the birds are so overanxious, though you may be pretty far off, and so shy about visiting their nests while you are there, that you watch them in vain. The female flies close past and perches near you on a rock or stump and chirps *whit tit, whit tit, whit it tit tit te* incessantly.

August 18, 1858　Miss Caroline Pratt saw the white bobolink yesterday where Channing saw it the day before, in the midst of a large flock. I go by the place this afternoon and see very large flocks of them, certainly several hundreds in all, and one has a little white on his back, but I do not see *the* white one. Almost every bush along this brook is now alive with these birds. You wonder where they were all hatched, for you may have failed to find a single nest. I know eight or ten active boys who have been searching for these nests the past season quite busily, and they have found but two at most. Surely but a small fraction of these birds will ever return from the South. Have they so many foes there? Hawks must fare well at present. They go off in a straggling flock, and it is a long time before the last loiterer has left the bushes near you.

July 15, 1860 I hear this forenoon the *link link* of the first bobolink going over our garden,—though I hear several full strains of bobolinks to-day, as in May, carrying me back to Apple Sunday, but they have been rare a long time. Now as it were the very cope of the dark-glazed heavens yields a slightly metallic sound when struck.

COWBIRD
(COW BLACKBIRD)
(COW TROOPIAL)

July 16, 1851 The red-wings and crow blackbirds are heard chattering on the trees, and the cow troopials are accompanying the cows in the pastures for the sake of the insects they scare up. Oftentimes the thoughtless sportsman has lodged his charge of shot in the cow's legs or body in his eagerness to obtain the birds.

September 4, 1853 In Potter's dry pasture I saw the ground black with blackbirds (troopials?). As I approach, the front rank rises and flits a little further back into the midst of the flock,—it rolls up on the edges,—and, being thus alarmed, they soon take to flight, with a loud rippling rustle, but soon alight again, the rear wheeling swiftly into place like well-drilled soldiers. Instead of being an irregular and disorderly crowd, they appear to know and keep their places and wheel with the precision of drilled troops.

June 11, 1854   Saw in and near some woods four or five cow blackbirds, with their light-brown heads,—their strain an imperfect, milky, gurgling *conqueree*, an unsuccessful effort. It made me think, for some reason, of streams of milk bursting out a sort of music between the staves of a keg.

July 13, 1856   In Hubbard's euphorbia pasture, cow blackbirds about cows. At first the cows were resting and ruminating in the shade, and no birds were seen. Then one after another got up and went to feeding, straggling into the midst of the field. With a chattering appeared a cowbird, and, with a long slanting flight, lit close to a cow's nose, within the shadow of it, and watched for insects, the cow still eating along and almost hitting it, taking no notice of it. Soon it is joined by two or three more birds.

September 6, 1858   Going over Clamshell Plain, I see a very large flock of a hundred or more cowbirds about some cows. They whirl away on some alarm and alight on a neighboring rail fence, close together on the rails, one above another. Then away they whirl and settle on a white oak top near me. Half of them are evidently quite young birds, having glossy black breasts with a drab line down middle. The heads of all are light-colored, perhaps a slaty drab, and some apparently wholly of this color.

RED-WINGED BLACKBIRD

October 5, 1851   I hear the red-wing blackbirds by the riverside again, as if it were a new spring. They appear to have come to bid farewell. The birds appear to depart with the coming of the frosts, which kill vegetation and, directly or indirectly, the insects on which they feed.

April 22, 1852   The strain of the red-wing on the willow spray over the water to-night is liquid, bubbling, watery, almost like a tinkling fountain, in perfect harmony with the meadow. It oozes, trickles, tinkles, bubbles from his throat,—*bob-y-lee-e-e*, and then its shrill, fine whistle.

May 7, 1852   The red-wing's shoulder, seen in a favorable light, throws all epaulets into the shade. It is General Abercrombie, methinks, when they wheel partly with the red to me.

May 8, 1852   The blackbirds have a rich *sprayey* warble now, sitting on the top of a willow or an elm. They possess the river now, flying back and forth across it.

March 19, 1853   This morning I hear the blackbird's fine clear whistle and also his sprayey note, as he is swayed back and forth on the twigs of the elm or of the black willow over the river. His first note may be a chuck, but his second is a rich gurgle or warble.

May 14, 1853   The still dead-looking willows and button-bushes are alive with red-wings, now perched on a yielding twig, now pursuing a female swiftly over the meadow, now darting across the stream. No two have epaulets equally brilliant. Some are small and almost white, and others a brilliant vermilion. They are hand-somer than the golden robin, methinks. The yellowbird, kingbird, and pewee, beside many swallows, are also seen. But the rich colors and the rich and varied notes of the blackbirds surpass them all.

June 24, 1853 Also got a blackbird's nest whose inhabitants had flown, hung by a kind of small dried rush (?) between two button-bushes which crossed above it; of meeadow-grass and sedge, dried *Mikania scandens* vine, horse-tail, fish-lines, and a strip apparently of a lady's bathing-dress, lined with a somewhat finer grass; of a loose and ragged texture to look at. Green mikania running over it now.

April 18, 1854 Heard a red-wing sing his *bobylee* in new wise, as if he tossed up a fourpence and it rattled on some counter in the air as it went up.

May 16, 1854 Looked into several red-wing blackbirds' nests which are now being built, but no eggs yet. They are generally hung between two twigs, say of button-bush. I noticed at one nest what looked like a tow string securely tied about a twig at each end about six inches apart, left loose in the middle. It was not a string, but I think a strip of milkweed pod, etc.,—water asclepias proba-bly,—maybe a foot long and very strong. How remarkable that this bird should have found out the strength of this, which I was so slow to find out![1]

[1][See under Yellow Warbler, Chapter 18.]

May 13, 1855 I heard from a *female* red-wing that peculiar rich screwing warble—not *o gurgle ee*—made with *r*, not with *l*.

June 14, 1855 See young red-wings; like grizzly-black vultures, they are still so bald.

June 1, 1857 A red-wing's nest, four eggs, low in a tuft of sedge in an open meadow. What Champollion can translate the hieroglyphics on these eggs? It is always writing of the same character, though much diversified. While the bird picks up the material and lays the egg, who determines the style of the marking? When you approach, away dashes the dark mother, betraying her nest, and then chatters her anxiety from a neighboring bush, where she is soon joined by the red-shouldered male, who comes scolding over your head, chattering and uttering a sharp *phe phee-e.*

March 19, 1858 By the river, see distinctly red-wings and hear their *conqueree.* They are not associated with grackles.[1] They are an age before their cousins, have attained to clearness and liquidity. They are officers, epauletted; the others are rank and file. I distinguish one even by its flight, hovering slowly from tree-top to tree-top, as if ready to utter its liquid notes. Their whistle is very clear and sharp, while the grackle's is ragged and split.

It is a fine evening, as I stand on the bridge. The waters are quite smooth; very little ice to be seen. The red-wing and song sparrow are singing, and a flock of tree sparrows is pleasantly war-

[1][That is, rusty blackbirds. See note on p. 288.]

bling. A new era has come. The red-wing's *gurgle-ee* is heard when smooth waters begin; they come together.

March 11, 1859 I see and hear a red-wing. It sings almost steadily on its perch there, sitting all alone, as if to attract companions (and I see two more, also solitary, on different tree-tops within a quarter of a mile), calling the river to life and tempting ice to melt and trickle like its own sprayey notes. Another flies over on high, with a *tchuck* and at length a clear whistle. The birds anticipate the spring; they come to melt the ice with their songs.

March 15, 1860 Here is a flock of red-wings. I heard one yesterday, and I see *a female* among these.[1] These are easily distinguished from grackles by the richness and clarity of their notes, as if they were a more developed bird. How handsome as they go by in a checker, each with a bright scarlet shoulder! They are not so very shy, but mute when we come near. I think here are four or five grackles with them, which remain when the rest fly. They cover the apple trees like a black fruit.

March 17, 1860 How handsome a flock of red-wings, ever changing its oval form as it advances, by the rear birds passing the others!

April 29, 1860 I listen to a concert of red-wings,—their rich sprayey notes, amid which a few more liquid and deep in a lower

---

[1] [The date is, of course, a very early one for female red-winged blackbirds, which ordinarily do not arrive till some time after the males.]

tone or undertone, as if it bubbled up from the very water beneath the button-bushes; as if those singers sat lower. Some old and skillful performer touches these deep and liquid notes, and the rest seem to get up a concert just to encourage him. Yet it is ever a prelude or essay with him, as are all good things, and the melody he is capable of and which we did not hear this time is what we remember. The future will draw him out. The different individuals sit singing and pluming themselves and not appearing to have any conversation with one another. They are only tuning all at once; they never seriously perform; the hour has not arrived. Then all go off with a hurried and perhaps alarmed *tchuck tchuck*.

MEADOWLARK
(LARK)

July 16, 1851   The lark sings in the meadow; the very essence of the afternoon is in his strain. This is a New England sound, but the cricket is heard under all sounds.

October 6, 1851[1]   (I hear a lark singing this morn [October 7th], and yesterday saw them in the meadows. Both larks and blackbirds are heard again now occasionally, seemingly after a short absence, as if come to bid farewell.)

April 14, 1852   Going down the railroad at nine A.M., I hear the lark singing from over the snow. This for steady singing comes

[1][Entered under this date, though written the next day.]

next to the robin now. It will come up very sweet from the meadows ere long.

May 3, 1852   Some of the notes, the trills, of the lark sitting amid the tussocks and stubble are like my seringo-bird.[1] May these birds that live so low in the grass be called the cricket birds? and does their song resemble the cricket's, an earth-song?

April 6, 1853   I cannot describe the lark's song. I used these syllables in the morning to remember it by,—*heetar-su-e-oo.*

November 1, 1853   Now that the sun is fairly risen, I see and hear a flock of larks in Wheeler's meadow on left of the Corner road, singing exactly as in spring and twittering also, but rather faintly or suppressedly, as if their throats had grown up or their courage were less.

March 26, 1855   The lark sings, perched on the top of an apple tree, *seel-yah seel-yah*, and then perhaps *seel-yah-see-e*, and several other strains, quite sweet and plaintive, contrasting with the cheerless season and the bleak meadow. Further off I hear one like *ah-tick-seel-yah.*

March 28, 1858   The first lark of the 23d sailed through the meadow with that peculiar prolonged chipping or twittering sound, perhaps sharp clucking.

[1][See note to Savannah Sparrow, Chapter 15.]

BALTIMORE ORIOLE
(GOLDEN ROBIN)
(FIERY HANGBIRD)

May 8, 1852 Two gold robins; they chatter like blackbirds; the fire bursts forth on their backs when they lift their wings.

May 18, 1852 These days the golden robin is the important bird in the streets, on the elms.

May 10, 1853 You hear the clear whistle and see the red or fiery orange of the oriole darting through Hosmer's orchard. But its note is not melodious and rich. It is at most a clear tone, the healthiest of your city beaux and belles.

May 25, 1855 The golden robin keeps whistling something like *Eat it, Potter, eat it!*

June 28, 1857 I hear on all hands these days, from the elms and other trees, the twittering peep of young gold robins, which have recently left their nests, and apparently indicate their locality to their parents by thus incessantly peeping all day long.

December 22, 1859 As we passed under the elm beyond George Heywood's, I looked up and saw a fiery hangbird's nest dangling over the road. What a reminiscence of summer, a fiery hangbird's nest dangling from an elm over the road when perhaps the thermometer is down to −20 (?), and the traveller goes beating his arms beneath it! It is hard to recall the strain of that bird then.

RUSTY BLACKBIRD
(RUSTY GRACKLE)
(GRACKLE[1])

April 9, 1855 Wilson says that the only note of the rusty grackle is a *chuck*, though he is told that at Hudson's Bay, at the breeding-time, they sing with a fine note.[2] Here they utter not only a *chuck*, but a *fine* shrill whistle. They cover the top of a tree

[1] [So usually called by Thoreau, who used only the name crow blackbird for the bird now commonly called the bronzed grackle.]
[2] [The only song they are known to possess is the whistle that Thoreau here describes.]

now, and their concert is of this character: They all seem laboring together to get out a clear strain, as it were wetting their whistles against their arrival at Hudson's Bay. They begin as it were by disgorging or spitting it out, like so much tow, from a full throat, and conclude with a clear, fine, shrill, ear-piercing whistle. Then away they go, all chattering together.

April 11, 1856   Going up the railroad, I see a male and female rusty grackle alight on an oak near me, the latter apparently a flaxen brown, with a black tail. She looks like a different species of bird. Wilson had heard only a *tchuck* from the grackle, but this male, who was courting his mate, broke into incipient warbles, like a bubble burst as soon as it came to the surface, it was so aerated. Its air would not be fixed long enough.

October 14, 1857   I see a large flock of grackles, probably young birds, quite near me on William Wheeler's apple trees, pruning themselves and trying to sing. They *never* succeed; make a sort of musical spluttering. Most, I think, have brownish heads and necks, and some purple reflections from their black bodies.

October 16, 1857   I saw some blackbirds, apparently grackles, singing, after their fashion, on a tree by the river. Most had those grayish-brown heads and necks; some, at least, much ferruginous or reddish brown reflected. They were pruning themselves and splitting their throats in vain, trying to sing as the other day. All the melody flew off in splinters. Also a robin sings once or twice, just as in spring!

March 18, 1858 The blackbird—probably grackle this time—wings his way direct above the swamp northward, with a regular *tchuck*, carrier haste, calling the summer months along, like a hen her chickens.

October 16, 1858 See a large flock of grackles steering for a bare elm-top near the meadows. As they fly athwart my view, they appear successively rising half a foot or a foot above one another, though the flock is moving straight forward. I have not seen redwings for a long while, but these birds, which went so much further north to breed, are still arriving from those distant regions, fetching the year about.

March 14, 1859 I see a large flock of grackles searching for food along the water's edge, just below Dr. Bartlett's. Some wade in the water. They are within a dozen rods of me and the road. It must be something just washed up that they are searching for, for the water has just risen and is still rising fast. Is it not insects and worms washed out of the grass? and perhaps the snails? When a grackle sings, it is as if his mouth were full of cotton, which he was trying to spit out.

March 8, 1860 See a small flock of grackles on the willow-row above railroad bridge. How they sit and make a business of chattering! for it cannot be called singing, and no improvement from age to age perhaps. Yet, as *nature* is a *becoming*, their notes may become melodious at last. At length, on my very near approach, they flit suspiciously away, uttering a few subdued notes as they hurry off.

BRONZED GRACKLE
(CROW BLACKBIRD)

May 11, 1854   Now at last I see crow blackbirds without doubt. . . . They fly as if carrying or dragging their precious long tails, broad at the end, through the air. Their note is like a great rusty spring, and also a hoarse chuck.

June 6, 1854   A crow blackbird's nest in a white maple this side the Leaning Hemlocks, in a crotch seven or eight feet from ground; somewhat like a robin's, but larger, made of coarse weed stems, mikania, and cranberry vines (without leaves), fish-lines, etc., without, and of mud lined with finer fibres or roots within; four large but blind young covered with dark down.

April 14, 1855   I see half a dozen crow blackbirds uttering their coarse rasping *char char*, like great rusty springs, on the top of an elm by the riverside; and often at each *char* they open their great tails. They also attain to a clear whistle with some effort, but seem to have some difficulty in their throats yet.

May 11, 1855   A crow blackbird's nest, about eight feet up a white maple over water,—a large, loose nest without, some eight inches high, between a small twig and main trunk, composed of coarse bark shreds and dried last year's grass, without mud; within deep and size of robin's nest; with four pale-green eggs, streaked and blotched with black and brown. Took one. Young bird not begun to form.

February 3, 1856   Analyzed the crow blackbird's nest from which I took an egg last summer, eight or ten feet up a white maple by river, opposite Island. Large, of an irregular form, appearing as if wedged in between a twig and two large contiguous trunks. From outside to outside it measures from six to eight inches; inside, four; depth, two; height, six. The foundation is a loose mass of coarse strips of grape-vine bark chiefly, some eighteen inches long by five eighths of an inch wide; also slender grass and weed stems, mikania stems, a few cellular river weeds, as rushes, sparganium, pipe-grass, and some soft, coarse, fibrous roots. The same coarse grape-vine bark and grass and weed stems, together with some harder, wiry stems, form the sides and rim, the bark being passed around the twig. The nest is lined with the finer grass and weed stems, etc. The solid part of the nest is of half-decayed vegetable matter and mud, full of fine fibrous roots and wound internally with grass stems, etc., and some grape bark, being an inch and a half thick at bottom. Pulled apart and lying loose, it makes a great mass of material. This, like similar nests, is now a great haunt for spiders.

April 15, 1856   Coming up from the riverside, I hear the harsh rasping *char-r char-r* of the crow blackbird, like a very coarsely vibrating metal, and, looking up, see three flying over.

BLACKBIRDS (MISCELLANEOUS)

May 8, 1852 The blackbirds fly in flocks and sing in concert on the willows,—what a lively, chattering concert! a great deal of chattering with many liquid and rich warbling notes and clear whistles,—till now a hawk sails low, beating the bush, and they are silent or off, but soon begin again. Do any other birds sing in such deafening concert?

March 18, 1853 Several times I hear and see blackbirds flying north singly, high overhead, chucking as if to find their mates, migrating; or are they even now getting near their own breeding-place? Perchance these are blackbirds that were hatched here,—that know me!

March 29, 1853 It would be worth the while to attend more to the different notes of the blackbirds. Methinks I may have seen the female red-wing within a day or two; or what are these purely black ones without the red shoulder?[1] It is pleasant to see them scattered about on the drying meadow. The red-wings will stand close to the water's edge, looking larger than usual, with their red shoulders very distinct and handsome in that position, and sing *okolee*, or *bob-y-lee*, or what-not. Others, on the tops of trees over your head, out of a fuzzy beginning spit forth a clear, shrill whistle incessantly, for what purpose I don't know. Others, on the elms over the water, utter still another note, each time lifting their wings

---

[1][This was before he had learned to distinguish the rusty blackbird.]

slightly. Others are flying across the stream with a loud *char-r, char-r.*

April 4, 1853 After turning Lee's Cliff I heard, methinks, more birds singing even than in fair weather,—tree sparrows, whose song has the character of the canary's, *F. hyemalis's chill-lill,* the sweet strain of the fox-colored sparrow, song sparrows, a nut-hatch, jays, crows, bluebirds, robins, and a large congregation of blackbirds. They suddenly alight with great din in a stubble-field just over the wall, not perceiving me and my umbrella behind the pitch pines, and there feed silently; then, getting uneasy or anxious, they fly up on to an apple tree, where being reassured, commences a rich but deafening concert, *o-gurgle-ee-e, o-gurgle-ee-e,* some of the most liquid notes ever heard, as if produced by some of the water of the Pierian spring, flowing through some kind of musical water-pipe and at the same time setting in motion a multitude of fine vibrating metallic springs. Like a shepherd merely meditating most enrapturing glees on such a water-pipe. A more liquid bag-pipe or clarionet, immersed like bubbles in a thousand sprayey notes, the bubbles half lost in the spray. When I show myself, away they go with a loud harsh *charr-r, charr-r.* At first I had heard an in-undation of blackbirds approaching, some beating time with a loud *chuck, chuck,* while the rest played a hurried, gurgling fugue.

June 11, 1853 Probably blackbirds were never less numerous along our river than in these years. They do not depend on the clearing of the woods and the cultivation of orchards, etc. Streams and meadows, in which they delight, always existed. Most of the towns, soon after they were settled, were obliged to set a price upon their heads. In 1672, according to the town records of Concord, instruction was given to the selectmen, "That incorigment be given for the destroying of blackbirds and jaies." (Shattuck,[1] page 45.)

April 3, 1856   Hear also squeaking notes of an advancing flock of red-wings,[2] somewhere high in the sky. At length detect them high overhead, advancing northeast in loose array, with a broad extended front, competing with each other, winging their way to some northern meadow which they remember. The note of some is like the squeaking of many signs, while others accompany them with a steady dry *tchuck, tchuck.*

August 18, 1858   I also see large flocks of blackbirds, blackish birds with chattering notes. It is a fine sight when you can look down on them just as they are settling on the ground with outspread wings,—a hovering flock.

March 13, 1859   I see a small flock of blackbirds flying over, some rising, others falling, yet all advancing together, one flock but many birds, some silent, others tchucking,—incessant alternation. This harmonious movement as in a dance, this agreeing to differ, makes the charm of the spectacle to me. One bird looks frac-

---

[1][Lemuel Shattuck's *History of Concord.*]
[2]Or grackles; am uncertain which makes that squeak.

tional, naked, like a single thread or ravelling from the web to which it belongs. Alternation! Alternation! Heaven and hell! Here again in the flight of a bird, its ricochet motion, is that undulation observed in so many materials, as in the mackerel sky.

March 28, 1859 As we were paddling over the Great Meadows, I saw at a distance, high in the air above the middle of the meadow, a very compact flock of blackbirds advancing against the sun. Though there were more than a hundred, they did not appear to occupy more than six feet in breadth, but the whole flock was dashing first to the right and then to the left. When advancing straight toward me and the sun, they made but little impression on the eye,—so many fine dark points merely, seen against the sky,—but as often as they wheeled to the right or left, displaying their wings flatwise and the whole length of their bodies, they were a very conspicuous black mass. This fluctuation in the amount of dark surface was a very pleasing phenomenon. It reminded me of those blinds whose sashes [*sic*] are made to move all together by a stick, now admitting nearly all the light and now entirely excluding it; so the flock of blackbirds opened and shut. But at length they suddenly spread out and dispersed, some flying off this way, and others that, as, when a wave strikes against a cliff, it is dashed upward and lost in fine spray. So they lost their compactness and impetus and broke up suddenly in mid-air.

April 25, 1860 I hear the greatest concerts of blackbirds—red-wings and crow blackbirds—nowadays, especially of the former (also the 22d and 29th). The maples and willows along the river, and the button-bushes, are all alive with them. They look like a black fruit on the trees, distributed over the top at pretty equal distances. It is worth while to see how slyly they hide at the base of the thick and shaggy button-bushes at this stage of the water. They will suddenly cease their strains and flit away and secrete themselves low amid these bushes till you are past; or you scare up an unexpectedly large flock from such a place, where you had seen none.

I pass a large quire in full blast on the oaks, etc., on the island in the meadow northwest of Peter's. Suddenly they are hushed, and I hear the loud rippling rush made by their wings as they dash away, and, looking up, I see what I take to be a sharp-shinned hawk just alighting on the trees where they were, having failed to catch one. They retreat some forty rods off, to another tree, and renew their concert there. The hawk plumes himself, and then flies off, rising gradually and beginning to circle, and soon it joins its mate, and soars with it high in the sky and out of sight, as if the thought of so terrestrial a thing as a blackbird had never entered its head. It appeared to have a plain reddish-fawn breast. The size more than anything made me think it a sharp-shin.

FINCHES

PINE GROSBEAK

December 24, 1851   Saw also some pine grosbeaks, magnificent winter birds, among the weeds and on the apple trees; like large catbirds at a distance, but, nearer at hand, some of them, when they flit by, are seen to have gorgeous heads, breasts, and rumps (?), with red or crimson reflections, more beautiful than a steady bright red would be. The note I heard, a rather faint and innocent whistle of two bars.

July 15, 1858   When half-way down the mountain,[1] amid the spruce, we saw two pine grosbeaks, male and female, close by the path, and looked for a nest, but in vain. They were remarkably tame, and the male a brilliant red orange,—neck, head, breast beneath, and rump,—blackish wings and tail, with two white bars on wings. (Female, yellowish.) The male flew nearer inquisitively, uttering a low twitter, and perched fearlessly within four feet of us,

[1][Mt. Lafayette.]

eying and pluming himself and plucking and eating the leaves of the *Amelanchier oligocarpa* on which he sat, for several minutes. The female, meanwhile, was a rod off. They were evidently breeding there. Yet neither Wilson nor Nuttall speak of their breeding in the United States.[1]

PURPLE FINCH

October 7, 1842 A little girl has just brought me a purple finch, or American linnet. These birds are now moving south. It reminds me of the pine and spruce, and the juniper and cedar on whose berries it feeds. It has the crimson hues of the October evenings, and its plumage still shines as if it had caught and preserved some of their tints (beams?). We know it chiefly as a traveller. It reminds me of many things I had forgotten. Many a serene evening lies snugly packed under its wing.

April 15, 1854 The arrival of the purple finches appears to be coincident with the blossoming of the elm, on whose blossom it feeds.

[1][The pine grosbeak breeds very sparingly in the White Mountain region. Mr. J. E. Cabot's statement in the *Atlantic* for December, 1857, that he had seen the bird "at the White Mountains in August" seems to have escaped Thoreau's attention. Perhaps the descendants of these birds of Thoreau's still haunt the mountain. Thirty years later at least, in June, 1888, the writer, in company with Mr. Bradford Torrey, found several pine grosbeaks high up on Lafayette and heard from two of them their beautiful song.]

May 24, 1855   Heard a purple finch sing more than one minute without pause, loud and rich, on an elm over the street. Another singing very faintly on a neighboring elm.

April 12, 1856   There suddenly flits before me and alights on a small apple tree in Mackay's field, as I go to my boat, a splendid purple finch. Its glowing redness is revealed when it lifts its wings, as when the ashes is blown from a coal of fire. Just as the oriole displays its gold.

April 3, 1858   Going down-town this morning, I am surprised by the rich strain of the purple finch from the elms. Three or four have arrived and lodged against the elms of our street, which runs east and west across their course, and they are now mingling their loud and rich strains with that of the tree sparrows, robins, bluebirds, etc. The hearing of this note implies some improvement in the acoustics of the air. It reminds me of that genial state of the air when the elms are in bloom. They sit still over the street and make a business of warbling. They advertise me surely of some additional warmth and serenity. How their note rings over the roofs of the village! You wonder that even the sleepers are not awakened by it to inquire who is there, and yet probably not another than myself in all the town observes their coming, and not half a dozen ever distinguished them in their lives. And yet the very mob of the town know the hard names of Germanians or Swiss families which once sang here or elsewhere.

RED CROSSBILL

April 13, 1860 At first I had felt disinclined to
make this excursion up the Assabet, but it distinctly occurred to me
that, perhaps, if I came against my will, as it were, to look at the
sweet-gale as a matter of business, I might discover something else
interesting, as when I discovered the sheldrake. As I was paddling
past the uppermost hemlocks I saw two peculiar and plump birds
near me on the bank there which reminded me of the cow blackbird and of the oriole at first. I saw at once that they were new to
me, and guessed that they were crossbills, which was the case,—
male and female. The former was dusky-greenish (through a
glass), orange, and red, the orange, etc., on head, breast, and
rump, the vent white; dark, large bill; the female more of a dusky
slate-color, and yellow instead of orange and red. They were very
busily eating the seeds of the hemlock, whose cones were strewn
on the ground, and they were very fearless, allowing me to approach quite near.

When I returned this way I looked for them again, and at the
larger hemlocks heard a peculiar note, *cheep, cheep, cheep, cheep,* in
the rhythm of a fish hawk but faster and rather loud, and looking
up saw them fly to the north side and alight on the top of a swamp
white oak, while I sat in my boat close under the south bank. But
immediately they recrossed and went to feeding on the bank within
a rod of me. They were very parrot-like both in color (especially the

male, greenish and orange, etc.) and in their manner of feeding,—holding the hemlock cones in one claw and rapidly extracting the seeds with their bills, thus trying one cone after another very fast. But they kept their bills a-going so that, near as they were, I did not distinguish the cross. I should have looked at them in profile. At last the two hopped within six feet of me, and one within four feet, and they were coming still nearer, as if partly from curiosity, though nibbling the cones all the while, when my chain fell down and rattled loudly,—for the wind shook the boat,—and they flew off a rod. In Bechstein[1] I read that "it frequents fir and pine woods, but only when there are abundance of the cones." It may be that the abundance of white pine cones last fall had to do with their coming here. The hemlock cones were very abundant too, methinks.

LESSER REDPOLL
(LINARIA)

November 12, 1852 Saw a flock of little passenger birds[2] by Walden, busily pecking at the white birch catkins; about the size of a chickadee; *distinct* white bar on wings; most with dark pencilled breast, some with whitish; forked tail; bright chestnut or crimson (?) frontlet; yellowish shoulders or sack. When startled,

---

[1][J. M. Bechstein, M.D., *Cage and Chamber-Birds*, translated from the German and edited by H. G. Adams, London, 1853, p. 174.]
[2]*Fringilla linaria* [now called *Acanthis linaria*, the redpoll].

they went off with a jingling sound somewhat like emptying a bag of coin. Is it the yellow redpoll?

December 9, 1852   Those little ruby-crowned wrens (?)[1] still about. They suddenly dash away from this side to that in flocks, with a tumultuous note, half jingle, half rattle, like nuts shaken in a bag, or a bushel of nutshells, soon returning to the tree they had forsaken on some alarm. They are oftenest seen on the white birch, apparently feeding on its seeds, scattering the scales about.

January 3, 1853   The red-crowns here still. They appear to frequent one clump of birches a long time, for here the snow beneath is covered with the seeds they have loosened, while elsewhere there are none. They hang by the twigs while they peck the catkins, and others are busy on the snow beneath, picking up what drops. They are continually in motion, with a jingling twitter and occasional mew, and suddenly, when disturbed, go off with a loud jingle like the motion of a whole bag of nuts.

March 5, 1853   F. Brown[2] showed me to-day some lesser redpolls which he shot yesterday. They turn out to be my falsely-called chestnut-frontleted bird of the winter. "*Linaria minor*, Ray. Lesser Redpoll Linnet. From Pennsylvania and New Jersey to Maine, in winter; inland to Kentucky. Breeds in Maine, Nova Sco-

[1]Lesser redpolls.
[2][Frank Brown, of Concord, who made a collection of mounted birds.]

tia,[1] Newfoundland, Labrador, and the Fur Countries."—Audubon's Synopsis. They have a sharp bill, black legs and claws, and a bright-crimson crown or frontlet, in the male reaching to the base of the bill, with, in his case, a delicate rose or carmine on the breast and rump. Though this is described by Nuttall as an occasional visitor in the winter, it has been the prevailing bird here this winter.

December 19, 1854 Off Clamshell I heard and saw a large flock of *Fringilla linaria* over the meadow. . . . Suddenly they turn aside in their flight and dash across the river to a large white birch fifteen rods off, which plainly they had distinguished so far. I afterward saw many more in the Potter swamp up the river. They were commonly brown or dusky above, streaked with yellowish white or ash, and more or less white or ash beneath. Most had a crimson crown or frontlet, and a few a crimson neck and breast, very handsome. Some with a bright-crimson crown and clear-white breasts. I suspect that these were young males. They keep up an incessant twittering, varied from time to time with some mewing notes, and occasionally, for some unknown reason, they will all suddenly dash away with that universal loud note (twitter) like a bag of nuts. They are busily clustered in the tops of the birches, picking the seeds out of the catkins, and sustain themselves in all

[1][There are no authentic records of the bird's breeding in Maine or Nova Scotia.]

kinds of attitudes, sometimes head downwards, while about this. Common as they are now, and were winter before last, I saw none last winter.

January 19, 1855 It may be that the linarias come into the gardens now not only because all nature is a wilderness to-day, but because the woods where the wind has not free play are so snowed up, the twigs are so deeply covered, that they cannot readily come at their food.

January 20, 1855 I see the tracks of countless little birds, probably redpolls, where these have run over broad pastures and visited every weed,—johnswort and coarse grasses,—whose oat-like seed-scales or hulls they have scattered about. It is surprising they did not sink deeper in the light snow. Often the impression is so faint that they seem to have been supported by their wings.

January 24, 1860 See a large flock of lesser redpolls, eating the seeds of the birch (and perhaps alder) in Dennis Swamp by railroad. They are distinct enough from the goldfinch, their note more shelly and general as they fly, and they are whiter, without the black wings, beside that some have the crimson head or head and breast. They alight on the birches, then swarm on the snow beneath, busily picking up the seed in the copse.

January 27, 1860 Half a dozen redpolls busily picking the seeds out of the larch cones behind Monroe's. They are pretty tame, and I stand near. They perch on the slender twigs which are

beaded with cones, and swing and teeter there while they perse-
veringly peck at them, trying now this one, now that, and sometimes appearing to pick out and swallow them quite fast. I notice
no redness or carmine at first, but when the top of one's head
comes between me and the sun it unexpectedly glows.

January 29, 1860   To-day I see quite a flock of the lesser redpolls eating the seeds of the alder, picking them out of the cones
just as they do the larch, often head downward; and I see, under the
alders, where they have run and picked up the fallen seeds, making
chain-like tracks, two parallel lines.

AMERICAN GOLDFINCH

July 24, 1852   I heard this afternoon the cool water
twitter of the goldfinch, and saw the bird. They come with the
springing aftermath. It is refreshing as a cup of cold water to a
thirsty man to hear them, now only one at a time.

August 26, 1856   As I stand there, a young male goldfinch
darts away with a twitter from a spear thistle top close to my side,
and, alighting near, makes frequent returns as near to me and the
thistle as it dares pass, not yet knowing man well enough to fear
him.

August 28, 1856   A goldfinch twitters away from every thistle now, and soon returns to it when I am past. I see the ground
strewn with the thistle-down they have scattered on every side.

April 19, 1858 I hear the pine warbler there, and also what I thought a variation of its note, quite different, yet I thought not unfamiliar to me. Afterwards, along the wall under the Middle Conantum Cliff, I saw many goldfinches, male and female, the males singing in a very sprightly and varied manner, sitting still on bare trees. Also uttered their watery twitter and their peculiar mewing. In the meanwhile I heard a faint thrasher's note, as if faintly but perfectly imitated by some bird twenty or thirty rods off. This surprised me very much. It was equally rich and varied, and yet I did not believe it to be a thrasher. Determined to find out the singer, I sat still with my glass in hand, and at length detected the singer, a goldfinch sitting within gunshot all the while. This was the most varied and sprightly performer of any bird I have heard this year, and it is strange that I never heard the strain before. It may be this note which is taken for the thrasher's before the latter comes.

August 9, 1858 Edward Bartlett shows me this morning a nest which he found yesterday. It is saddled on the lowest horizontal branch of an apple tree in Abel Heywood's orchard, against a small twig, and answers to Nuttall's description of the goldfinch's nest, which it probably is. The eggs were five, pure white or with a faint bluish green tinge, just begun to be developed. I did not see the bird.

It is but little you learn of a bird in this irregular way,—having its nest and eggs shown you. How much more suggestive the sight of the goldfinch going off on a jaunt over the hills, twittering to its plainer consort by its side.

★   ★   ★

The goldfinch nest of this forenoon is saddled on a horizontal twig of an apple, some seven feet from ground and one third of an inch in diameter, supported on one side by a yet smaller branch, also slightly attached to another small branch. It measures three and one half inches from outside to outside, one and three quarters inside, two and one-half from top to bottom, or to a little below the twig, and one and one half inside. It is a very compact, thick, and warmly lined nest, slightly incurving on the edge within. It is composed of fine shreds of bark—grape-vine and other—and one piece of twine, with, more externally, an abundance of pale-brown slender catkins of oak(?) or hickory (?), mixed with effete apple blossoms and their peduncles, showing little apples, and the petioles of apple leaves, sometimes with half-decayed leaves of this year attached, last year's heads of lespedeza, and some other heads of weeds, with a little grass stem or weed stem, all more or less disguised by a web of white spider or caterpillar silk, spread over the outside. It is thickly and very warmly lined with (apparently) short thistle-down, mixed with which you see some grape-vine bark, and the rim is composed of the same shreds of bark, catkins, and some fine fibrous stems, and two or three hairs (of horse) mixed with wool (?); for only the hollow is lined with the looser or less tenacious thistle-down. This nest shows a good deal of art.

August 11, 1858 Heard a fine, sprightly, richly warbled strain from a bird perched on the top of a bean-pole. It was at the same time novel yet familiar to me. I soon recognized it for the strain of the purple finch, which I have not heard lately. But though it appeared as large, it seemed a different-colored bird. With my glass, four rods off, I saw it to be a goldfinch. It kept repeating this warble of the purple finch for several minutes. A very surprising note to be heard now, when birds generally are so silent. Have not heard the purple finch of late. I conclude that the goldfinch is a very fine and powerful singer, and the most successful and remarkable mocking-bird that we have. In the spring I heard it imitate the thrasher exactly, before that bird had arrived, and now it imitates the purple finch as perfectly, after the latter bird has ceased to sing! It is a surprising vocalist. It did not cease singing till I disturbed it by my nearer approach, and then it went off with its usual *mew*, succeeded by its watery twitter in its *ricochet* flight.

August 14, 1858 The Canada thistle down is now begun to fly, and I see the goldfinch upon it. *Carduelis*.[1] Often when I watch one go off, he flies at first one way, rising and falling, as if skimming close over unseen billows, but directly makes a great circuit

---

[1] [Nuttall placed the American goldfinch with the European bird in the subgenus *Caduelis*, from *carduus*, thistle.]

as if he had changed his mind, and disappears in the opposite direction, or is seen to be joined there by his mate.

December 22, 1858 P.M.—To Walden.

I see in the cut near the shanty-site quite a flock of *F. hyemalis*[1] and goldfinches together, on the snow and weeds and ground. Hear the well-known mew and watery twitter of the last and the drier *chilt chilt* of the former. These burning yellow birds with a little black and white on their coat-flaps look warm above the snow. There may be thirty goldfinches, very brisk and pretty tame. They hang head downwards on the weeds. I hear of their coming to pick sunflower seeds in Melvin's garden these days.

March 24, 1859 Returning, above the railroad causeway, I see a flock of goldfinches, first of *spring*, flitting along the causeway-bank. They have not yet the bright plumage they will have, but in some lights might be mistaken for sparrows. There is considerable difference in color between one and another, but the flaps of their coats are black, and their heads and shoulders more or less yellow. They are eating the seeds of the mullein and the large primrose, clinging to the plants sidewise in various positions and pecking at the seed-vessels.

November 15, 1859 About the 23d of October I saw a large flock of goldfinches (judging from their motions and notes) on the tops of the hemlocks up the Assabet, apparently feeding on their

---

[1] [Now called *Junco hyemalis*, the slate-colored snowbird.]

seeds, then falling. They were collected in great numbers on the very tops of these trees and flitting from one to another. Rice has since described to me the same phenomenon as observed by him there since (says he saw the birds picking out the seeds), though he did not know what birds they were. William Rice says that these birds get so much of the lettuce seed that you can hardly save any. They get sunflower seeds also. Are called "lettuce-birds" in the books.

SNOW BUNTING
(ARCTIC SNOWBIRD)

December 29, 1853 The driving snow blinds you, and where you are protected, you can see but little way, it is so thick. Yet in spite, or on account, of all, I see the first flock of arctic snowbirds (*Emberiza nivalis*)[1] near the depot, white and black, with a sharp, whistle-like note. . . . These are the true winter birds for you, these winged snowballs. I could hardly see them, the air was so full of driving snow. What hardy creatures! Where do they spend the night?

January 2, 1854 A flock of snow buntings flew over the fields with a rippling whistle, accompanied sometimes by a tender peep and a ricochet motion.

January 2, 1856 Crossing the railroad at the Heywood meadow, I saw some snow buntings rise from the side of the em-

[1][Now called *Plectrophenax nivalis*.]

bankment, and with surging, rolling flight wing their way up through the cut.

* * *

Returning, I saw, near the back road and railroad, a small flock of eight snow buntings feeding on the seeds of the pigweed, picking them from the snow,—apparently flat on the snow, their legs so short,—and, when I approached, alighting on the rail fence. They were pretty black, with white wings and a brown crescent on their breasts. They have come with this deeper snow and colder weather.

January 6, 1856 While I am making a path to the pump, I hear hurried *rippling* notes of birds, look up, and see quite a flock of snow buntings coming to alight amid the currant-tops in the yard. It is a sound almost as if made with their wings. What a pity our yard was made so tidy in the fall with rake and fire, and we have now no tall crop of weeds rising above this snow to invite these birds!

January 21, 1857 As I flounder along the Corner road against the root fence, a very large flock of snow buntings alight with a wheeling flight amid the weeds rising above the snow in Potter's heater piece,[1]—a hundred or two of them. They run restlessly amid

---

[1] [A "heater piece," in the parlance of old New England, is a triangular plot of ground, so called from its resemblance in shape to a flat-iron heater, a triangular piece of cast iron which was heated and put into the old-fashioned flat-iron.]

the weeds, so that I can hardly get sight of them through my glass; then suddenly all arise and fly only two or three rods, alighting within three rods of me. (They keep up a constant twittering.) It was as if they were any instant ready for a longer flight, but their leader had not so ordered it. Suddenly away they sweep again, and I see them alight in a distant field where the weeds rise above the snow, but in a few minutes they have left that also and gone further north. Beside their *rippling* note, they have a vibratory twitter, and from the loiterers you hear quite a tender peep, as they fly after the vanishing flock.

What independent creatures! They go seeking their food from north to south. If New Hampshire and Maine are covered deeply with snow, they scale down to Massachusetts for their breakfasts. Not liking the grain in this field, away they dash to another distant one, attracted by the weeds rising above the snow. Who can guess in what field, by what river or mountain they breakfasted this morning. They did not seem to regard me so near, but as they went off, their wave actually broke over me as a rock. They have the pleasure of society at their feasts, a hundred dining at once, busily talking while eating, remembering what occurred at Grinnell Land. As they flew past me they presented a pretty appearance, somewhat like broad bars of white alternating with bars of black.

March 2, 1858 See a large flock of snow buntings, the white birds of the winter, rejoicing in the snow. I stand near a flock in an open field. They are trotting about briskly over the snow amid the weeds,—apparently pigweed and Roman wormwood,—as it were to keep their toes warm, hopping up to the weeds. Then they restlessly take to wing again, and as they wheel about one, it is a very rich sight to see them dressed in black and white uniforms, alternate black and white, very distinct and regular. Perhaps no colors would be more effective above the snow, black tips (considerably more) to wings, then clear white between this and the back, which is black or very dark again. One wonders if they are aware what a pleasing uniform appearance they make when they show their backs thus. They alight again equally near. Their track is much like a small crow's track, showing a long heel and furrowing the snow between with their toes.

November 7, 1858 Going up the lane beyond Farmer's, I was surprised to see fly up from the white, stony road, two snow buntings, which alighted again close by, one on a large rock, the other on the stony ground. They had pale-brown or tawny touches on the white breast, on each side of the head, and on the top of the head, in the last place with some darker color. Had light-yellowish bills. They sat quite motionless within two rods, and allowed me to approach within a rod, as if conscious that the white rocks, etc., concealed them. It seemed as if they were attracted to surfaces of the same color with themselves,—white and black (or quite dark) and tawny. One squatted *flat*, if not both. Their soft rippling notes as they went off reminded me of the northeast snow-storms to which ere long they are to be an accompaniment.

December 12, 1858 P.M.—Up river on ice to Fair Haven Hill.

Crossing the fields west of our Texas[1] house, I see an immense flock of snow buntings, I think the largest that I ever saw. There must be a thousand or two at least. There is but three inches, at most, of crusted and dry frozen snow, and they are running amid the weeds which rise above it. The weeds are chiefly *Juncus tenuis* (?), but its seeds are apparently gone. I find, however, the glumes of the piper grass[2] scattered about where they have been. The flock is at first about equally divided into two parts about twenty rods apart, but birds are incessantly flitting across the interval to join the pioneer flock, until all are united. They are very restless, running amid the weeds and continually changing their ground. They will suddenly rise again a few seconds after they have alighted, as if alarmed, but after a short wheel settle close by. Flying from you, in some positions, you see only or chiefly the black part of their bodies, and then, as they wheel, the white comes into view, contrasted prettily with the former, and in all together at the same time. Seen flying higher against a cloudy sky, they look like large snowflakes. When they rise all together their note is like the rattling of nuts in a bag, as if a whole binful were rolled from side to side. They also utter from time to time—*i.e.*, individuals

---

[1] ["Texas" was a part of Concord where the Thoreau family lived from 1844 to 1850.]

[2] [A local name for the couch, quitch, or witch grass (*Agropyron repens*). See *Walden*, Riverside Literature Series, Notes, p. 391.]

do—a clear rippling note, perhaps of alarm, or a call. It is remarkable that their notes above described should resemble the lesser redpoll's! Away goes this great wheeling, rambling flock, rolling through the air, and you cannot easily tell where they will settle. Suddenly the pioneers (or a part not foremost) will change their course when in full career, and when at length they know it, the rushing flock on the other side will be fetched about as it were with an undulating jerk, as in the boys' game of snap-the-whip, and those that occupy the place of the snapper are gradually off after their leaders on the new tack. As far as I observe, they confine themselves to upland, not alighting in the meadows. Like a snowstorm they come rushing down from the north. The extremities of the wings are black, while the parts next their bodies are black [*sic*]. They are unusually abundant now.

January 6, 1859 Near Nut Meadow Brook, on the Jimmy Miles road, I see a flock of snow buntings. They are feeding exclusively on . . . Roman wormwood. Their tracks where they sink in the snow are very long, *i.e.*, have a very long heel, thus:

or sometimes almost in a single straight line. They made notes when they went,—sharp, rippling, like a vibrating spring. They had run about to every such such [*sic*], leaving distinct tracks raying from and to them, while the snow immediately about the weed was so tracked and pecked where the seeds fell that no track was distinct.

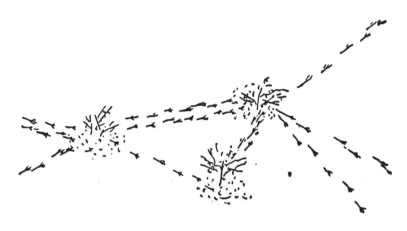

AND MUCH MORE TRACKED UP

March 3, 1859 Going by the solidago oak[1] at Clamshell Hill bank, I heard a faint rippling note and, looking up, saw about fifteen snow buntings sitting in the top of the oak, all with their breasts toward me,—sitting so still and quite white, seen against the white cloudy sky, they did not look like birds but the ghosts of birds, and their boldness, allowing me to come quite near, enhanced this impression. These were almost as white as snowballs,

[1][A particular tree so named by Thoreau.]

and from time to time I heard a low, soft rippling note from them. I could see no features, but only the general outline of plump birds in white. It was a very spectral sight, and after I had watched them for several minutes, I can hardly say that I was prepared to see them fly away like ordinary buntings when I advanced further. At first they were almost concealed by being almost the same color with the cloudy sky.

December 23, 1859   In this slight snow I am surprised to see countless tracks of small birds, which have run over it in every direction from one end to the other of this great meadow since morning. By the length of the hind toe I know them to be snow buntings. Indeed, soon after I see them running still on one side of the meadow. I was puzzled to tell what they got by running there. Yet I [saw them] stopping repeatedly and picking up something. Of course I thought of those caterpillars which are washed out by a rain and freshet at this season, but I could not find one of them. It rained on the 18th and again the 20th, and over a good part of the meadow the top of the stubble left by the scythe rises a little above the ice, *i.e.* an inch or two, not enough to disturb a skater. The birds have run here chiefly, visiting each little collection or tuft of stubble, and found their food chiefly in and about this thin stubble. I examined such places a long time and very carefully, but I could not find there the seed of any plant whatever. It was merely the stubble of sedge, with never any head left, and a few cranberry leaves projecting. All that I could find was pretty often (in some places very often) a little black, or else a brown, spider (sometimes quite a large one) motionless on the snow or ice; and therefore I am constrained to think that they eat them, for I saw them running and picking in exactly such places a little way from me, and here were their tracks all around. Yet they are called graminivorous [*sic*]. Wilson says that he has seen them feeding on the seeds of aquatic plants on the Seneca River, clinging to their heads. I think he means wool-grass. Yet its seeds are too minute and involved in the wool. Though there was wool-grass hereabouts, the birds did not go near it. To be sure, it has but little seed now. If they are so common at the extreme north, where there is so little vegetation but perhaps a great many spiders, is it not likely that they feed on these insects?

It is interesting to see how busy this flock is, exploring this great meadow to-day. If it were not for this slight snow, revealing their tracks but hardly at all concealing the stubble, I should not suspect it, though I might see them at their work. Now I see them running briskly over the ice, most commonly near the shore, where there is most stubble (though very little); and they explore the ground so fast that they are continually changing their ground, and if I do not keep my eye on them I lose the direction. Then here they come, with a stiff *rip* of their wings as they suddenly wheel, and those peculiar rippling notes, flying low quite across the meadow, half a mile even, to explore the other side, though that too is already tracked by them. Not the fisher nor skater range the meadow a thousandth part so much in a week as these birds in a day. They hardly notice me as they come on. Indeed, the flock, flying about as high as my head, divides, and half passes on each side of me. Thus they sport over these broad meadows of ice this pleasant winter day. The spiders lie torpid and plain to see on the snow, and if it is they that they are after they never know what kills them.

January 3, 1860 Saw four snow buntings by the railroad causeway, just this side the cut, quite tame. They arose and alighted on the rail fence as we went by. Very stout for their length. Look very pretty when they fly and reveal the clear white space on their wings next the body,—white between the blacks. They were busily eating the seed of the piper grass on the embankment there, and it was strewn over the snow by them like oats in a stable. Melvin speaks of seeing flocks of them on the river meadows in the fall, when they are of a different color.

VESPER SPARROW
(GRASS FINCH)
(BAY-WING)

January 1, 1854 The white-in-tails, or grass finches, linger pretty late, flitting in flocks before, but they come so near winter only as the white in their tail indicates. They let it come near enough to whiten their tails, perchance, and they are off.

The snow buntings and the tree sparrows are the true spirits of the snow-storm; they are the animated beings that ride upon it and have their life in it.

July 15, 1854   I hear a bay-wing on the wall near by, sounding far away,—a fainter song sparrow strain, somewhat. I see its open mouth and quivering throat, yet can hardly believe the seemingly distant strain proceeds from it, *yaw yaw, twee twee, twitter twitter, te twee twe tw tw tw*, and so ends with a short and rapid trill.

April 29, 1855   This morning it snows, but the ground is not yet whitened. This will probably take the cold out of the air. Many chip-birds are feeding in the yard, and one bay-wing. The latter incessantly scratches like a hen, all the while looking about for foes. The bay on its wings is not obvious except when it opens them. The white circle about the eye is visible afar. Now it makes a business of pluming itself, doubling prettily upon itself, now touching the root of its tail, now thrusting its head under its wing, now between its wing and back above, and now between its legs and its belly; and now it drops flat on its breast and belly and spreads and shakes its wings, now stands up and repeatedly shakes its wings. It is either cleaning itself of dirt acquired in scratching and feeding,— for its feet are black with mud,—or it is oiling its feathers thus. It is rather better concealed by its color than the chip-bird with its chestnut crown and light breast. The chip-bird scratches but slightly and rarely; it finds what it wants on the surface, keeps its head down more steadily, not looking about. I see the bay-wing eat some worms.

April 13, 1856   I hear a bay-wing on the railroad fence sing— the rhythm—somewhat like, *char char* (or *here here*), *che che, chip chip chip* (fast), *chitter chitter chitter chit* (very fast and jingling), *tchea tchea* (jinglingly). It has another strain, considerably different, but a second also sings the above. Two on different posts are steadily singing the same, as if contending with each other, notwithstanding the cold wind.

June 23, 1856   Bay-wings sang morning and evening about R.'s house,[1] often sitting on a bean-pole and dropping down and running and singing on the bare ground amid the potatoes. Its note somewhat like *Come, here here, there there,—quick quick quick* (fast),—*or I'm gone.*

May 12, 1857   While dropping beans in the garden at Texas[2] just after sundown (May 13th), I hear from across the fields the note of the bay-wing, *Come here here there there quick quick quick or I'm gone,* (which I have no doubt sits on some fence-post or rail there), and it instantly translates me from the sphere of my work and re- pairs all the world that we jointly inhabit. It reminds me of so many country afternoons and evenings when this bird's strain was

---

[1] [Mr. Daniel Ricketson's house in New Bedford, where Thoreau was visiting.]
[2] [See note on p. 316.]

heard far over the fields, as I pursued it from field to field. The spirit of its earth-song, of its serene and true philosophy, was breathed into me, and I saw the world as through a glass, as it lies eternally. Some of its aboriginal contentment, even of its domestic felicity, possessed me. What he suggests is permanently true. As the bay-wing sang many a thousand years ago, so sang he to-night. In the beginning God heard his song and pronounced it good, and hence it has endured. It reminded me of many a summer sunset, of many miles of gray rails, of many a rambling pasture, of the farmhouse far in the fields, its milk-pans and well-sweep, and the cows coming home from pasture.

I would thus from time to time take advice of the birds, correct my human views by listening to their volucral (?). He is a brother poet, this small gray bird (or bard), whose muse inspires mine. His lay is an idyl or pastoral, older and sweeter than any that is classic. He sits on some gray perch like himself, on a stake, perchance, in the midst of the field, and you can hardly see him against the plowed ground. You advance step by step as the twilight deepens, and lo! he is gone, and in vain you strain your eyes to see whither, but anon his tinkling strain is heard from some other quarter. One with the rocks and with us.

Methinks I hear these sounds, have these reminiscences, only when well employed, at any rate only when I have no reason to be ashamed of my employment. I am often aware of a certain compensation of this kind for doing something from a sense of duty, even unconsciously. Our past experience is a never-failing capital which can never be alienated, of which each kindred future event reminds us. If you would have the song of the sparrow inspire you a thousand years hence, let your life be in harmony with its strain to-day.

I ordinarily plod along a sort of whitewashed prison entry, subject to some indifferent or even grovelling mood. I do not distinctly realize my destiny. I have turned down my light to the merest glimmer and am doing some task which I have set myself. I take incredibly narrow views, live on the limits, and have no recollection of absolute truth. Mushroom institutions hedge me in. But suddenly, in some fortunate moment, the voice of eternal wisdom reaches me, even in the strain of the sparrow, and liberates me, whets and clarifies my senses, makes me a competent witness.

April 2, 1858   On the side of Fair Haven Hill I go looking for bay-wings, turning my glass to each sparrow on a rock or tree. At last I see one, which flies right up straight from a rock eighty or one hundred feet and warbles a peculiar long and pleasant strain, after the manner of the skylark, methinks, and close by I see another, apparently a bay-wing, though I do not see its white in tail, and it utters while sitting the same subdued, rather peculiar strain.

April 15, 1859   The bay-wing now sings—the first I have been able to hear—both about the Texas house and the fields this side of Hayden's, both of them similar dry and open pastures. I heard it just before noon, when the sun began to come out, and at

3 P.M., singing loud and clear and incessantly. It sings with a pleasing deliberation, contrasting with the spring vivacity of the song sparrow, whose song many would confound it with. It comes to revive with its song the dry uplands and pastures and grass-fields about the skirts of villages. Only think how finely our life is furnished in all its details,—sweet wild birds provided to fill its interstices with song! It is provided that while we are employed in our corporeal, or intellectual, or other, exercises we shall be lulled and amused or cheered by the singing of birds. When the laborer rests on his spade to-day, the sun having just come out, he is not left wholly to the mercy of his thoughts, nature is not a mere void to him, but he can hardly fail to hear the pleasing and encouraging notes of some newly arrived bird. The strain of the grass finch is very likely to fall on his ear and convince him, whether he is conscious of it or not, that the world is beautiful and life a fair enterprise to engage in. It will make him calm and contented. If you yield for a moment to the impressions of sense, you hear some bird giving expression to its happiness in a pleasant strain. We are provided with singing birds and with ears to hear them. What an institution that! Nor are we obliged to catch and cage them, nor to be bird-fanciers in the common sense. Whether a man's work be hard or easy, whether he be happy or unhappy, a bird is appointed to sing to a man while he is at his work.

SAVANNAH SPARROW
(SERINGO-BIRD)

May 1, 1852 I hear the note of the shy Savannah sparrow (*F. Savanna*),[1] that plump bird with a dark-streaked breast that runs and hides in the grass, whose note sounds so like a cricket's in the grass. (I used to hear it when I walked by moonlight last summer.) I hear it now from deep in the sod,—for there is hardly grass yet. The bird keeps so low you do not see it. You do not suspect how many there are till at length their heads appear. The word *seringo* reminds me of its note,—as if it were produced by some kind of fine metallic spring. It is an earth-sound.

March 18, 1853 With regard to my seringo-bird (and others), I think that my good genius withheld his name that I might learn his character.

April 22, 1856 The seringo also sits on a post, with a very distinct yellow line over the eye, and the *rhythm* of its strain is *ker*

---

[1]Probably have seen it before,—seringo. [Though here, where the "seringo-bird" makes its first appearance in the *Journal*, its identity with the Savannah sparrow seems to have been unquestioned by Thoreau, it proved afterwards to be almost as puzzling to him as the ever elusive "night-warbler." The probability is that the "seringo" in this and most other cases was the Savannah sparrow, but it may sometimes have been the yellow-winged, or grasshopper, sparrow, or even, as Thoreau once suspected, the grass finch, or vesper sparrow. It is quite likely that at times the bird he saw was not the bird he heard. *Passerculus sandwichensis savanna* is the scientific name now in use. Only a few of the many references to the bird in the *Journal* are here given.]

chick | *ker che* | *ker-char-r-r-r* | *chick,* the last two bars being the part chiefly heard.

TREE SPARROW

April 2, 1853   The tree sparrows and a few blue snowbirds in company sing (the former) very sweetly in the garden this morning. I now see a faint spot on the breast. It says something like *a twee twee, chit chit, chit chit chee var-r.*

January 1, 1854 The snow is the great betrayer. It not only shows the tracks of mice, otters, etc., etc., which else we should rarely if ever see, but the tree sparrows are more plainly seen against its white ground, and they in turn are attracted by the dark weeds which it reveals. It also drives the crows and other birds out of the woods to the villages for food.

March 30, 1854 Great flocks of tree sparrows and some *F. hyemalis* on the ground and trees on the Island Neck, making the air and bushes ring with their jingling. The former—some of them—say somewhat like this: *a che che, ter twee twee, tweer tweer twa.* It sounded like a new bird.

April 19, 1854 Hear the tree sparrows at willow hedgerow this morning,—*ah ha ha yip yip yip yip*, or *twitter twitter twe twe twe,* or *ah ha ha twitter twitter twe,*—very canary-like, yet clear, as if aspirated vowels alone,—no *t* or *r*.

December 4, 1856 Saw and heard cheep faintly one little tree sparrow, the neat chestnut crowned and winged and white-barred bird, perched on a large and solitary white birch. So clean and tough, made to withstand the winter. This color reminds me of the upper side of the shrub oak leaf. I love the few homely colors of Nature at this season,—her strong wholesome browns, her sober and primeval grays, her celestial blue, her vivacious green, her pure, cold, snowy white.

December 17, 1856 A flock of a dozen or more tree sparrows flitting through the edge of the birches, etc., by the meadow front of Puffer's. They make excursions into the open meadow and, as I approach, take refuge in the brush. I hear their faint *cheep*, a very feeble evidence of their existence, and also a pretty little suppressed warbling from them.

*   *   *

That feeble *cheep* of the tree sparrow, like the tinkling of an icicle, or the chafing of two hard shrub oak twigs, is probably a call to their mates, by which they keep together. These birds, when perched, look larger than usual this cold and windy day; they are puffed up for warmth, have added a porch to their doors.

January 6, 1857 Though there is an extremely cold, cutting northwest wind, against which I see many travellers turning their backs, and so advancing, I hear and see an unusual number of merry little tree sparrows about the few weeds that are to be seen. They look very chipper, flitting restlessly about and jerking their long tails.

October 13, 1857 See a pretty large flock of tree sparrows, very lively and tame, drifting along and pursuing each other along a bushy fence and ditch like driving snow. Two pursuing each other would curve upward like a breaker in the air and drop into the hedge again.

November 20, 1857 The hardy tree sparrow has taken the place of the chipping and song sparrow, so much like the former that most do not know it is another. His faint lisping chip will keep our spirits up till another spring.

January 6, 1858 The North River[1] is not frozen over. I see tree sparrows twittering and moving with a low creeping and jerking motion amid the chenopodium in a field, upon the snow, so chubby or puffed out on account of the cold that at first I took them for the arctic birds, but soon I see their bright-chestnut crowns and clear white bars; as the poet says, "a thousand feeding like one,"[2]— though there are not more than a dozen here.

January 7, 1858 P.M.—I see some tree sparrows feeding on the fine grass seed above the snow, near the road on the hillside below the Dutch house. They are flitting along one at a time, their feet commonly sunk in the snow, uttering occasionally a low sweet warble and seemingly as happy there, and with this wintry prospect before them for the night and several months to come, as any man by his fireside. One occasionally hops or flies toward another, and the latter suddenly jerks away from him. They are reaching or hopping up to the fine grass, or oftener picking the seeds from the snow. At length the whole ten have collected within a space a dozen feet square, but soon after, being alarmed, they utter a different and less musical chirp and flit away into an apple tree.

[1][The Assabet, or North Branch of the Concord River.]
[2][Wordsworth said, "There are forty feeding like one."]

March 20, 1858 A.M.—By river.

The tree sparrow is perhaps the sweetest and most melodious warbler at present and for some days. It is peculiar, too, for singing in concert along the hedgerows, much like a canary, especially in the mornings. Very clear, sweet, melodious notes, between a twitter and a warble, of which it is hard to catch the strain, for you commonly hear many at once.

December 17, 1859 I see on the pure white snow what looks like dust for half a dozen inches under a twig. Looking closely, I find that the twig is hardhack and the dust its slender, light-brown, chaffy-looking seed, which falls still in copious showers, dusting the snow, when I jar it; and here are the tracks of a sparrow[1] which has jarred the twig and picked the minute seeds a long time, making quite a hole in the snow. The seeds are so fine that it must have got more snow than seed at each peck. But they probably look large to its microscopic eyes. I see, when I jar it, that a meadow-sweet close by has quite similar, but larger, seeds. This the reason, then, that these plants rise so high above the snow and retain their seed, dispersing it on the least jar over each successive layer of snow beneath them; or it is carried to a distance by the wind. What abundance and what variety in the diet of these small granivorous birds, while I find only a few nuts still! These stiff weeds which no snow can break down hold their provender. What the cereals are to men,

[1][Very likely the tree sparrow, which feeds largely on weed seeds.]

these are to the sparrows. The only threshing they require is that the birds fly against their spikes or stalks. A little further I see the seed-box (?) (*Ludwigia*) full of still smaller, yellowish seeds. And on the ridge north is the track of a partridge amid the shrubs. It has hopped up to the low clusters of smooth sumach berries, sprinkled the snow with them, and eaten all but a few. Also, here only, or where it has evidently jarred them down—whether intentionally or not, I am not sure—are the large oval seeds of the stiff-stalked lespedeza, which I suspect it ate, with the sumach berries. There is much solid food in them. When the snow is deep the birds could easily pick the latter out of the heads as they stand on the snow.

December 31, 1859   There is a great deal of hemlock scales scattered over the recent snow (at the Hemlocks), evidently by birds on the trees, and the wind has blown them southeast,— scales, seeds, and cones,—and I see the tracks of small birds that have apparently picked the seeds from the snow also. It may have been done by goldfinches. I see a tree sparrow hopping close by, and perhaps they eat them on the snow. Some of the seeds have blown at least fifteen rods southeast. So the hemlock seed is important to some birds in the winter.

January 16, 1860   I see a flock of tree sparrows busily picking something from the surface of the snow amid some bushes. I watch one attentively, and find that it is feeding on the very fine brown chaffy-looking seed of the panicled andromeda. It understands how to get its dinner, to make the plant *give down*, perfectly. It flies up and alights on one of the dense brown panicles of the hard berries, and gives it a vigorous shaking and beating with its claws and bill, sending down a shower of the fine chaffy-looking seed on to the snow beneath. It lies very distinct, though fine almost as dust, on the spotless snow. It then hops down and briskly picks up from the snow what it wants. How very clean and agreeable to the imagination, and withal abundant, is this kind of food! How delicately they fare! These dry persistent seed-vessels hold their crusts of bread until shaken. The snow is the white table-cloth on which they fall. No anchorite with his water and his crust fares more simply. It shakes down a hundred times as much as it wants at each shrub, and shakes the same or another cluster after each successive snow. How bountifully Nature feeds them! No wonder they come to spend the winter with us, and are at ease with regard to their food. These shrubs ripen an abundant crop of seeds to supply the wants of these immigrants from the far north which annually come to spend the winter with us. How neatly and simply it feeds!

This shrub grows unobserved by most, only known to botanists, and at length matures its hard, dry seed-vessels, which, if noticed, are hardly supposed to contain seed. But there is no shrub nor weed which is not known to some bird. Though you may have never noticed it, the tree sparrow comes from the north in the winter straight to this shrub, and confidently shakes its panicle, and then feasts on the fine shower of seeds that falls from it.

January 24, 1860   As I stand at the south end of J. P. B.'s moraine, I watch six tree sparrows, which come from the wood and alight and feed on the ground, which is there bare. They are only two or three rods from me, and are incessantly picking and eating an abundance of the fine grass (short-cropped pasture grass) on that knoll, as a hen or goose does. I see the stubble an inch or two long in their bills, and how they stuff it down. Perhaps they select chiefly the green parts. So they vary their fare and there is no danger of their starving. These six hopped round for five minutes over a space a rod square before I put them to flight, and then I noticed, in a space only some four feet square in that rod, at least eighteen droppings (white at one end, the rest more slate-colored). So wonderfully active are they in their movements, both external and internal. They do not suffer for want of a good digestion, surely. No doubt they eat some earth or gravel too. So do partridges eat a great deal. These birds, though they have bright brown and buff backs, hop about amid the little inequalities of the pasture almost unnoticed, such is their color and so humble are they.

CHIPPING SPARROW
(CHIP-BIRD)

May 1, 1852   5 A.M.—A smart frost in the night, the ploughed ground and platforms white with it. I hear the little forked-tail chipping sparrow (*Fringilla socialis*)[1] shaking out his rapid *tchi-tchi-tchi-tchi-tchi-tchi*, a little jingle, from the oak behind the Depot.

July 21, 1852 4 A.M.—Robins sing as loud as in spring, and the chip-bird breathes in the dawn.

July 25, 1852 4 A.M.—This early twitter or breathing of chip-birds in the dawn sounds like something organic in the earth. This is a morning celebrated by birds. Our bluebird sits on the peak of the house, and warbles as in the spring, but as he does not now by day.

March 22, 1853 As soon as those spring mornings arrive in which the birds sing, I am sure to be an early riser. I am waked by my genius. I wake to inaudible melodies and am surprised to find myself expecting the dawn in so serene and joyful and expectant a mood. I have an appointment with spring. She comes to the window to wake me, and I go forth an hour or two earlier than usual. It is by especial favor that I am waked,—not rudely but gently, as infants should be waked. Though as yet the trill of the chip-bird is not heard,—added,—like the sparkling bead which bursts on bottled cider or ale.

April 9, 1853 The chipping sparrow, with its ashy-white breast and white streak over eye and undivided chestnut crown, holds up its head and pours forth its *che che che che che che*.

[1][Now known as *Spizella passerina*.]

June 2, 1853 3.30 A.M.—When I awake I hear the low universal chirping or twittering of the chip-birds, like the bursting bead on the surface of the uncorked day. First come, first served! You must taste the first glass of the day's nectar, if you would get all the spirit of it. Its fixed air begins to stir and escape. Also the robin's morning song is heard as in the spring, earlier than the notes of most other birds, thus bringing back the spring; now rarely heard or noticed in the course of the day.

April 17, 1860 I hear this forenoon the soothing and simple, though monotonous, notes of the chip-bird, telling us better than our thermometers what degree of summer warmth is reached; adds its humble but very pleasant contribution to the steadily increasing quire of the spring. It perches on a cherry tree, perchance, near the house, and unseen, by its steady *che-che-che-che-che-che*, affecting us often without our distinctly hearing it, it blends all the other and previous sounds of the season together. It invites us to walk in the yard and inspect the springing plants.

FIELD SPARROW
(RUSH SPARROW)
(HUCKLEBERRY-BIRD)
July 16, 1851 The rush sparrow jingles her small change, pure silver, on the counter of the pasture.

April 27, 1852   Heard the field or rush sparrow this morning (*Fringilla juncorum*),[1] George Minott's "huckleberry-bird." It sits on a birch and sings at short intervals, apparently answered from a distance. It is clear and sonorous heard afar; but I found it quite impossible to tell from which side it came; sounding like *phe, phe, phe, pher-pher-tw-tw-tw-t-t-t-t,*—the first three slow and loud, the next two syllables quicker, and the last part quicker and quicker, becoming a clear, sonorous trill or rattle, like a spoon in a saucer.

April 30, 1852   Half an hour before sunset. The robins sing powerfully on the elms; the little frogs peep; the woodpecker's harsh and long-continued cry is heard from the woods; the huckleberry-bird's simple, sonorous trill.

May 1, 1852   The tinkle of the huckleberry-bird comes up from the shrub oak plain. He commonly lives away from the habitations of men, in retired bushy fields and sprout-lands.

April 13, 1854   On the hill near Moore's hear the *F. juncorum,*—*phē-phē-phē-phē-phē, pher-phē-ē-ē-ē-ē-ē-ē.* How sweet it sounds in a clear warm morning in a wood-side pasture amid the old corn-hills, or in sprout-lands, a [*sic*] clear and distinct, "like a spoon in a cup," the last part very fast and ringing.

June 24, 1857   Returning, heard a fine, clear note from a bird on a white birch near me,—*whit whit, whit whit, whit whit,* (very

---

[1][Rush sparrow and *Fringilla juncorum* are Nuttall's names, which he got from earlier authors. They seem singularly inappropriate for a bird of the upland pastures. The scientific name now in use for the field sparrow is *Spizella pusilla.*]

fast) *ter phe phe phe,*—sounding perfectly novel. Looking round, I saw it was the huckleberry-bird, for it was near and plain to be seen.

April 22, 1859 When setting the pines at Walden the last three days, I was sung to by the field sparrow. For music I heard their jingle from time to time. That the music the pines were set to, and I have no doubt they will build many a nest under their shelter. It would seem as if such a field as this—a dry open or half-open pasture in the woods, with small pines scattered in it—was well-nigh, if not quite, abandoned to this one alone among the sparrows. The surface of the earth is portioned out among them. By a beautiful law of distribution, one creature does not too much interfere with another. I do not hear the song sparrow here. As the pines gradually increase, and a wood-lot is formed, these birds will withdraw to new pastures, and the thrushes, etc., will take their place. Yes, as the walls of cities are fabled to have been built by music, so my pines were established by the song of the field sparrow. They commonly place their nests here under the shelter of a little pine in the field.

SLATE-COLORED JUNCO (SLATE-COLORED SNOWBIRD) (FRINGILLA HYEMALIS [Junco Hyemalis])

April 14, 1852 The slate-colored snowbird's (for they are still about) is a somewhat shrill jingle, like the sound of ramrods when the order has been given to a regiment to "return ramrods" and they obey stragglingly.

March 25, 1853   The *Fringilla hyemalis* sing *most* in concert of any bird nowadays that I hear. Sitting near together on an oak or pine in the woods or an elm in the village, they keep up a very pleasant, enlivening, and incessant jingling and twittering *chill-lill-lill*, so that it is difficult to distinguish a single bird's note,—parts of it much like a canary. This sound advances me furthest toward summer, unless it be the note of the lark, who, by the way, is the most steady singer at present. Notwithstanding the raw and windy mornings, it will sit on a low twig or tussock or pile of manure in the meadow and sing for hours, as sweetly and plaintively as in summer.

March 28, 1853   The woods ring with the cheerful jingle of the *F. hyemalis*. This is a very trig and compact little bird, and appears to be in good condition. The straight edge of slate on their breasts contrasts remarkably with the white from beneath; the short, light-colored bill is also very conspicuous amid the dark slate; and when they fly from you, the two white feathers in their tails are very distinct at a good distance. They are very lively, pursuing each other from bush to bush.

December 1, 1856   Slate-colored snowbirds flit before me in the path, feeding on the seeds on the snow, the countless little brown seeds that begin to be scattered over the snow, so much the more obvious to bird and beast. A hundred kinds of indigenous grain are harvested now, broadcast upon the surface of the snow. Thus at a critical season these seeds are shaken down on to a clean white napkin, unmixed with dirt and rubbish, and off this the little pensioners pick them. Their clean table is thus spread a few inches or feet above the ground. Will wonder become extinct in me? Shall I become insensitive as a fungus?

October 26, 1857   At the hewing-place on the flat above, many sparrows are flitting past amid the birches and sallows. They are chiefly *Fringilla hyemalis*. How often they may be seen thus flitting along in a straggling manner from bush to bush, so that the hedgerow will be all alive with them, each uttering a faint *chip* from time to time, as if to keep together, bewildering you so that you know not if the greater part are gone by or still to come! One rests but a moment on the tree before you and is gone again. You wonder if they know whither they are bound, and how their leader is appointed.

★   ★   ★

Those sparrows, too, are thoughts I have. They come and go; they flit by quickly on their migrations, uttering only a faint *chip*, I know not whither or why exactly. One will not rest upon its twig for me to scrutinize it. The whole copse will be alive with my rambling thoughts, bewildering me by their very multitude, but they will be all gone directly without leaving me a feather. My loftiest thought is somewhat like an eagle that suddenly comes into the field of view, suggesting great things and thrilling the beholder, as if it were bound hitherward with a message for me; but it comes no nearer, but circles and soars away, growing dimmer, disappointing me, till it is lost behind a cliff or a cloud.

May 20, 1858   The note of the *F. hyemalis*, or *chill-lill*, is a jingle, with also a shorter and drier *crackling* or shuffling chip as it flits by.

June 2, 1858   Some forty or fifty rods below the very apex southeast, or quite on the top of the mountain,[1] I saw a little bird flit out from beneath a rock close by the path on the left of it, where there were only very few scattered dwarf black spruce[2] about, and, looking, I found a nest with three eggs. It was the *Fringilla hyemalis*, which soon disappeared around a projecting rock. It was near by a conspicuous spruce, six or eight feet high, on the west edge of a sort of hollow, where a vista opened south over the precipice, and the path ascended at once more steeply. The nest was sunk in the ground by the side of a tuft of grass, and was pretty deep, made of much fine dry grass or sedge (?) and lined with a little of a delicate bluish hair-like fibre (?) two or three inches long. The eggs were three, of a regular oval form, faint bluish-white, sprinkled with fine pale-brown dots, in two of the three condensed into a ring

[1][Mt. Monadnock.]
[2][The red spruce of the uplands of northern New England was not generally distinguished from the black in Thoreau's day.]

about the larger end. They had apparently just begun to develop. The nest and tuft were covered by a projecting rock. Brewer says that only one nest is known to naturalists.[1] We saw many of these birds flitting about the summit, perched on the rocks and the dwarf spruce, and disappearing behind the rocks. It is the prevailing bird now up there, *i.e.* on the summit. They are commonly said to go to the fur countries to breed, though Wilson says that some breed in the Alleghanies. The New York Reports make them breed on the mountains of Oswego County and the Catskills.[2] This was a quite interesting discovery. They probably are never seen in the surrounding low grounds at this season. The ancestors of this bird had evidently perceived on their flight northward that here was a small piece of arctic region, containing all the conditions they require,— coolness and suitable food, etc., etc.,—and so for how long have builded here. For ages they have made their home here with the *Arenaria Grœnlandica* and *Potentilla tridentata*. They discerned arctic isles sprinkled in our southern sky. I did not see any of them below the rocky and generally bare portion of the mountain. It finds here the same conditions as in the north of Maine and in the fur countries,—Labrador mosses, etc. Now that the season is advanced, migrating birds have gone to the extreme north or gone to the

[1] ["Synopsis of the Birds of North America," appended to the 1840 Boston edition of Wilson's *American Ornithology* (p. 703).]

[2] Prevail in Novia Scotia according to Bryant and Cabot.

mountain-tops. By its color it harmonized with the gray and brownish-gray rocks. We felt that we were so much nearer to perennial spring and winter.

SONG SPARROW

1837—47[1] The song sparrow, whose voice is one of the first heard in the spring, sings occasionally throughout the season,—from a greater depth in the summer, as it were behind the notes of other birds.

July 16, 1851 The song sparrow, the most familiar and New England bird, is heard in fields and pastures, setting this midsummer day to music, as if it were the music of a mossy rail or fence post; a little stream of song, cooling, rippling through the noon,— the usually unseen songster usually unheard like the cricket, it is so common,—like the poet's song, unheard by most men, whose ears are stopped with business, though perchance it sang on the fence before the farmer's house this morning for an hour. There are little strains of poetry in our animals.

March 18, 1852 This snow has not driven back the birds. I hear the song sparrow's simple strain, most genuine herald of the spring, and see flocks of chubby northern birds with the habit of snowbirds, passing north.

[1][Undated paragraph in Journal transcript covering this period.]

April 1, 1852   As I come over the Turnpike, the song sparrow's jingle comes up from every part of the meadow, as native as the tinkling rills or the blossoms of the spirea, the meadow-sweet, soon to spring. Its cheep is like the sound of opening buds. The sparrow is continually singing on the alders along the brook-side, while the sun is continually setting.

April 1, 1853   The three spots on breast of the song sparrow seem to mark a difference of sex.[1] At least, the three-spotted is the one I oftenest hear sing of late. The accompanying one is lighter beneath and one-spotted. One of the former by J. P. Brown's meadow-side, selecting the top of a bush, after lurking and feeding under the alders, sang *olit olit olit* | (faster) *chip chip chip che char* | (fast) *che wiss wiss wiss*. The last bar was much varied, and sometimes one *olit* omitted in the first. This, I have no doubt, is my bird of March 18th. Another three-spotted sang *vit chit chit char* | *weeter char* | *tee chu*.

April 2, 1853   The song sparrows, the three-spotted, away by the meadow-sides, are very shy and cunning: instead of flying will frequently trot along the ground under the bushes, or dodge through a wall like a swallow; and I have observed that they generally bring some object, as a rail or branch, between themselves and the face of the walker,—often with outstretched necks will peep at him anxiously for five or ten minutes.

[1][No sexual difference is recognized in the song sparrow's markings.]

May 11, 1853   I nearly stepped upon a song sparrow and a striped snake at the same time. The bird fluttered away almost as if detained. I thought it was a case of charming, without doubt, and should think so still if I had not found her nest with five eggs there, which will account for her being so near the snake that was about to devour her.

October 30, 1853   By the bathing-place, I see a song sparrow. . . . He drops stealthily behind the wall and skulks amid the bushes; now sits behind a post, and peeps round at me, ever restless and quirking his tail, and now and then uttering a faint *chip*.

March 11, 1854   Song sparrows toward the water, with at least two kinds or variations of their strain hard to imitate.

QUICK

Ozit, ozit, ozit, psa te te te te te ter twe ter

is one; the other began *chip chip che we*, etc., etc.

March 16, 1854   A.M.—Another fine morning.

Willows and alders along watercourses all alive these mornings and ringing with the trills and jingles and warbles of birds, even as the waters have lately broken loose and tinkle below,— song sparrows, blackbirds, not to mention robins, etc., etc. The song sparrows are very abundant, peopling each bush, willow, or alder for a quarter of a mile, and pursuing each other as if now selecting their mates. It is their song which especially fills the air, made an incessant and undistinguishable trill and jingle by their numbers.

March 20, 1855   A flurry of snow at 7 A.M. I go to turn my boat up. Four or five song sparrows are flitting along amid the willows by the waterside. Probably they came yesterday with the bluebirds. From distant trees and bushes I hear a faint tinkling *te te te te té* and at last a full strain whose rhythm is *whit whit whit, ter tche, tchear tche,* deliberately sung, or measuredly, while the falling snow is beginning to whiten the ground,—not discouraged by such a reception.

March 21, 1855   The song sparrow is now seen dodging behind the wall, with a quirk of its tail, or flitting along the alders or other bushes by the side of the road, especially in low ground, and its pleasant strain is heard at intervals in spite of the cold and blustering wind. It is the most steady and resolute singer as yet, its strain being heard at intervals throughout the day, more than any as yet *peopling* the hedgerows.

March 22, 1855   I hear a song sparrow on an alder-top sing *ozit ozit oze-e-e* | (quick) *tchip tchip tchip tchip tchay* | *te tchip ter che ter tchay*; also the same shortened and *very much* varied. Heard one sing uninterruptedly, *i.e.* without a pause, almost a minute.

April 22, 1855   See a song sparrow getting its breakfast in the water on the meadow like a wader.

April 6, 1856   Apparently song sparrows may have the dark splash on each side of the throat but be more or less brown on the breast and head. Some are quite light, some quite dark. Here is one of the light-breasted on the top of an apple tree, sings unweariedly at regular intervals something like *tchulp | chilt chilt, chilt chilt,* (faster and faster) *chilt chilt, chilt chilt | tuller tchay ter splay-ee.* The last, or third, bar I am not sure about. It flew too soon for me. I only remember that the last part was sprinkled on the air like drops from a rill, as if its strain were moulded by the spray it sat upon.

June 22, 1856   Ricketson says that they say at New Bedford that the song sparrow says, *Maids, maids, maids,—hang on your tea-kettle-ettle-ettle-ettle-ettle.*

January 21, 1857   Minott tells me that Sam Barrett told him once when he went to mill that a song sparrow took up its quarters in his grist-mill and stayed there all winter. When it did not help itself he used to feed it with meal, for he was glad of its company; so, what with the dashing water and the crumbs of meal, it must have fared well.

January 28, 1857   Am again surprised to see a song sparrow sitting for hours on our wood-pile in the yard, in the midst of snow in the yard. It is unwilling to move. People go to the pump, and the cat and dog walk round the wood-pile without starting it. I examine it at my leisure through a glass. Remarkable that the coldest of all winters these summer birds should remain. Perhaps it is no more comfortable this season further south, where they are accustomed to abide. In the afternoon this sparrow joined a flock of tree sparrows on the bare ground west of the house. It was amusing to see the tree sparrows wash themselves, standing in the puddles and tossing the water over themselves. Minott says they wade in to where it is an inch deep and then "splutter splutter," throwing the water over them. They have had no opportunity to wash for a month, perhaps, there having been no thaw. The song sparrow did not go off with them.

February 2, 1858 Still rains, after a rainy night with a little snow, forming slosh. As I return from the post-office, I hear the hoarse, robin-like chirp of a song sparrow on Cheney's ground, and see him perched on the topmost twig of a heap of brush, look-ing forlorn and drabbled and solitary in the rain.

March 18, 1858 7 A.M.—By river.

Almost every bush has its song sparrow this morning, and their tinkling strains are heard on all sides. You see them just hop-ping under the bush or into some other covert, as you go by, turn-ing with a jerk this way and that, or they flit away just above the ground, which they resemble. It is the prettiest strain I have heard yet.

June 13, 1858 I see a song sparrow's nest here in a little spruce just by the mouth of the ditch.[1] It rests on the thick branches fifteen inches from the ground, firmly made of coarse sedge without, lined with finer, and then a little hair, small within,—a very thick, firm, and portable nest, an inverted cone;—four eggs. They build

[1][At Ledum Swamp, in Concord.]

them in a peculiar manner in these sphagnous swamps, elevated apparently on account of water and of different materials. Some of the eggs have quite a blue ground.

March 3, 1860   The first song sparrows are very inconspicuous and shy on the brown earth. You hear some weeds rustle, or think you see a mouse run amid the stubble, and then the sparrow flits low away.

FOX SPARROW
(FOX-COLORED SPARROW)

March 31, 1852   Methinks I would share every creature's suffering for the sake of its experience and joy. The song sparrow and the transient fox-colored sparrow,—have they brought me no message this year? Do they go to lead heroic lives in Rupert's Land? They are so small, I think their destinies must be large. Have I heard what this tiny passenger has to say, while it flits thus from tree to tree? Is not the coming of the fox-colored sparrow something more earnest and significant than I have dreamed of? Can I forgive myself if I let it go to Rupert's Land before I have appreciated it? God did not make this world in jest; no, nor in indifference. These migrating sparrows all bear messages that concern my life. I do not pluck the fruits in their season. I love the birds and beasts because they are mythologically in earnest. I see that the sparrow cheeps and flits and sings adequately to the great design of the universe; that man does not communicate with it, understand its language, because he is not at one with nature. I reproach myself because I have regarded with indifference the passage of the birds; I have thought them no better than I.

March 14, 1854 A large company of fox-colored sparrows in Heywood's maple swamp close by. I heard their loud, sweet, canary-like whistle thirty or forty rods off, sounding richer than anything yet; some on the bushes singing, *twee twee twa twa ter tweer tweer twa,*—this is the scheme of it only, there being no dental grit to it. They were shy, flitting before me, and I heard a slight susurrus where many were busily scratching amid the leaves of the swamp, without seeing them, and also saw many indistinctly. Wilson never heard but one sing, their common note there being a *cheep.*

March 25, 1858 P.M.—To bank of Great Meadows by Peter's.
Cold northwest wind as yesterday and before. . . .

Going across A. Clark's field behind Garfield's, I see many fox-colored sparrows flitting past in a straggling manner into the birch and pitch pine woods on the left, and hear a sweet warble there from time to time. They are busily scratching like hens amid the dry leaves of that wood (not swampy), from time to time the rearmost moving forward, one or two at a time, while a few are perched here and there on the lower branches of a birch or other tree; and I hear a very clear and sweet whistling strain, commonly half-finished, from one every two or three minutes. It is too irregular to be readily caught, but methinks begins like *ar tche tche tchear, te tche tchear*, etc., etc., but is more clear than these words would indicate. The whole flock is moving along pretty steadily.

TOWHEE
(CHEWINK)
(GROUND-ROBIN)

1850 Many a time I have expected to find a woodchuck, or rabbit, or a gray squirrel, when it was the ground-robin rustling the leaves.

1850 I noticed a singular instance of ventriloquism to-day in a male chewink singing on the top of a young oak. It was difficult to believe that the last part of his strain, the concluding jingle, did not proceed from a different quarter, a woodside many rods off. *Hip-you, he-he-he-he.* It was long before I was satisfied that the last part was not the answer of his mate given in exact time. I endeavored to get between the two; indeed, I seemed to be almost between them already.

May 1, 1852 I hear the first towhee finch. He says *to-wee, to-wee,* and another, much farther off than I supposed when I went in search of him, says *whip your ch-r-r-r-r-r,* with a metallic ring.

May 23, 1853 How different the ramrod jingle of the chewink or any bird's note sounds now at 5 P.M. in the cooler, stiller air, when also the humming of insects is more distinctly heard, and perchance some impurity has begun to sink to earth strained by the air! Or is it, perchance, to be referred to the cooler, more clarified and pensive state of the mind, when dews have begun to descend in it and clarify it? Chaste eve! A certain lateness in the sound, pleasing to hear, which releases me from the obligation to return in any particular season. I have passed the Rubicon of staying out. I have said to myself, that way is not homeward; I will wander further from what I have called my home—to the home which is forever inviting me. In such an hour the freedom of the woods is offered me, and the birds sing my dispensation.

June 9, 1855   A chewink's nest sunk in ground under a bank covered with ferns, dead and green, and huckleberry bushes; composed of dry leaves, then grass stubble, and lined with a very few slender, reddish moss stems; four eggs, rather fresh; merely enough moss stems to indicate its choice.

May 17, 1858   I see a chewink flit low across the road with its peculiar flirting, undulating motion.

September 19, 1858   Hear a chewink's *chewink*. But how ineffectual is the note of a bird now! We hear it as if we heard it not, and forget it immediately. In spring it makes its due impression, and for a long time will not have done echoing, as it were, through our minds. It is even as if the atmosphere were in an unfavorable condition for this kind of music. Every musician knows how much depends on this.

ROSE-BREASTED GROSBEAK

June 13, 1853 What was that rare and beautiful bird in the dark woods under the Cliffs, with black above and white spots and bars, a large triangular blood-red spot on breast, and sides of breast and beneath white? Note a warble like the oriole, but softer and sweeter. It was quite tame. I cannot find this bird described. I think it must be a grosbeak.[1] At first I thought I saw a chewink, as it sat within a rod sideways to me, and I was going to call Sophia to look at it, but then it turned its breast full toward me and I saw the blood-red breast, a *large* triangular painted spot occupying the greater part of the breast. It was in the cool, shaded underwood by the old path just under the Cliff. It is a memorable event to meet with so rare a bird. Birds answer to flowers, both in their abundance and in their rareness. The meeting with a rare and beautiful bird like this is like meeting with some rare and beautiful flower, which you may never find again, perchance, like the great purple fringed orchis, at least. How much it enhances the wildness and the richness of the forest to see in it some beautiful bird which you never detected before!

May 24, 1855 Hear a rose-breasted grosbeak. At first thought it a tanager, but soon I perceived its more *clear* and instru-

---

[1]Probably a rose-breasted grosbeak. [Though the rose-breasted grosbeak was formerly much less common about houses than it is now, being chiefly confined to the woods, it is doubtful if it was quite so rare in Concord as Thoreau thought at the time.]

mental—should say whistle, if one could whistle like a flute; a noble singer, reminding me also of a robin; clear, loud and flute-like; on the oaks, hillside south of Great Fields. Black all above except white on wing, with a triangular red mark on breast but, as I saw, all white beneath this. Female quite different, yellowish olivaceous above, more like a muscicapa. Song not so sweet as clear and strong. Saw it fly off and catch an insect like a flycatcher.

May 21, 1856   Saw two splendid rose-breasted grosbeaks with females in the young wood in Emerson's lot. What strong-colored fellows, black, white, and fiery rose-red breasts! Strong-natured, too, with their stout bills. A clear, sweet singer, like a tanager but hoarse somewhat,[1] and not shy.

July 15, 1858   At the base of the mountain,[2] over the road, heard (and saw), at the same place where I heard him the evening before, a splendid rose-breasted grosbeak singing. I had before mistaken him at first for a tanager, then for a red-eye, but was not satisfied; but now, with my glass, I distinguished him sitting quite still, high above the road at the entrance of the mountain-path in the deep woods, and singing steadily for twenty minutes. It was remarkable for sitting so still and where yesterday. It was much richer and sweeter and, I think, more powerful than the note of the tanager or red-eye. It had not the hoarseness of the tanager, and

[1][The song, of course, is not really hoarse as compared with the tanager's. See below.]

[2][Mt. Lafayette.]

more sweetness and fullness than the red-eye. Wilson does not give their breeding-place. Nuttall quotes Pennant as saying that some breed in New York but most further north. They, too, appear to breed about the White Mountains.

June 2, 1859 Found within three rods of Flint's Pond a rose-breasted grosbeak's nest. It was in a thicket where there was much cat-briar, in a high blueberry bush, some five feet from the ground, in the forks of the bush, and of very loose construction, being made of the dead gray extremities of the cat-briar, with its tendrils (and some of this had dropped on the ground beneath), and this was lined merely with fine brown stems of weeds like pinweeds, without any leaves or anything else,—a slight nest on the whole. Saw the birds. The male uttered a very peculiar sharp clicking or squeaking note of alarm while I was near the nest.

June 14, 1859 The rose-breasted grosbeak is common now in the Flint's Pond woods. It is not at all shy, and our richest singer, perhaps, after the wood thrush. The rhythm is very like that of the tanager, but the strain is perfectly clear and sweet. One sits on the bare dead twig of a chestnut, high over the road, at Gourgas Wood, and over my head, and sings clear and loud at regular intervals,— the strain about ten or fifteen seconds long, rising and swelling to the end, with various modulations. Another, singing in emulation, regularly answers it, alternating with it, from a distance, at least a quarter of a mile off. It sings thus long at a time, and I leave it singing there, regardless of me.

July 9, 1860   See two handsome rose-breasted grosbeaks on the Corner causeway. One utters a peculiar squeaking or snapping note, and, both by form of bill and this note, and color, reminds me of some of those foreign birds with great bills in cages.

INDIGO-BIRD

June 9, 1857   In the sprout-land beyond the red huckleberry, an indigo-bird, which *chips* about me as if it had a nest there. This is a splendid and marked bird, high-colored as is the tanager, looking strange in this latitude. Glowing indigo. It flits from top of one bush to another, chirping as if anxious. Wilson says it sings, not like most other birds in the morning and evening chiefly, but also in the middle of the day. In this I notice it is like the tanager, the other fiery-plumaged bird. They seem to love the heat. It probably had its nest in one of those bushes.

SPARROWS, ETC. (MISCELLANEOUS)

1837–47   It is a marvel how the birds contrive to survive in this world. These tender sparrows that flit from bush to bush this evening, though it is so late, do not seem improvident, [but appear] to have found a roost for the night. They must succeed by weakness and reliance, for they are not bold and enterprising, as their mode of life would seem to require, but very weak and tender creatures. I have seen a little chipping sparrow, come too early in the spring, shivering on an apple twig, drawing in its head and striving to warm it in its muffled feathers; and it had no voice to intercede with nature, but peeped as helpless as an infant, and was ready to yield up its spirit and die without any effort. And yet this was no new spring in the revolution of the seasons.

November 9, 1850   A rusty sparrow or two only remains to people the drear spaces. It goes to roost without neighbors.

June 30, 1851   The cuckoo is faintly heard from a neighboring grove. Now that it is beginning to be dark, as I am crossing a pasture I hear a happy, cricket-like, shrill little lay from a sparrow, either in the grass or else on that distant tree, as if it were the vibrations of a watch-spring; its vespers.

September 28, 1851   Flocks of small birds—apparently sparrows, bobolinks (or some bird of equal size with a pencilled breast which makes a musical clucking), and piping goldfinches—are flitting about like leaves and hopping up on to the bent grass stems in the garden, letting themselves down to the heavy heads, either shaking or picking out a seed or two, then alighting to pick it up. I am amused to see them hop up on to the slender, drooping grass stems; then slide down, or let themselves down, as it were foot over foot, with great fluttering, till they can pick at the head and release a few seeds; then alight to pick them up. They seem to prefer a coarse grass which grows like a weed in the garden between the potato-hills, also the amaranth.

March 20, 1852   As to the winter birds,—those which came here in the winter,—I saw first that rusty sparrow-like bird flying in flocks with the smaller sparrows early in the winter and sliding down the grass stems to their seeds, which clucked like a hen, and F. Brown thought to be the young of the purple finch; then I saw, about Thanksgiving time and later in the winter, the pine grosbeaks, large and carmine, a noble bird; then, in midwinter, the snow bunting, the white snowbird, sweeping low like snowflakes from field to field over the walls and fences. And now, within a day or two, I have noticed the chubby slate-colored snowbird (*Fringilla hyemalis?*), and I drive the flocks before me on the railroad causeway as I walk. It has two white feathers in its tail.

January 20, 1853   I see where snowbirds[1] in troops have visited each withered chenopodium that rises above the snow in the yard—and some are large and bushlike—for its seeds, their well-filled granary now. There are a few tracks reaching from weed to weed, where some have run, but under the larger plants the snow is entirely trodden and blackened, proving that a large flock has been there and flown.

March 31, 1853   I afterward heard a fine concert of little songsters along the edge of the meadow. Approached and watched and listened for more than half an hour. There were many little

---

[1][Thoreau used the term snowbird indefinitely, of any small sparrow-like bird, seen in winter.]

sparrows, difficult to detect, flitting and hopping along and scratching the ground like hens, under the alders, willows, and cornels in a wet leafy place, occasionally alighting on a low twig and preening themselves. They had bright-bay crowns, two rather indistinct white bars on wings, an ashy breast and dark tail. These twittered sweetly, some parts very much like a canary and many together, making it the fullest and sweetest I have heard yet,—like a shopful of canaries. The blackbirds may make more noise. About the size of a song sparrow. I think these are the tree sparrow. Also, mixed with them, and puzzling me to distinguish for a long time, were many of the fox-colored (?) sparrows mentioned above, with a creamy cinnamon-tinged ashy breast, cinnamon shoulderlet, ashy about side head and throat, a fox-colored tail; a size larger than the others; the spot on breast very marked. Were evidently two birds intimately mixed. Did not Peabody confound them when he mentioned the mark on the breast of the tree sparrow?[1] The rich strain of the fox-colored sparrow, as I think it is, added much to the quire. The latter solos, the former in concert. I kept off a hawk by my presence. These were for a long time invisible to me, except when they flitted past.

February 13, 1855   One of these pigweeds in the yard lasts the snowbirds all winter, and after every new storm they revisit it. How inexhaustible their granary!

---

[1] [Thoreau afterwards detected the breast spot of the tree sparrow.]

March 14, 1855 I observe the tracks of sparrows leading to every little sprig of blue-curls amid the other weeds which (its seemingly empty pitchers) rises above the snow. There seems, however, to be a little seed left in them. This, then, is reason enough why these withered stems still stand,—that they may raise these granaries above the snow for the use of the snowbirds.

October 11, 1856 The sprout-land and stubble behind the Cliffs are all alive with restless flocks of sparrows of various species. I distinguish *F. hyemalis*, song sparrow, apparently *F. juncorum* or maybe tree sparrow,[1] and chip-birds (?). They are continually flitting past and surging upward, two or more in pursuit of each other, in the air, where they break like waves, and pass along with a faint cheep. On the least alarm many will rise from a juniper bush on to a shrub oak above it, and, when all is quiet, return into the juniper perhaps for its berries. It is often hard to detect them as they sit on the young trees, now beginning to be bare, for they are very nearly the color of the bark and are very cunning to hide behind the leaves.

October 19, 1856 The fall, now and for some weeks, is the time for flocks of sparrows of various kinds flitting from bush to bush and tree to tree—and both bushes and trees are thinly leaved or bare—and from one seared meadow to another. They are mingled together, and their notes, even, being faint, are, as well as their

[1]Probably not. [Too early in the season.]

colors and motions, much alike. The sparrow youth are on the wing. They are still further concealed by their resemblance in color to the gray twigs and stems, which are now beginning to be bare.

*   *   *

I have often noticed the inquisitiveness of birds, as the other day of a sparrow, whose motions I should not have supposed to have any reference to me, if I had not watched it from first to last. I stood on the edge of a pine and birch wood. It flitted from seven or eight rods distant to a pine within a rod of me, where it hopped about stealthily and chirped awhile, then flew as many rods the other side and hopped about there a spell, then back to the pine again, as near me as it dared, and again to its first position, very restless all the while. Generally I should have supposed that there was more than one bird, or that it was altogether accidental,—that the chipping of this sparrow eight or ten rods [away] had no reference to me,—for I could see nothing peculiar about it. But when I brought my glass to bear on it, I found that it was almost steadily eying me and was all alive with excitement.

March 20, 1859 P.M.—I see under the east side of the house, amid the evergreens, where they were sheltered from the cold northwest wind, quite a parcel of sparrows, chiefly *F. hyemalis*, two or three tree sparrows, and one song sparrow, quietly feeding together. I watch them through a window within six or eight feet. They evidently love to be sheltered from the wind, and at least are not averse to each other's society. The tree sparrows *sing* a little. One perches on a bush to sing, while others are feeding on the ground, but he is very restless on his perch, hopping about and stooping as if dodging those that fly over. He must perch on some bit of stubble or twig to sing. They are evidently picking up the seeds of weeds which lie on the surface of the ground invisible to our eyes. They suffer their wings to hang rather loose. The *F. hyemalis* is the largest of the three. They have remarkably distinct light-colored bills, and when they stretch, show very distinct clear-white lateral tail-feathers. This stretching seems to be contagious among them, like yawning with us. They have considerable brown on the quill-feathers. The tree sparrows are much brighter brown and white than the song sparrow. The latter alone scratches once or twice, and is more inclined to hop or creep close to the ground, under the fallen weeds. Perhaps it deserves most to be called the *ground*-bird.

April 8, 1859   These windy days the sparrows resort to the pines and peach trees on the east side of our house for shelter, and there they sing all together,—tree sparrows, fox-colored sparrows, and song sparrows. The *F. hyemalis* with them do not sing so much of late. The first two are most commonly heard together, the fine canary-like twitter of the tree sparrow appearing to ripen or swell from time to time into the clear, rich whistle of the fox-colored sparrow, so that most refer both notes to one bird.

TANAGERS

SWALLOWS

SCARLET TANAGER

July 8, 1852   I hear many scarlet tanagers, the first I have seen this season, which some might mistake for a red-eye. A hoarse, rough strain, comparatively, but more easily caught owing to its simplicity and sameness; something like *heer chip-er-way-heer chory chay.*

May 20, 1853   Saw a tanager in Sleepy Hollow. It most takes the eye of any bird. You here have the red-wing reversed,—the deepest scarlet of the red-wing spread over the whole body, not on the wing-coverts merely, while the wings are black. It flies through the green foliage as if it would ignite the leaves.

May 23, 1853   At Loring's Wood heard and saw a tanager. That contrast of a *red* bird with the green pines and the blue sky! Even when I have heard his note and look for him and find the bloody fellow, sitting on a dead twig of a pine, I am always startled. (They seem to love the darkest and thickest pines.) That incredible red, with the green and blue, as if these were the trinity we wanted. Yet with his hoarse note he pays for his color. I am transported; these are not the woods I ordinarily walk in. He sunk Concord in his thought. How he enhances the wildness and wealth of the woods! This and the emperor moth make the tropical phenomena of our zone. There is warmth in the pewee's strain, but this bird's colors and his note tell of Brazil.

May 29, 1853 At A. Hosmer's hill on the Union Turnpike I see the tanager hoarsely warbling in the shade; the surprising red bird, a small morsel of Brazil, advanced picket of that Brazilian army,—parrot-like. But no more shall we see; it is only an affair of outposts. It appears as if he loved to contrast himself with the green of the forest.

May 23, 1854 We soon get through with Nature. She excites an expectation which she cannot satisfy. The merest child which has rambled into a copsewood dreams of a wilderness so wild and strange and inexhaustible as Nature can never show him. The redbird which I saw on my companion's string on election days[1] I

[1]["Old election day" in Massachusetts came on the last Wednesday in May. It was the day when the Legislature met, to organize, to count the vote for governor and lieutenant-governor, and to hear an "election sermon" in one of the Boston churches. The actual voting for governor, lieutenant-governor, and State senators came on the first Monday in April, and the representatives to the General Court were elected at different times in the different towns. The last of these May "elections" was held in 1831, but "old election day" was observed as a sort of holiday for years after, and it was the custom to conduct shooting-matches on that day, when birds of all kinds were shot indiscriminately. See Chapter 18.]

thought but the outmost sentinel of the wild, immortal camp,—of the wild and dazzling infantry of the wilderness,—that the deeper woods abounded with redder birds still; but, now that I have threaded all our woods and waded the swamps, I have never yet met with his compeer, still less his wilder kindred. The red-bird which is the last of Nature is but the first of God. The White Mountains, likewise, were smooth molehills to my expectation. We *condescend* to climb the crags of earth. It is our weary legs alone that praise them. That forest on whose skirts the red-bird flits is not of earth. I expected a fauna more infinite and various, birds of more dazzling colors and more celestial song.

May 28, 1855 I see a tanager, the most brilliant and tropical-looking bird we have, bright-scarlet with black wings, the scarlet appearing on the rump again between wing-tips. He brings heat, or heat him. A remarkable contrast with the green pines. At this distance he has the aspect and manners of a parrot, with a fullness about the head and throat and beak, indolently inspecting the limbs and twigs—leaning over to it—and sitting still a long time. The female, too, is a neat and handsome bird, with the same indolent ways, but very differently colored from the male; all yellow below with merely dusky wings, and a sort of clay (?)-color on back.

June 24, 1857 Looked over Farmer's eggs and list of names. He has several which I have not. Is not his "chicklisee," after all, the Maryland yellow-throat? The eggs were numbered with a pen,— 1, 2, 3, etc.,—and corresponding numbers written against the names on the cover of the pasteboard box in which were the eggs. Among the rest I read, "*Fire never redder.*" That must be the tanager. He laughed and said that this was the way he came to call it by that name: Many years ago, one election-day, when he and other boys, or young men, were out gunning to see how many birds they could kill, Jonathan Hildreth, who lived near by, saw one of these birds on the top of a tree before him in the woods, but he did not see a deep ditch that crossed his course between him and it. As he raised his gun, he exclaimed, "Fire never redder!" and, taking a step or two forward, with his eye fixed on the bird, fell headlong into the ditch, and so the name became a byword among his fellows.

June 23, 1858 The tanager's nest of the 19th is four and a half to five inches wide and an inch or more deep, considerably open to look through; the outside, of many very slender twigs, apparently of hemlock, some umbelled pyrola with seed-vessels, everlasting, etc.; within, quite round and regular, of very slender or fine stems, apparently pinweed or the like, and pine-needles; hardly any grass stubble about it. The egg is a regular oval, nine tenths of an inch long by twenty-seven fortieths, pale-blue, sprinkled with purplish-brown spots, thickest on the larger end. To-day there are three rather fresh eggs in this nest. Neither going nor returning do we see anything of the tanager, and conclude it to be deserted, but perhaps she stays away from it long.

May 24, 1860 As I sit just above the northwest end of the Cliff, I see a tanager perched on one of the topmost twigs of a hickory, holding by the tender leafets, now five inches long, and evidently come to spy after me, peeping behind a leafet. He is between me and the sun, and his plumage is incredibly brilliant, all aglow. It is our highest-colored bird,—a deep scarlet (with a yellower reflection when the sun strikes him), in the midst of which his pure-black wings look high-colored also. You can hardly believe that a living creature can wear such colors. A hickory, too, is the fittest perch for him.

PURPLE MARTIN

June 15, 1852 The chuckling warble of martins heard over the meadow, from a village box.

CLIFF SWALLOW
(REPUBLICAN SWALLOW)

1850 Returning, I saw in Sudbury twenty-five nests of the new (cliff?) swallow[1] under the eaves of a barn. They

---

[1][This bird was then a comparatively recent addition to the avifauna of eastern Massachusetts, whither it had spread from its early home in the West. The name "republican" was given to it by Audubon on account of its social nesting habits. The notion that its irruption into the East was coincident with the rise of the Republican Party, and that this gave it its popular name, is, of course, a false one.]

seemed particularly social and loquacious neighbors, though their voices are rather squeaking. Their nests, built side by side, looked somewhat like large hornets' nests, enough so to prove a sort of connection. Their activity, sociability, and chattiness make them fit pensioners and neighbors of man—summer companions—for the barn-yard.

November 9, 1857   Mr. Farmer tells me that one Sunday he went to his barn, having nothing to do, and thought he would watch the swallows, republican swallows. The old bird was feeding her young, and he sat within fifteen feet, overlooking them. There were five young, and he was curious to know how each received its share; and as often as the bird came with a fly, the one at the door (or opening) took it, and then they all hitched round one notch, so that a new one was presented at the door, who received the next fly; and this was the invariable order, the same one never receiving two flies in succession. At last the old bird brought a very small fly, and the young one that swallowed it did not desert his ground but waited to receive the next, but when the bird came with another, of the usual size, she commenced a loud and long scolding at the little one, till it resigned its place, and the next in succession received the fly.

BARN SWALLOW
May 19, 1852   A barn swallow accompanied me across the Depot Field, methinks attracted by the insects which I

started, though I saw them not, wheeling and tacking incessantly on all sides and repeatedly dashing within a rod of me. It is an agreeable sight to watch one. Nothing lives in the air but is in rapid motion.

April 30, 1855 I observed yesterday that the barn swallows confined themselves to one place, about fifteen rods in diameter, in Willow Bay, about the sharp rock. They kept circling about and flying up the stream (the wind easterly), about six inches above the water,—it was cloudy and almost raining,—yet I could not perceive any insects there. Those myriads of little fuzzy gnats mentioned on the 21st and 28th must afford an abundance of food to insectivorous birds. Many new birds should have arrived about the 21st. There were plenty of myrtle-birds and yellow redpolls[1] where the gnats were. The swallows were confined to this space when I passed up, and were still there when I returned, an hour and a half later. I saw them nowhere else. They uttered only a slight twitter from time to time and when they turned out for each other on meeting. Getting their meal seemed to be made a social affair. Pray, how long will they continue to circle thus without resting?

TREE SWALLOW
(WHITE-BELLIED SWALLOW)

June 12, 1852 Small white-bellied (?) swallows in a row (a dozen) on the telegraph-wire over the water by the bridge.

[1][Myrtle warblers and yellow palm warblers.]

This perch is little enough departure from unobstructed air to suit them. Pluming themselves. If you could furnish a perch aerial enough, even birds of paradise would alight. Swallows have forked tails, and wings and tails are about the same length. They do not alight on trees, methinks, unless on dead and bare boughs, but stretch a wire over water and they perch on it. This is among the phenomena that cluster about the telegraph.

June 14, 1855 I told C.[1] to look into an old mortise-hole in Wood's Bridge for a white-bellied swallow's nest, as we were paddling under; but he laughed, incredulous. I insisted, and when he climbed up he scared out the bird. Five eggs. "You see the feathers about, do you not?" "Yes," said he.

BANK SWALLOW

May 23, 1854 Saw in Dakin's land, near the road, at the bend of the river, fifty-nine bank swallows' holes in a small upright bank within a space of twenty by one and a half feet (in the middle), part above and part below the sand-line. This would give over a hundred birds to this bank. They continually circling about over the meadow and river in front, often in pairs, one pursuing the other, and filling the air with their twittering.

May 7, 1856 In the first hollow in the bank this side of Clamshell, where sand has been dug for the meadow, are a hundred or

[1][W. E. Channing.]

more bank swallows at 2 P.M. (I suspect I have seen them for some time) engaged in prospecting and digging their holes and circling about. It is a snug place for them,—though the upright portion of the bank is only four or five feet high,—a semi-circular recess facing the southeast. Some are within scratching out the sand,—I see it cast out of the holes behind them,—others hanging on to the entrance of the holes, others on the flat sandy space beneath in front, and others circling about, a dozen rods off over the meadow. Theirs is a low, dry, grating twitter, or rather rattle, less metallic or musical than the *vite vite* and twittering notes of barn and white-bellied swallows. They are white-bellied, dark winged and tailed, with a crescent of white [*sic*] nearly around the lower part of the neck, and mouse-colored heads and backs. The upper and greater part of this bank is a coarse sliding gravel, and they build only in the perpendicular and sandy part (I sit and watch them within three or four rods) and close to the upper part of it. While I am looking, they all suddenly with one consent take to wing, and circle over the hillside and meadow, as if they chose to work at making their holes a little while at a time only. I find the holes on an average about a foot deep only as yet, some but a few inches.

May 12, 1856   I see, in the road beyond Luther Hosmer's, in different places, two bank swallows which were undoubtedly killed by the four days' northeast rain we have just had.

May 13, 1856   In the swallows' holes behind Dennis's, I find two more dead bank swallows, and one on the sand beneath, and the feathers of two more which some creature has eaten. This makes at least seven dead bank swallows in consequence of the long, cold northeast rain. A male harrier, skimming low, had nearly reached this sandpit before he saw me and wheeled. Could it have been he that devoured the swallows?

The swallows were 10¾+ alar extent, 4¾ inches long; a wing 4¾+ by 1¾. Above they were a light brown on their backs, wings blackish, beneath white, with a dark-brown band over the breast and again white throat and side of neck; bill small and black; reddish-brown legs, with long, sharp, slender claws. It chanced that each one of two I tried weighed between five and six sixteenths of an ounce, or between five and six drams avoirdupois. This seems to be the average weight, or say six drams because they have pined a little. A man who weighs one hundred and fifty pounds weighs sixty-four hundred times as much as one. The wing of one contains about seven square inches, the body about five, or whole bird nineteen. If a man were to be provided with wings, etc., in proportion to his weight, they would measure about 844 square feet, and one wing would cover 311 feet, or be about 33 feet long by 14 wide. This is to say nothing of his muscles.

December 4, 1856 I notice that the swallow-holes in the bank behind Dennis's, which is partly washed away, are flat-elliptical, three times or more as wide horizontally as they are deep vertically, or about three inches by one.

November 20, 1857   Some bank swallows' nests are exposed by the caving of the bank at Clamshell. The very smallest hole is about two and a half inches wide horizontally, by barely one high. All are much wider than high (vertically). One nest, with an egg in it still, is completely exposed. The cavity at the end is shaped like a thick hoe-cake or lens, about six inches wide and two plus thick, vertically. The nest is a regular but shallow one made simply of stubble, about five inches in diameter, and three quarters of an inch deep.

January 24, 1858   The inside of the swallow-holes there appears quite firm yet and regular, with marks where it was pecked or scratched by the bird, and the top is mottled or blotched, almost as if made firm in spots by the saliva of the bird. There is a low oven-like expansion at the end, and a good deal of stubble for the nest. I find in one an empty black cherry stone and the remains of a cricket or two. Probably a mouse left them there.

June 23, 1858   Get an egg out of a deserted bank swallow's nest, in a bank only about four feet high dug in the spring for a bank wall near Everett's. The nest is flattish and lined abundantly with the small, somewhat downy, naturally curved feathers of poultry. Egg pure white, long, oval, twenty-seven fortieths by eighteen fortieths of an inch.

SWALLOWS
(GENERAL AND MISCELLANEOUS)

July 16, 1851   The twittering of swallows is in the air, reminding me of water.

July 23, 1851   The swallow's twitter is the sound of the lapsing waves of the air, or when they break and burst, as his wings represent the ripple. He has more air in his bones than other birds; his feet are defective. The fish of the air. His note is the voice of the air. As fishes may hear the sound of waves lapsing on the surface and see the outlines of the ripples, so we hear the note and see the flight of swallows.

August 17, 1851   The birds seem to know that it will not rain just yet. The swallows skim low over the pastures, twittering as they fly near me with forked tail, dashing near me as if I scared up insects for them. I see where a squirrel has been eating hazelnuts on a stump.

August 4, 1855   Just after bathing at the rock near the Island this afternoon, after sunset, I saw a flock of thousands of barn swallows and some white-bellied, and perhaps others, for it was too dark to distinguish them. They came flying over the river in loose array, wheeled and flew round in a great circle over the bay there, about eighty feet high, with a loud twittering as if seeking a resting-place, then flew up the stream. I was very much surprised at their numbers. Directly after, hearing a buzzing sound, we found them all alighted on the dense golden willow hedge at Shattuck's shore, parallel with the shore, quite densely leaved and eighteen feet high. They were generally perched five or six feet from the top, amid the thick leaves, filling it for eight or ten rods. They were very restless, fluttering from one perch to another and about one another, and kept up a loud and remarkable buzzing or squeaking, breathing or hum, with only occasionally a regular twitter, now and then flitting alongside from one end of the row to the other. It was so dark we had to draw close to see them. At intervals they were perfectly still for a moment, as if at a signal. At length, after twenty or thirty minutes of bustle and hum, they all settled quietly to rest on their perches, I supposed for the night. We had rowed up within a rod of one end of the row, looking up so as to bring the birds between us and the sky, but they paid not the slightest attention to us. What was remarkable was: first, their numbers; second, their perching on densely leaved willows; third, their buzzing or humming, like a hive of bees, even squeaking notes; and fourth, their disregarding our nearness. I supposed that they were preparing to migrate, being the early broods.

August 5, 1855   4 A.M.—On river to see swallows.

They are all gone; yet Fay saw them there last night after we passed. Probably they started very early. I asked Minott if he ever saw swallows migrating, not telling him what I had seen, and he said that he used to get up and go out to mow very early in the morning on his meadow, as early as he could see to strike, and once, at that hour, hearing a noise, he looked up and could just distinguish high overhead fifty thousand swallows. He thought it was in the latter part of August.

April 30, 1856   About 3.30 P.M., when it was quite cloudy as well as raw, and I was measuring along the river just south of the bridge, I was surprised by the great number of swallows—white-bellied and barn swallows and perhaps republican—flying round and round, or skimming very low over the meadow, just laid bare, only a foot above the ground. Either from the shape of the hollow or their circling, they seemed to form a circular flock three or four rods in diameter and one swallow deep. There were two or three of these centres and some birds equally low over the river. It looked like rain, but did not rain that day or the next. Probably their insect food was flying at that height over the meadow at that time. There were a thousand or more of swallows, and I think that they had recently arrived together on their migration. Only this could account for there being so many together. We were measuring through one little circular meadow, and many of them were not driven off by our nearness. The noise of their wings and their twittering was quite loud.

May 11, 1856   There are many swallows circling low over the river behind Monroe's,—bank swallows, barn, republican, chimney, and white-bellied. These are all circling together a foot or two over the water, passing within ten or twelve feet of me in my boat. It is remarkable how social the different species of swallow are one with another. They recognize their affinity more than usual.

July 29, 1856   Pratt says he one day walked out with Wesson, with their rifles, as far as Hunt's Bridge. Looking down-stream, he saw a swallow sitting on a bush very far off, at which he took aim and fired with ball. He was surprised to see that he had touched the swallow, for it flew directly across the river toward Simon Brown's barn, always descending toward the earth or water, not being able to maintain itself; but what surprised him most was to see a second swallow come flying behind and repeatedly strike the other with all his force beneath, so as to toss him up as often as he approached the ground and enable him to continue his flight, and thus he continued to do till they were out of sight. Pratt said he resolved that he would never fire at a swallow again.

August 26, 1856   The flooded meadow, where the grasshoppers cling to the grass so thickly, is alive with swallows skimming just over the surface amid the grass-tops and *apparently* snapping up insects there. Are they catching the grasshoppers as they cling to bare poles? (I see the swallows equally thick there at 5 P.M. when I return also.)

May 20, 1858   P.M.—Up Assabet.

A cloudy afternoon, with a cool east wind, producing a mist. Hundreds of swallows are now skimming close over the river, at its broadest part, where it is shallow and runs the swiftest, just below the Island, for a distance of twenty rods. There are bank, barn, cliff, and chimney swallows, all mingled together and continually scaling back and forth,—a very lively sight. They keep descending or stooping to within a few inches of the water on a curving wing, without quite touching it, and I suppose are attracted by some small insects which hover close over it. They also stoop low about me as I stand on the flat island there, but I do not perceive the insects. They rarely rise more than five feet above the surface, and a general twittering adds to the impression of sociability. The principal note is the low grating sound of the bank swallow, and I hear the *vit vit* of the barn swallow. The cliff swallow, then, is here. Are the insects in any measure confined to that part of the river? Or are they congregated for the sake of society? I have also in other years noticed them over another swift place, at Hubbard's Bath, and also, when they first come, in smaller numbers, over the still and smooth water under the lee of the Island wood. They are thick as the gnats which perhaps they catch. Swallows are more confident and fly nearer to man than most birds. It may be because they are more protected by the sentiment and superstitions of men.

WAXWINGS
SHRIKES
VIREOS

CEDAR WAXWING
(CHERRY-BIRD)

June 21, 1852 Cherry-birds. I have not seen, though I think I have heard them before,—their *fine* seringo note, like a vibrating spring in the air. They are a handsome bird, with their crest and chestnut breasts. There is no keeping the run of their goings and comings, but they will be ready for the cherries when they shall be ripe.

June 16, 1854 The note of the cherry-bird is fine and ringing, but peculiar and very noticeable. With its crest it is a resolute and combative-looking bird.

June 14, 1855 A cherry-bird's nest and two eggs in an apple tree, fourteen feet from ground. One egg, round black spots and a few oblong, about equally but thinly dispersed over the whole, and a dim, internal, purplish tinge about the large end. It is difficult to see anything of the bird, for she steals away early, and you may neither see nor hear anything of her while examining the nest, and so think it deserted. Approach very warily and look out for them a dozen or more rods off.

March 1, 1856   Goodwin says that somewhere where he lived they called cherry-birds "port-royals."

March 20, 1858   On that same tree by Conant's orchard, I see a flock of cherry-birds with that alert, chieftain-like look, and hear their *seringo* note, as if made by their swift flight through the air. They have been seen a week or two.

NORTHERN SHRIKE
February 25, 1839

THE SHRIKE
Hark! hark! from out the thickest fog
Warbles with might and main
The fearless shrike, as all agog
To find in fog his gain.

His steady sails he never furls
At any time o' year,
And, perchèd now on Winter's curls,
He whistles in his ear.

December 24, 1850 Saw a shrike pecking to pieces a small bird, apparently a snowbird. At length he took him up in his bill, almost half as big as himself, and flew slowly off with his prey dangling from his beak. I find that I had not associated such actions with my idea of birds. It was not birdlike.

February 3, 1856 Returning, saw near the Island a shrike glide by, cold and blustering as it was, with a remarkably even and steady sail or gliding motion like a hawk, eight or ten feet above the ground, and alight in a tree, from which at the same instant a small bird, perhaps a creeper or nuthatch, flitted timidly away. The shrike was apparently in pursuit.

November 29, 1858 I see a living shrike caught to-day in the barn of the Middlesex House.

November 30, 1858 The shrike was very violent for a long time, beating itself against the bars of its cage at Stacy's. To-day it is quiet and has eaten raw meat. Its plain dark ash-colored crown and back are separated by a very distinct line from the black wings. It has a powerful hawk-like beak, but slender legs and claws. Close to, it looks more like a muscicapa[1] than anything.

March 7, 1859 6:30 A.M.—To Hill.

I come out to hear a spring bird, the ground generally covered with snow yet and the channel of the river only partly open. On

[1][That is, a flycatcher.]

the Hill I hear first the tapping of a small woodpecker. I then see a
bird alight on the dead top of the highest white oak on the hilltop,
on the topmost point. It is a shrike. While I am watching him eight
or ten rods off, I hear robins down below, west of the hill. Then,
to my surprise, the shrike begins to sing. It is at first a wholly ineffectual and inarticulate sound without any solid tone to it, a mere
hoarse breathing, as if he were clearing his throat, unlike any bird
that I know,—a shrill hissing. Then he uttered a kind of mew, a
very decided mewing, clear and wiry, between that of a catbird and
the note of the nuthatch, as if to lure a nuthatch within his reach;
then rose into the sharpest, shrillest vibratory or tremulous whistling or chirruping on the very highest key. This high gurgling jingle was like some of the notes of a robin singing in summer. But
they were very short spurts in all these directions, though there was
all this variety. Unless you saw the shrike it would be hard to tell
what bird it was. This variety of notes covered considerable time,
but were sparingly uttered with intervals. It was a decided chink-
ing sound—the clearest strain—suggesting much ice in the stream.
I heard this bird sing once before, but that was also in early spring,
or about this time. It is said that they imitate the notes of the birds
in order to attract them within their reach. Why, then, have I never
heard them sing in the winter? (I have seen seven or eight of them
the past winter quite near.) The birds which it imitated—if it imitated any this morning—were the catbird and the robin, neither of

which probably would it catch,—and the first is not here to be caught. Hearing a peep, I looked up and saw three or four birds passing rather [*sic*], which suddenly descended and settled on this oak-top. They were robins, but the shrike instantly hid himself behind a bough and in half a minute flew off to a walnut and alighted, as usual, on its very topmost twig, apparently afraid of its visitors. The robins kept their ground, one alighting on the very point which the shrike vacated. Is not this, then, probably the spring note or pairing note or notes of the shrike?

December 18, 1859 I see three shrikes in different places to-day,—two on the top of apple trees, sitting still in the storm, on the lookout. They fly low to another tree when disturbed, much like a bluebird, and jerk their tails once or twice when they alight.

December 30, 1859 Going by Dodd's, I see a shrike perched on the tip-top of the topmost upright twig of an English cherry tree before his house, standing square on the topmost bud, balancing himself by a slight motion of his tail from time to time. I have noticed this habit of the bird before. You would suppose it inconvenient for so large a bird to maintain its footing there. Scared by my passing [?] in the road, it flew off, and I thought I would see if it alighted on a similar place. It flew toward a young elm, whose higher twigs were much more slender, though not quite so upright as those of the cherry, and I thought he might be excused if he alighted on the side of one; but no, to my surprise, he alighted without any trouble upon the very top of one of the highest of all, and looked around as before.

YELLOW-THROATED VIREO

May 19, 1856 Hear and see a yellow-throated vireo, which methinks I have heard before. Going and coming, he is in the top of the same swamp white oak and singing indolently, *ullia—eelya,* and sometimes varied to *eelyee.*

VIREOS
(UNSPECIFIED AND UNIDENTIFIED)

May 7, 1852 The vireo comes with warm weather, midwife to the leaves of the elms.

January 13, 1856 Took to pieces a pensile nest which I found the 11th on the south shore of Walden on an oak sapling (red or black), about fifteen feet from the ground. Though small, it measures three inches by three in the extreme, and was hung between two horizontal twigs or in a fork forming about a right angle, the third side being regularly rounded without any very stiff material. The twigs extended two or three inches beyond the nest. The bulk of it is composed of fine shreds or fibres, pretty long (say three to six inches), of apparently inner oak (?) bark, judging from some scraps of the epidermis adhering. It looks at first sight like sedge or grass. The bottom, which I accidentally broke off and disturbed the arrangement of, was composed of this and white and pitch pine needles and little twigs about the same size and form, rough with little leaf-stalks or feet (probably hemlock (?)[1]), and also strips and curls of paper birch epidermis, and some hornet or other wasp nest used like the last. I mention the most abundant material first. Probably the needles and twigs were used on account of their curved form[2] and elasticity, to give shape to the bottom. The sides, which were not so thick, were composed of bark shreds, paper birch, and hornet-nest (the two latter chiefly outside, probably to bind and conceal and keep out the wind), agglutinated together. But most pains was taken with the thin edge and for three quarters of an inch down, where, beside the bark-fibres, birch paper, and hornets' nest, some silky reddish-brown and also white fibre was used to bind all with, almost spun into threads and passed over the twigs and agglutinated to them, or over the bark edge. The shreds of birch paper were smaller there, and the hornets' nest looked as if it had been reduced to a pulp by the bird and spread very thinly here and there over all, mixed with the brown silk. This last looked like cow's hair, but as I found a piece of a small brown cocoon, though a little paler, I suspect it was from that.[3] The white may have been from a cocoon, or else vegetable silk. Probably a vireo's nest, maybe red-eye's.

[1]Yes, they are.
[2]Perhaps bent by the bird.
[3]Some of the same on my red-eye's nest.

In our workshops we pride ourselves on discovering a use for what had previously been regarded as waste, but how partial and accidental our economy compared with Nature's. In Nature nothing is wasted. Every decayed leaf and twig and fibre is only the better fitted to serve in some other department, and all at last are gathered in her compost-heap. What a wonderful genius it is that leads the vireo to select the tough fibres of the inner bark, instead of the more brittle grasses, for its basket, the elastic pine-needles and the twigs, curved as they dried to give it form, and, as I suppose, the silk of cocoons, etc., etc., to bind it together with! I suspect that extensive use is made of these abandoned cocoons by the birds, and they, if anybody, know where to find them. There were at least seven materials used in constructing this nest, and the bird visited as many distinct localities many times, always with the purpose or design to find some particular one of these materials, as much as if it had said to itself, "Now I will go and get some old hornets' nest from one of those that I saw last fall down in the maple swamp—perhaps thrust my bill into them—or some silk from those cocoons I saw this morning."

WARBLERS

BLACK AND WHITE WARBLER
(BLACK AND WHITE CREEPER)

May 12, 1855 Watched a black and white creeper from Bittern Cliff, a very neat and active bird, exploring the limbs on all sides and looking three or four ways almost at once for insects. Now and then it raises its head a *little*, opens its bill, and, without closing it, utters its faint *seeser seeser seeser*.

May 30, 1857 In the midst of the shower, though it was not raining very hard, a black and white creeper came and inspected the limbs of a tree before my rock, in his usual zigzag, prying way, head downward often, and when it thundered loudest, heeded it not. Birds appear to be but little incommoded by the rain. Yet they do not often sing in it.

May 16, 1860 Near Peter's I see a small creeper hopping along the branches of the oaks and pines, ever turning this way and that as it hops, making various angles with the bough; then flies across to another bough, or to the base of another tree, and traces that up, zigzag and prying into the crevices. Think how thoroughly the trees are thus explored by various birds! You can hardly sit near one for five minutes now, but either a woodpecker or

creeper comes and examines its bark rapidly, or a warbler—a summer yellowbird, for example—makes a pretty thorough exploration about all its expanding leafets, even to the topmost twig. The whole North American forest is being thus explored for insect food now by several hundred (?) species of birds. Each is visited by many kinds, and thus the equilibrium of the insect and vegetable kingdom is preserved. Perhaps I may say that each opening bud is thus visited before it has fully expanded.

YELLOW WARBLER
(SUMMER YELLOWBIRD)

May 7, 1852   The first summer yellowbirds on the willow causeway. The birds I have lately mentioned come not singly, as the earliest, but all at once, *i.e.* many yellowbirds all over town. Now I remember the yellowbird comes when the willows begin to leave out. So yellow. They bring summer with them and the sun, *tche-tche-tche-tcha tcha-tchar.* Also they haunt the oaks, white and swamp white, where are not leaves.

May 10, 1853   At this season the traveller passes through a golden gate on causeways where these willows are planted, as if he were approaching the entrance to Fairyland; and there will surely be found the yellowbird, and already from a distance is heard his note, a *tche tche tche tcha tchar tcha*,—ah, willow, willow. Could not he truly arrange for us the difficult family of the willows better than Borrer, or Barratt of Middletown? And as he passes between the portals, a sweet fragrance is wafted to him; he not only breathes but scents and tastes the air, and he hears the low humming or susurrus of a myriad insects which are feeding on its sweets. It is, apparently, these that attract the yellowbird.

May 12, 1853   The yellowbird has another note, *tchut tchut tchar te tchit e war.*

June 24, 1853   A yellowbird's nest in a fork of a willow on Hubbard's Causeway, resting chiefly on the leading branch; of fine grass, lined with hair, bottom outside puffing out with a fine, light, flax-like fibre, perhaps the bark of some weed, by which also it is fastened to the twigs. It is surprising that so many birds find hair enough to line their nests with. If I wish for a horsehair for my compass sights I must go to the stable, but the hair-bird,[1] with her sharp eyes, goes to the road.

January 18, 1856   Analyzed a nest which I found January 7th in an upright fork of a red maple sapling on the edge of Hubbard's

---

[1][The chipping sparrow.]

Swamp Wood, north side, near river, about eight feet from the ground, the deep grooves made by the twigs on each side. It *may* be a yellowbird's.

Extreme breadth outside, three inches; inside, one and a half. Extreme height outside, three inches; inside, one and five eighths; sides, three quarters of an inch thick.

It is composed of seven principal materials. (I name the most abundant first; I mean most abundant when compressed.)

1. Small compact lengths of silvery pappus about seven eighths of an inch long, perhaps of erechthites, one half inch deep and nearly pure, a very warm bed, chiefly concealed, just beneath the lining inside.

2. Slender catkins, often with the buds and twig ends (of perhaps hazel), throughout the whole bottom and sides, making it thick but open and light, mixed with

(3) milkweed silk, *i.e.* fibres like flax, but white, being bleached, also in sides and rim, some of it almost threadlike, white with some of the dark epidermis. From the pods?[1]

4. Thin and narrow strips of grape-vine bark, chiefly in the rim and sides for three quarters of an inch down, and here and there throughout.

---

[1]No, I am about certain, from comparison, that it is the fibres of the bark of the stem. *Vide* 19th *inst.*

5. Wads of apparently brown fern wool, mixed with the last three.

6. Some finer pale-brown and thinner shreds of bark within the walls and bottom, apparently not grape. If this were added to the grape, these five materials would be not far from equally abundant.

7. Some very fine pale-brown wiry fibres for a lining, just above the pappus and somewhat mixed with it, perhaps for coolness, being springy.

Directly beneath the pappus were considerable other shreds of grape and the other bark, short and broken. In the rim and sides some cotton ravellings and some short shreds of fish-line or crow-fence. A red maple leaf within the bottom; a kernel of corn just under the lining of fibres (perhaps dropped by a crow or blackbird or jay or squirrel while the nest was building). A few short lengths of stubble or weed stems in the bottom and sides. A very little brown wool, like, apparently, that in the nest last described, which may be brown fern wool. The milkweed and fern wool conspicuous without the rim and about the twigs. I was most struck by that mass of pure pappus under the inside lining.

January 19, 1856 Gathered some dry water milkweed stems to compare with the materials of the bird's nest of the 18th. The bird used, I am almost certain, the fibres of the bark of the stem,— not the pods,—just beneath the epidermis; only the bird's is older and more fuzzy and finer, like worn twine or string. The fibres and bark have otherwise the same appearance under the microscope. I stripped off some bark about one sixteenth of an inch wide and six inches long and, separating ten or twelve fibres from the epidermis, rolled it in my fingers, making a thread about the ordinary size. This I could not break by direct pulling, and no man could. I doubt if a thread of flax or hemp of the same size could be made so strong. What an admirable material for the Indian's fish-line! I can easily get much longer fibres. I hold a piece of the dead weed in my hands, strip off a narrow shred of the bark before my neighbor's eyes and separate ten or twelve fibres as fine as a hair, roll them in my fingers, and offer him the thread to try its strength. He is surprised and mortified to find that he cannot break it. Probably both the Indian and the bird discovered for themselves this same (so to call it) wild hemp. The corresponding fibres of the mikania seem not so divisible, become not so fine and fuzzy; though somewhat similar, are not nearly so strong. I have a hang-bird's nest from the riverside, made almost entirely of this, in narrow shreds or strips with the epidermis on, wound round and round the twigs and woven into a basket. That is, this bird has used perhaps the strongest fibre which the fields afforded and which most civilized men have not detected.

* * *

Knocked down the bottom of that summer yellowbird's nest made on the oak at the Island last summer. It is chiefly of fern wool and also, *apparently*, some sheep's wool (?), with a fine green moss (apparently that which grows on button-bushes) inmixed, and some milkweed fibre, and all very firmly agglutinated together. Some shreds of grape-vine bark about it. Do not know what portion of the whole nest it is.

MYRTLE WARBLER
(MYRTLE-BIRD)

May 6, 1855   Myrtle-birds very numerous just beyond Second Division. They sing like an instrument, *teee teee te, ttt, ttt,* on very various keys, *i.e.* high or low, sometimes beginning like *phe-be.*[1] As I sat by roadside one drew near, perched within ten feet, and dived once or twice with a curve to catch the little black flies about my head, coming once within three feet, not minding me much. I could not tell at first what attracted it toward me. It saw them from twenty-five feet off. There was a little swarm of small flies, regularly fly-like with large shoulders, about my head. Many white-throated sparrows there.

October 19, 1856   See quite a flock of myrtle-birds,—which I might carelessly have mistaken for slate-colored snowbirds,—flitting about on the rocky hillside under Conantum Cliff. They show

---

[1][The song that Thoreau heard was, of course, that of the white-throated sparrows he saw at the same place. He was long in learning the real authorship of this song, which he at first credited to the chickadee and then for several years to the "myrtle-bird."]

about three white or light-colored spots when they fly, *commonly* no bright yellow, though some are pretty bright. They perch on the side of the dead mulleins, on rocks, on the ground, and directly dart off, apparently in pursuit of some insect. I hear no note from them. They are thus near or on the ground, then, not as in spring.

October 21, 1857 I see many myrtle-birds now about the house this forenoon, on the advent of cooler weather. They keep flying up against the house and the window and fluttering there, as if they would come in, or alight on the wood-pile or pump. They would commonly be mistaken for sparrows, but show more white when they fly, beside the yellow on the rump and sides of breast seen near to and two white bars on the wings. Chubby birds.

PINE WARBLER

April 23, 1852 I hear this morning, in the pine woods above the railroad bridge, for the first time, that delicious cool-sounding *wetter-wetter-wetter-wetter-wet'* from that small bird (pine warbler?) in the tops of the pines. I associate it with the *cool, moist, evergreen spring* woods.

April 2, 1853 Heard and saw what I call the pine warbler,— *vetter vetter vetter vetter vet,*—the cool woodland sound. The first this year of the higher-colored birds, after the bluebird and the black-bird's wing; is it not? It so affects me as something more tender.

April 8, 1853 Saw and heard my small pine warbler shaking out his trills, or jingle, even like money coming to its bearings.

They appear much the smaller from perching high in the tops of white pines and flitting from tree to tree at that height.

April 9, 1853   On a pitch [pine] on side of J. Hosmer's river hill, a pine warbler, by ventriloquism sounding farther off than it was, which was seven or eight feet, hopping and flitting from twig to twig, apparently picking the small flies at and about the base of the needles at the extremities of the twigs. Saw two afterward on the walls by roadside.

April 9, 1856   While I am looking at the hazel, I hear from the old locality, the edge of the great pines and oaks in the swamp by the railroad, the note of the pine warbler. It sounds far off and faint, but, coming out and sitting on the iron rail, I am surprised to see it within three or four rods, on the upper part of a white oak, where it is busily catching insects, hopping along toward the extremities of the limbs and looking off on all sides, twice darting off like a wood pewee two rods over the railroad after an insect and returning to the oak, and from time to time uttering its simple, rapidly iterated, cool-sounding notes. When heard a little within the wood, as he hops to that side of the oak, they sound particularly cool and inspiring, like a part of the evergreen forest itself, the trickling of the sap. Its bright-yellow or golden throat and breast, etc., are conspicuous at this season,—a greenish yellow above, with two white bars on its bluish-brown wings. It sits often with loose-hung wings and forked tail.

April 11, 1856   Hear in the old place, the pitch pine grove on the bank by the river, the pleasant ringing note of the pine warbler. Its *a-che, vitter vitter, vitter vitter, vitter vitter, vitter vitter, vet* rings through the open pine grove very rapidly. I also heard it at the old place by the railroad, as I came along. It is remarkable that I have so often heard it first in these two localities, *i.e.* where the railroad skirts the north edge of a small swamp densely filled with tall old white pines and a few white oaks, and in a young grove composed wholly of pitch pines on the otherwise bare, very high and level bank of the Assabet. When the season is advanced enough, I am pretty sure to hear its ringing note in both those places.

April 15, 1859   The warm pine woods are all alive this afternoon with the jingle of the pine warbler, the for the most part invisible minstrel. That wood, for example, at the Punk Oak, where we sit to hear it. It is surprising how quickly the earth, which was covered half an inch deep this morning, and since so wet, has become comparatively dry, so that we sit on the ground or on the dry leaves in woods at 3 P.M. and smell the pines and see and hear the flies, etc., buzz about, though the sun did not come out till 12 P.M. This morning, the aspect of winter; at mid-forenoon, the ground reeking with moisture; at 3 P.M., sit on dry leaves and hear the flies buzz and smell the pines! That wood is now very handsome seen from the westerly side, the sun falling far through it, though some trunks are wholly in shade. This warbler impresses me as if it were calling the trees to life. I think of springing twigs. Its jingle rings through the wood at short intervals, as if, like an electric shock, it imparted a fresh spring life to them. You hear the same bird, now here now there, as it incessantly flits about, commonly invisible and uttering its simple jingle on very different keys, and from time to time a companion is heard farther or nearer. This is a peculiarly summer-like sound. Go to a warm pine wood-side on a pleasant day at this season after storm, and hear it ring with the jingle of the pine warbler.

OVEN-BIRD
(GOLDEN-CROWNED THRUSH)
("NIGHT-WARBLER")[1]

June 11, 1851   I hear the night-warbler breaking out as in his dreams, made so from the first for some mysterious reason.

June 29, 1851   The night-warbler sings the same strain at noon.

May 10, 1853   P.M.—Hear the night-warbler now distinctly. It does not soon repeat its note, and disappears with the sound.

June 19, 1853   Heard my night-warbler on a solitary white pine in the Heywood Clearing by the Peak. Discovered it at last, looking like a small piece of black bark curving partly over the limb. No fork to its tail. It appeared black beneath; was very shy, not bigger than a yellowbird, and very slender.

May 28, 1854   The night-warbler, after his strain, drops down almost perpendicularly into a tree-top and is lost.

May 29, 1854   Saw what I thought my night-warbler,—sparrow-like with chestnut (?) stripes on breast, white or whitish below and about eyes, and perhaps chestnut (??) head.

---

[1][Practically all of Thoreau's references, however slight, to his mysterious "night-warbler" are here printed. He never satisfied himself as to the identity of the bird, but the accumulated evidence makes it clear that the night-warbler's song was no other than the flight-song of the oven-bird, though the somewhat similar aerial song of the Maryland yellow-throat deceived him on one occasion.]

May 3, 1857   Emerson says that Brewer tells him my "night warbler" is probably the Nashville warbler.

May 12, 1857   A night-warbler, plainly light beneath. It always flies to a new perch immediately after its song.

May 16, 1858   A golden-crowned thrush hops quite near. It is quite small, about the size of the creeper, with the upper part of its breast thickly and distinctly pencilled with black, a tawny head; and utters now only a sharp cluck for a *chip*. See and hear a redstart, the rhythm of whose strain is *tse'-tse, tse'-tse, tse'*, emphasizing the last syllable of all and not ending with the common *tsear*. Hear the night-warbler.

May 17, 1858 Just after hearing my night-warbler I see two birds on a tree. The one which I examined—as well as I could without a glass—had a white throat with a white spot on his wings, was dark above and moved from time to time like a creeper, and it was about the creeper's size. The other bird, which I did not examine particularly, was a little larger and more tawny.[1]

May 19, 1858 Hear the night-warbler *begin* his strain just like an oven-bird! I have noticed that when it drops down into the woods it darts suddenly *one side* to a perch when low.

August 5, 1858 While passing there, I heard what I should call my night-warbler's note, and, looking up, saw the bird dropping to a bush on the hillside. Looking through the glass, I saw that it was the Maryland yellow-throat!! and it afterward flew to the button-bushes in the meadow.

May 8, 1860 The night-warbler's note.

May 18, 1860 The night-warbler is a powerful singer for so small a bird. It launches into the air above the forest, or over some

---

[1]Perhaps golden-crowned thrush.

hollow or open space in the woods, and challenges the attention of the woods by its rapid and impetuous warble, and then drops down swiftly into the tree-tops like a performer withdrawing behind the scenes, and he is very lucky who detects where it alights.

August 28, 1860   Hear the night-warbler and the whip-poor-will.

AMERICAN REDSTART

May 10, 1853   I hear, and have for a week, in the woods, the note of one or more small birds somewhat like a yellowbird's. What is it? Is it the redstart? I now see one of these. The first I have distinguished. And now I feel pretty certain that my black and yellow warbler of May 1st was this. As I sit, it inquisitively hops nearer and nearer. It is one of the election-birds[1] of rare colors which I can remember, mingled dark and reddish. This reminds me that I supposed much more variety and fertility in nature before I had learned the numbers and the names of each order. I find that I had expected such fertility in our Concord woods alone as not even the completest museum of stuffed birds of all the forms and colors from all parts of the world comes up to.

[1][Birds shot on election day. See Chapter 16.]

WARBLERS (IN GENERAL)

April 19, 1854   Within a few days the warblers have begun to come. They are of every hue. Nature made them to show her colors with. There are as many as there are colors and shades. In certain lights, as yesterday against the snow, nothing can be more splendid and celestial than the color of the bluebird.

Nineteen

TITLARKS

THRASHERS

WRENS

AMERICAN PIPIT
(TITLARK)

October 26, 1853   I hear a faint twittering of the sparrows in the grass, like crickets. Those flitting sparrows[1] which we have had for some weeks, are they not the sober snowbirds (tree sparrows?)? They fly in a great drifting flock, wheeling and dashing about, as if preluding or acting a snow-storm, with rapid *te te te*. They are as dry and rustling as the grass.

November 6, 1853   It is remarkable how little we attend to what is passing before us constantly, unless our genius directs our attention that way. There are these little sparrows with white in

---

[1][From other entries in the Journal it is evident that these "sparrows" which Thoreau saw in large flocks in the fall were titlarks.]

tail, perhaps the prevailing bird of late, which have flitted before me so many falls and springs,[1] and yet they have been as it were strangers to me, and I have not inquired whence they came or whither they were going, or what their habits were. It is surprising how little most of us are contented to know about the sparrows which drift about in the air before us just before the first snows. I hear the downy woodpecker's metallic *tchip* or peep. Now I see where many a bird builded last spring or summer. These are leaves which do not fall.

MOCKINGBIRD

August 18, 1854   I think I saw a mockingbird on a black cherry near Pedrick's. Size of and like a catbird; bluish-black side-head, a white spot on closed wings, lighter breast and beneath; but he flew before I had fairly adjusted my glass. There were brown thrashers with it making their clicking note.

CATBIRD

May 8, 1852   I hear a catbird singing within a rod among the alders, but it is too dark to see him. How he stops and half angrily, half anxiously and inquisitively, inquires *char-char*, sounding like the caw of a crow, not like a cat.

---

[1][Though common in the autumn, the titlark is rare in the spring in New England. Thoreau was probably only taking it for granted that he had often seen these birds in the spring.]

May 21, 1852   The catbird sings like a robin sometimes, sometimes like a blackbird's sprayey warble. There is more of squeak or mew, and also of clear *whistle*, than in the thrasher's note.

BROWN THRASHER
May 3, 1852   Hear the first brown thrasher,—two of them. . . . They drown all the rest. He says *cherruwit, cherruwit; go ahead, go ahead; give it to him, give it to him*; etc., etc., etc.

May 16, 1852   The thrasher has a sort of laugh in his strain which the catbird has not.

May 18, 1852   This afternoon the brown thrashers are very numerous and musical. They plunge downward when they leave their perch, in a peculiar way. It is a bird that appears to make a business of singing for its own amusement. There is great variety in its strains. It is not easy to detect any repetition.

June 24, 1853   The brown thrasher's nest has been robbed, probably by some other bird. It rested on a branch of a swamp-pink and some grape-vines, effectually concealed and protected by grape-vines and green-briar in a matted bower above it. The foundation of pretty stout twigs, eight or nine inches in diameter, surmounted by coarse strips of grape bark, giving form to the nest, and then lined with some harsh, wiry root-fibres; within rather small and shallow, and the whole fabric of loose texture, not easy to remove.

April 30, 1856   A fine morning. I hear the first brown thrasher singing within three or four rods of me on the shrubby hillside in front of the Hadley place. I think I had a glimpse of one darting down from a sapling-top into the bushes as I rode by the same place on the morning of the 28th.

This, I think, is the very place to hear them early, a dry hillside sloping to the south, covered with young wood and shrub oaks. I am the more attracted to that house as a dwelling-place. To live where you would hear the first brown thrasher! First, perchance, you have a glimpse of one's ferruginous long brown back, instantly lost amid the shrub oaks, and are uncertain if it was a thrasher, or one of the other thrushes; and your uncertainty lasts commonly a day or two, until its rich and varied strain is heard. Surveying seemed a noble employment which brought me within hearing of this bird. I was trying to get the exact course of a wall thickly beset with shrub oaks and birches, making an opening through them with axe and knife, while the hillside seemed to quiver or pulsate with the sudden melody. Again, it is with the side of the ear that you hear. The music or the beauty belong not to your work itself but some of its accompaniments. You would fain devote yourself to the melody, but you will hear more of it if you devote yourself to your work.

May 4, 1859   We hear a thrasher sing for half an hour steadily,—a very rich singer and heard a quarter of a mile off very distinctly. This is first heard commonly at planting-time. He sings as if conscious of his power.

June 19, 1860 Observe a nest crowded full with four young brown thrashers half fledged. You would think they would die of heat, so densely packed and overflowing. Three head one way, and the other lies across. How quickly a fox would gobble them up!

WINTER WREN

July 10, 1858 The *Fringilla hyemalis* was most common in the upper part of the ravine,[1] and I saw a large bird of prey, perhaps an eagle, sailing over the head of the ravine. The wood thrush and veery[2] sang regularly, especially morning and evening. But, above all, the peculiar and memorable songster was that Monadnock-like one,[3] keeping up an exceedingly brisk and lively strain. It was remarkable for its incessant twittering flow. Yet we never got sight of the bird, at least while singing, so that I could not identify it, and my lameness[4] prevented my pursuing it. I heard

[1] [Tuckerman's Ravine on the side of Mt. Washington.]
[2] [Doubtless the olive-backed thrush and Bicknell's thrush, which are the only thrushes found on the upper slopes of Mt. Washington. See note on wood thrush, Chapter 21.]
[3] [On June 4 of the same year he had heard on Mt. Monadnock "a very peculiar lively and interesting strain from some bird," but had been unable to see the singer.]
[4] [He had sprained his ankle the day before.]

it afterward, even in the Franconia Notch. It was surprising for its steady and uninterrupted flow, for when one stopped, another appeared to take up the strain. It reminded me of a fine corkscrew stream issuing with incessant lisping tinkle from a cork, flowing rapidly, and I said that he had pulled out the spile and left it running.[1] That was the rhythm, but with a sharper tinkle of course. It had no more variety than that, but it was more remarkable for its continuance and monotonousness than any bird's note I ever heard. It evidently belongs only to cool mountainsides, high up amid the fir and spruce. I saw once flitting through the fir-tops restlessly a small white and dark bird, sylvia-like, which may have been it. Sometimes they appeared to be attracted by our smoke. The note was so incessant that at length you only noticed when it ceased.

SHORT-BILLED MARSH WREN

August 5, 1858   Just opposite this bay,[2] I heard a peculiar note which I thought at first might be that of a kingbird, but soon saw for the first time a wren within two or three rods perched on the tall sedge or the wool-grass and making it,—probably the short-billed marsh wren. It was peculiarly brisk and rasping, not at all musical, the rhythm something like *shar te dittle ittle ittle ittle ittle,*

[1][The song described is evidently that of the winter wren.]
[2][Lily Bay in the Sudbury River and in the town of Sudbury.]

but the last part was drier or less liquid than this implies. It was a small bird, quite dark above and apparently plain ashy-white beneath, and held its head up when it sang, and also commonly its tail. It dropped into the deep sedge on our approach, but did not go off, as we saw by the motion of the grass; then reappeared and uttered its brisk notes quite near us, and, flying off, was lost in the sedge again.

CREEPERS

NUTHATCHES

TITS

KINGLETS

BROWN CREEPER

November 26, 1859 I see here to-day one brown creeper busily inspecting the pitch pines. It begins at the base, and creeps rapidly upward by starts, adhering close to the bark and shifting a little from side to side often till near the top, then suddenly darts off downward to the base of another tree, where it repeats the same course. This has no black cockade, like the nuthatch.

WHITE-BELLIED NUTHATCH

April 6, 1856 I went to the oaks. Heard there a nuthatch's faint vibrating *tut-tut*, somewhat even like croaking of frogs, as it made its way up the oak bark and turned head down to peck. Anon it answered its mate with a *gnah gnah*.

December 5, 1856 As I walk along the side of the Hill, a pair of nuthatches flit by toward a walnut,[1] flying low in midcourse and then ascending to the tree. I hear one's faint *tut tut* or *gnah gnah*—no doubt heard a good way by its mate now flown into the next tree— as it is ascending the trunk or branch of a walnut in a zigzag manner, hitching along, prying into the crevices of the bark; and now it has found a savory morsel, which it pauses to devour, then flits to a new bough. It is a chubby bird, white, slate-color, and black.

January 5, 1859 As I go over the causeway, near the railroad bridge, I hear a fine busy twitter, and, looking up, see a nuthatch hopping along and about a swamp white oak branch, inspecting every side of it, as readily hanging head-downwards as standing upright, and then it utters a distinct *gnah*, as if to attract a companion. Indeed, that other, finer twitter seemed designed to keep some companion in tow, or else it was like a very busy man talking to himself. The companion was a single chickadee, which lisped six or eight feet off. There were, perhaps, no other birds than these two within a quarter of a mile. And when the nuthatch flitted to another tree two rods off, the chickadee unfailingly followed.

[1][Thoreau was accustomed to use the name walnut for the various species of hickory.]

March 5, 1859 Going down-town this forenoon, I heard a white-bellied nuthatch on an elm within twenty feet, uttering peculiar notes and more like a song than I remember to have heard from it. There was a chickadee close by, to which it may have been addressed. It was something like *to-what what what what what*, rapidly repeated, and not the usual *gnah gnah*; and this instant it occurs to me that this may be that earliest spring note which I hear, and have referred to a woodpecker! (This is before *I* have chanced to see a bluebird, blackbird, or robin in Concord this year.) It is the spring note of the nuthatch. It paused in its progress about the trunk or branch and uttered this lively but peculiarly inarticulate song, an awkward attempt to warble almost in the face of the chickadee, as if it were one of its kind. It was thus giving vent to the spring within it. If I am not mistaken, it is what I have heard in former springs or winters long ago, fabulously early in the season, when we men had just begun to anticipate the spring,—for it would seem that we, in our anticipations and sympathies, include in succession the moods and expressions of all creatures. When only the snow had begun to melt and no rill of song had broken loose, a note so dry and fettered still, so inarticulate and half thawed out, that you might (and would commonly) mistake for the tapping of a woodpecker. As if the young nuthatch in its hole had listened only to the tapping of woodpeckers and learned that music, and now, when it would sing and give vent to its spring ecstasy, it can modulate only some notes like that. That is its theme still. That is its ruling idea of song and music,—only a little clangor and liquidity added to the tapping of the woodpecker. It was the handle by which my thoughts took firmly hold on spring.

CHICKADEE

[Dated only 1838] Sometimes I hear the veery's silver clarion, or the brazen note of the impatient jay, or in secluded woods the chickadee doles out her scanty notes, which sing the praise of heroes, and set forth the loveliness of virtue evermore.— *Phe-be.*

November 9, 1850 The chickadees, if I stand long enough, hop nearer and nearer inquisitively, from pine bough to pine bough, till within four or five feet, occasionally lisping a note.

October 10, 1851 As I stood amid the witch-hazels near Flint's Pond, a flock of a dozen chickadees came flitting and singing about me with great ado,—a most cheering and enlivening sound,—with incessant *day-day-day* and a fine wiry strain between-whiles, flitting ever nearer and nearer and nearer, inquisitively, till the boldest was within five feet of me; then suddenly, their curiosity satiated, they flit by degrees further away and disappear, and I hear with regret their retreating *day-day-days.*

March 10, 1852 Heard the phœbe note of the chickadee to-day for the first time. I had at first heard their *day-day-day* ungratefully,—ah! you but carry my thoughts back to winter,—but anon I found that they too had become spring birds; they had changed their note. Even they feel the influence of spring.

October 23, 1852   The chickadees flit along, following me inquisitively a few rods with lisping, tinkling note,—flit within a few feet of me from curiosity, head downward on the pines.

March 22, 1853   I hear the phœbe note of the chickadee, one taking it up behind another as in a catch, *phe-bee phe-bee.*

December 1, 1853   Those trees and shrubs which retain their withered leaves through the winter—shrub oaks and young white, red, and black oaks, the lower branches of larger trees of the last-mentioned species, hornbeam, etc., and young hickories—seem to form an intermediate class between deciduous and evergreen trees. They may almost be called the ever-reds. Their leaves, which are falling all winter long, serve as a shelter to rabbits and partridges and other winter quadrupeds and birds. Even the little chickadees love to skulk amid them and peep out from behind them. I hear their faint, silvery, lisping notes, like tinkling glass, and occasionally a sprightly *day-day-day*, as they inquisitively hop nearer and nearer to me. They are our most honest and innocent little bird, drawing yet nearer to us as the winter advances, and deserve best of any of the walker.

February 9, 1854   I do not hear Therien's[1] axe far of late. The moment I came on his chopping-ground, the chickadees flew to

[1] [Aleck Therien, the French-Canadian woodchopper celebrated in *Walden.*]

me, as if glad to see me. They are a peculiarly honest and sociable little bird. I saw them go to his pail repeatedly and peck his bread and butter. They came and went a dozen times while I stood there. He said that a great flock of them came round him the other day while he was eating his dinner and lit on his clothes "just like flies." One roosted on his finger, and another pecked a piece of bread in his hand. They are considerable company for the woodchopper. I heard one wiry *phe-be*. They love to hop about wood freshly split. Apparently they do not leave his clearing all day They were not scared when he threw down wood within a few feet of them. When I looked to see how much of his bread and butter they had eaten, I did not perceive that any was gone. He could afford to dine a hundred.

January 7, 1855   Here comes a little flock of titmice, plainly to keep me company, with their black caps and throats making them look top-heavy, restlessly hopping along the alders, with a sharp, clear, lisping note.

December 15, 1855   This morning it has begun to snow apparently in earnest. The air is quite thick and the view confined. It is quite still, yet some flakes come down from one side and some from another, crossing each other like woof and warp apparently, as they are falling in different eddies and currents of air. In the midst of it, I hear and see a few little chickadees prying about the twigs of the locusts in the graveyard. They have come into town with the snow. They now and then break forth into a short, sweet strain, and then seem suddenly to check themselves, as if they had done it before they thought.

June 3, 1856   While running a line in the woods, close to the water, on the southwest side of Loring's Pond, I observed a chickadee sitting quietly within a few feet. Suspecting a nest, I looked and found it in a small hollow maple stump which was about five inches in diameter and two feet high. I looked down about a foot and could just discern the eggs. Breaking off a little, I managed to get my hand in and took out some eggs. There were seven, making by their number an unusual figure as they lay in the nest, a sort of egg rosette, a circle around with one (or more) in the middle. In the meanwhile the bird sat silent, though rather restless, within three feet. The nest was very thick and warm, of average depth, and made of the bluish-slate rabbit's (?) fur. The eggs were a perfect oval, five eighths inch long, white with small reddish-brown or rusty spots, especially about larger end, partly developed. The bird sat on the remaining eggs next day. I called off the boy in another direction that he might not find it.

October 17, 1856   As I stood looking at Emerson's bound under the railroad embankment, I heard a smart *tche-day-day-day* close to my ear, and, looking up, saw four of these birds, which had come to scrape acquaintance with me, hopping amid the alders within three and four feet of me. I had heard them further off at first, and they had followed me along the hedge. They *day-day*'d and lisped their faint notes alternately, and then, as if to make me think they had some other errand than to peer at me, they pecked the dead twigs with their bills,—the little top-heavy, black-crowned, volatile fellows.

December 3, 1856 Six weeks ago I noticed the advent of chickadees and their winter habits. As you walk along a wood-side, a restless little flock of them, whose notes you hear at a distance, will seem to say, "Oh, there he goes! Let's pay our respects to him." And they will flit after and close to you, and naïvely peck at the nearest twig to you, as if they were minding their own business all the while without any reference to you.

November 8, 1857 I do not know exactly what that sweet word is which the chickadee says when it hops near to me now in those ravines.

March 21, 1858 Standing by the mud-hole in the swamp, I hear the pleasant phebe note of the chickadee. It is, methinks, the most of a wilderness note of any yet. It is peculiarly interesting that this, which is one of our winter birds also, should have a note with which to welcome the spring.

November 7, 1858 We are left to the chickadee's familiar notes, and the jay for trumpeter. What struck me was a certain emptiness beyond, between the hemlocks and the hill, in the cool, washed air, as if I appreciated even here the absence of insects from it. It suggested agreeably to me a mere space in which to walk briskly. The fields are bleak, and they are, as it were, vacated. The very earth is like a house shut up for the winter, and I go knocking about it in vain. But just then I heard a chickadee on a hemlock, and was inexpressibly cheered to find that an old acquaintance was yet stirring about the premises, and was, I was assured, to be there all winter. All that is evergreen in me revived at once.

December 28, 1858   I notice a few chickadees there in the edge of the pines, in the sun, lisping and twittering cheerfully to one another, with a reference to me, I think,—the cunning and innocent little birds. One a little further off utters the phœbe note. There is a foot more or less of clear open water at the edge here, and, seeing this, one of these birds hops down as if glad to find any open water at this season, and, after drinking, it stands in the water on a stone up to its belly and dips its head and flirts the water about vigorously, giving itself a good washing. I had not suspected this at this season. No fear that it will catch cold.

October 15, 1859   The chickadees sing as if at home. They are not travelling singers hired by any Barnum.[1] Theirs is an honest, homely, heartfelt melody. Shall not the voice of man express as much content as the note of a bird?

November 26, 1859   The chickadee is the bird of the wood the most unfailing. When, in a windy, or in any, day, you have penetrated some thick wood like this, you are pretty sure to hear its cheery note therein. At this season it is almost their sole inhabitant.

---

[1][Jenny Lind made her American tour under an engagement with P. T. Barnum in 1850–1851.]

December 12, 1859 Seeing a little hole in the side of a dead white birch, about six feet from the ground, I broke it off and found it to be made where a rotten limb had broken off. The hole was about an inch over and was of quite irregular and probably natural outline, and, within, the rotten wood had been removed to the depth of two or three inches, and on one side of this cavity, under the hole, was quite a pile of bird-droppings. The diameter of the birch was little more than two inches,—if at all. Probably it was the roosting-place of a chickadee. The bottom was an irregular surface of the rotten wood, and there was nothing like a nest.

January 12, 1860 As I stand by the hemlocks, I am greeted by the lively and unusually prolonged *tche de de de de de* of a little flock of chickadees. The snow has ceased falling, the sun comes out, and it is warm and still, and this flock of chickadees, little birds that perchance were born in their midst, feeling the influences of this genial season, have begun to flit amid the snow-covered fans of the hemlocks, jarring down the snow,—for there are hardly bare twigs enough for them to rest on,—or they plume themselves in some snug recess on the sunny side of the tree, only pausing to utter their *tche de de de.*

January 18, 1860 Standing under Lee's Cliff, several chickadees, uttering their faint notes, come flitting near to me as usual. They are busily prying under the bark of the pitch pines, occasionally knocking off a piece, while they cling with their claws on any side of the limb. Of course they are in search of animal food, but I see one suddenly dart down to a seedless pine seed wing on the snow, and then up again. C.[1] says that he saw them busy about these wings on the snow the other day, so I have no doubt that they eat this seed.

January 20, 1860 The snow and ice under the hemlocks is strewn with cones and seeds and tracked with birds and squirrels. What a bountiful supply of winter food is here provided for them! No sooner has fresh snow fallen and covered up the old crop than down comes a new supply all the more distinct on the spotless snow. Here comes a little flock of chickadees, attracted by me as usual, and perching close by boldly; then, descending to the snow and ice, I see them pick up the hemlock seed which lies all around them. Occasionally they take one to a twig and hammer at it there under their claws, perhaps to separate it from the wing, or even the shell. The snowy ice and the snow on shore have been blackened with these fallen cones several times over this winter. The snow along the sides of the river is also all dusted over with birch and alder seed, and I see where little birds have picked up the alder seed.

RUBY-CROWNED KINGLET

April 25, 1854 Saw a golden-crested wren[2] in the woods near Goose Pond. It sounded far off and like an imitation of

[1] [W. E. Channing.]
[2] ["Golden" crossed out in pencil and "ruby" substituted.]

a robin,[1]—a long strain and often repeated. I was quite near it before I was aware of it, it sounding still like a faint imitation of a robin. Some chickadees and yellow redpolls were first apparent, then my wren on the pitch pines and young oaks. He appeared curious to observe me. A very interesting and active little fellow, darting about amid the tree-tops, and his song quite remarkable and rich and loud for his size. Begins with a very fine note, before its pipes are filled, not audible at a little distance, then *woriter weter*, etc., etc., winding up with *teter teter*, all clear and round.[2] This was at 4 P.M., when most birds do not sing. I saw it yesterday, pluming itself and stretching its little wings.

[1]And of a golden robin, which later I often mistook for him.
[2]His song is comical and reminds me of the thrasher.

Twenty-One

THRUSHES

WOOD THRUSH[1]

July 27, 1840   The wood thrush is a more modern philosopher than Plato and Aristotle. They are now a dogma, but he preaches the doctrine of this hour.

May 31, 1850   There is a sweet wild world which lies along the strain of the wood thrush—the rich intervals which border the stream of its song—more thoroughly genial to my nature than any other.

June 22, 1851   I hear around me, but never in sight, the many wood thrushes whetting their steel-like notes. Such keen singers!

---

[1][The hermit thrush as well as the wood thrush breeds in Concord, but Thoreau never learned to distinguish between the songs of the two species and they were all wood thrushes to him. In the White Mountains and the Maine woods he mistook the olive-backed thrush also for the wood thrush. It is not unlikely that some of the observations included under this head belong of right to the hermit thrush, but as they would apply equally well to the wood thrush they are retained here without question. Those that from the date or some other evidence clearly refer to the hermit are placed under that species.]

It takes a fiery heat, many dry pine leaves added to the furnace of the sun, to temper their strains! Always they are either rising or falling to a new strain. After what a moderate pause they deliver themselves again! saying ever a new thing, avoiding repetition, methinks answering one another. While most other birds take their siesta, the wood thrush discharges his song. It is delivered like a bolas, or a piece of jingling steel.

July 21, 1851 Never yet did I chance to sit in a house, except my own house in the woods, and hear a wood thrush sing. Would it not be well to sit in such a chamber within sound of the finest songster of the grove?

August 12, 1851 The birds utter a few languid and yawning notes, as if they had not left their perches, so sensible to light to wake so soon,—a faint peeping sound from I know not what kind, a slight, innocent, half-awake sound, like the sounds which a quiet housewife makes in the earliest dawn. Nature preserves her innocence like a beautiful child. I hear a wood thrush even now, long before sunrise, as in the heat of the day. And the pewee and the catbird and the vireo (red-eyed?). I do not hear—or do not mind, perchance—the crickets now. Now whip-poor-wills commence to sing in earnest, considerably *after* the wood thrush. The wood thrush, that beautiful singer, inviting the day once more to enter his pine woods. (So you may hear the wood thrush and whip-poor-will at the same time.) Now go by two whip-poor-wills, in haste seeking some coverts from the eye of day. And the bats are flying about on the edge of the wood, improving the last moments of their day in catching insects. The moon appears at length, not yet as a cloud, but with a frozen light, ominous of her fate. The early cars sound like a wind in the woods. The chewinks make a business now of waking each other up with their low *yorrick* in the neighboring low copse.

June 23, 1852   The wood thrush sings at all hours. I associate it with the cool morning, sultry noon, and serene evening. At this hour[1] it suggests a cool vigor.

July 5, 1852   Some birds are poets and sing all summer. They are the true singers. Any man can write verses during the love season. I am reminded of this while we rest in the shade on the Major Heywood road and listen to a wood thrush, now just before sunset. We are most interested in those birds who sing for the love of music and not of their mates; who meditate thier strains, and *amuse* themselves with singing; the birds, the strains, of deeper sentiment; not bobolinks, that lose their plumage, their bright colors, and their song so early. The robin, the red-eye, the veery, the wood thrush, etc., etc.

The wood thrush's is no opera music; it is not so much the composition as the strain, the tone,—cool bars of melody from the atmosphere of everlasting morning or evening. It is the quality of

[1][Early morning.]

the song, not the sequence. In the peawai's[1] note there is some sultriness, but in the thrush's, though heard at noon, there is the liquid coolness of things that are just drawn from the bottom of springs. The thrush alone declares the immortal wealth and vigor that is in the forest. Here is a bird in whose strain the story is told, though Nature waited for the science of æsthetics to discover it to man. Whenever a man hears it, he is young, and Nature is in her spring. Wherever he hears it, it is a new world and a free country, and the gates of heaven are not shut against him Most other birds sing from the level of my ordinary cheerful hours—a carol; but this bird never fails to speak to me out of an ether purer than that I breathe, of immortal beauty and vigor. He deepens the significance of all things seen in the light of his strain. He sings to make men take higher and truer views of things. He sings to amend their institutions; to relieve the slave on the plantation and the prisoner in his dungeon, the slave in the house of luxury and the prisoner of his own low thoughts.

July 27, 1852 How cool and assuaging the thrush's note after the fever of the day! I doubt if they have anything so richly wild in Europe. So long a civilization must have banished it. It will only be heard in America, perchance, while our star is in the ascendant. I should be very much surprised if I were to hear in the strain of the nightingale such unexplored wildness and fertility,

[1][The wood pewee.]

reaching to sundown, inciting to emigration. Such a bird must it-self have emigrated long ago. Why, then, was I born in America? I might ask.

May 17, 1853 The wood thrush has sung for some time. He touches a depth in me which no other bird's song does. He has learned to sing, and no thrumming of the strings or tuning disturbs you. Other birds may whistle pretty well, but he is the master of a finer-toned instrument. His song is musical, not from association merely, not from variety, but the character of its tone. It is all divine,—a Shakespeare among birds, and a Homer too.

June 12, 1853 The note of the wood thrush answers to some cool, unexhausted morning vigor in the hearer.

June 14, 1853 The wood thrush launches forth his evening strains from the midst of the pines. I admire the moderation of this master. There is nothing tumultuous in his song. He launches forth one strain with all his heart and life and soul, of pure and unmatchable melody, and then he pauses and gives the hearer and himself time to digest this, and then another and another at suitable intervals. Men talk of the *rich* song of other birds,—the thrasher, mockingbird, nightingale. But I doubt, I doubt. They know not what they say! There is as great an interval between the thrasher and the wood thrush as between Thomson's "Seasons" and Homer. The sweetness of the day crystallizes in this morning coolness.

June 22, 1853 As I come over the hill, I hear the wood thrush singing his evening lay. This is the only bird whose note affects me like music, affects the flow and tenor of my thought, my fancy and imagination. It lifts and exhilarates me. It is inspiring. It is a medicative draught to my soul. It is an elixir to my eyes and a fountain of youth to all my senses. It changes all hours to an eternal morning. It banishes all trivialness. It reinstates me in my dominion, makes me the lord of creation, is chief musician of my court. This minstrel sings in a time, a heroic age, with which no event in the village can be contemporary. How can they be contemporary when only the latter is *temporary* at all? How can the infinite and eternal be contemporary with the finite and temporal? So there is something in the music of the cow-bell, something sweeter and more nutritious, than in the milk which the farmers drink. This thrush's song is a *ranz des vaches* to me. I long for wildness, a nature which I cannot put my foot through, woods where the wood thrush forever sings, where the hours are early morning ones, and there is dew on the grass, and the day is forever unproved, where I might have a fertile unknown for a soil about me. I would go after the cows, I would watch the flocks of Admetus there forever, only for my board and clothes. A New Hampshire everlasting and unfallen.

★   ★   ★

All that was ripest and fairest in the wilderness and the wild man is preserved and transmitted to us in the strain of the wood thrush. It is the mediator between barbarism and civilization. It is unrepentant as Greece.

December 31, 1853   There are a few sounds still which never fail to affect me. The notes of the wood thrush and the sound of a vibrating chord, these affect me as many sounds once did often, and as almost all should. The strains of the æolian harp and of the wood thrush are the truest and loftiest preachers that I know now left on this earth. I know of no missionaries to us heathen comparable to them. They, as it were, lift us up in spite of ourselves. They intoxicate, they charm us.

May 28, 1855   While we sit by the path in the depths of the woods three quarters of a mile beyond Hayden's, confessing the influence of almost the first summer warmth, the wood thrush sings steadily for half an hour, now at 2.30 P.M., amid the pines,—loud and clear and sweet. While other birds are warbling betweenwhiles and catching their prey, he alone appears to make a business of singing, like a true minstrel.

July 31, 1858   Got the wood thrush's nest of June 19th (now empty). It was placed between many small upright shoots, against the main stem of the slender maple, and measures four and a half to five inches in diameter from outside to outside of the rim, and one and three quarters deep within. It is quite firm (except the external leaves falling off), the rim about three quarters of an inch thick, and it is composed externally of leaves, apparently chiefly chestnut, very much decayed, beneath which, in the place of the grass and stubble of which most nests are composed, are apparently the midribs of the same leaves, whose whole pulp, etc., is gone, arranged as compactly and densely (in a curving manner) as grass or stubble could be, upon a core, not of mud, but a pale-brown composition quite firm and smooth (within), looking like inside of a cocoanut-shell, and apparently composed of decayed leaf pulp (?), which the bird has perhaps mixed and cemented with its saliva. This is about a quarter of an inch thick and about as regular as a half of a cocoanut-shell. Within this, the lower part is lined with considerable rather coarse black root-fibre and a very little fine stubble. From some particles of fine white sand, etc., on the pale-brown composition of the nest, I thought it was obtained from the pond shore. This composition, viewed through a microscope, has almost a cellular structure.

August 9, 1858 The wood thrush's was a peculiarly woodland nest, made solely of such materials as that unfrequented grove afforded, the refuse of the wood or shore of the pond. There was no horsehair, no twine nor paper nor other relics of art in it.

VEERY
(WILSON'S THRUSH)

June 19, 1853 In the middle of the path to Wharf Rock at Flint's Pond, the nest of a Wilson's thrush, five or six inches high, between the green stems of three or four golden-rods, made of dried grass or fibres of bark, with dry oak leaves attached loosely, making the whole nine or ten inches wide, to deceive the eye. Two blue eggs. Like an accidental heap. Who taught it to do thus?

HERMIT THRUSH[1]

June 15, 1851   I sit in the shade of the pines to hear a wood thrush at noon. The ground smells of dry leaves; the heat is oppressive. The bird begins on a low strain, *i.e.* it first delivers a strain on a lower key, then a moment after another a little higher, then another still varied from the others,—no two successive strains alike, but either ascending or descending.[2] He confines himself to his few notes, in which he is unrivalled, as if his kind had learned this and no more anciently.

April 30, 1852   I hear a wood thrush[3] here, with a fine metallic ring to his note. This sound most adequately expresses the immortal beauty and wildness of the woods. I go in search of him. He sounds no nearer. On a low bough of a small maple near the brook in the swamp, he sits with ruffled feathers, singing more low

---

[1][See note to wood thrush, p. 426. The hermit thrush was a rare bird to Thoreau. He detected it occasionally in spring and autumn, but he seems never to have suspected that it was a regular summer resident in Concord and that he had often listened to its song.]

[2][The song described seems to be that of the hermit thrush.]

[3][Thoreau's April and very early May wood thrushes were all doubtless hermit thrushes.]

or with less power, as it were ventriloquizing; for though I am scarcely more than a rod off, he seems further off than ever.

May 1, 1852   I hear the first catbird also, mewing, and the wood thrush, which still thrills me,—a sound to be heard in a new country,—from one side of a clearing.

May 3, 1852   The wood thrush reminds me of cool mountain springs and morning walks.

April 27, 1854   The wood thrush afar,—so superior a strain to that of other birds. I was doubting if it would affect me as of yore, but it did measurably. I did not believe there could be such differences. This is the gospel according to the wood thrush. He makes a sabbath out of a week-day. I could go to hear him, could buy a pew in his church. Did he ever practice pulpit eloquence? He is right on the slavery question.

April 21, 1855   At Cliffs, I hear at a distance a wood thrush. It affects us as a part of our unfallen selves.

June 22, 1856   R. W. E. imitates the wood thrush by *he willy willy—ha willy willy—O willy O.*

AMERICAN ROBIN

March 26, 1846   The change from foul weather to fair, from dark, sluggish hours to serene, elastic ones, is a memorable crisis which all things proclaim. The change from foulness to serenity is instantaneous. Suddnely an influx of light, though it was late, filled my room. I looked out and saw that the pond was already calm and full of hope as on a summer evening, though the ice was dissolved but yesterday. There seemed to be some intelligence in the pond which responded to the unseen serenity in a distant horizon. I heard a robin in the distance,—the first I had heard this spring,—repeating the assurance. The green pitch pine suddenly looked brighter and more erect, as if now entirely washed and cleansed by the rain. I knew it would not rain any more. A serene summer-evening sky seemed darkly reflected in the pond, though the clear sky was nowhere visible overhead. It was no longer the end of a season, but the beginning. The pines and shrub oaks, which had before drooped and cowered the winter through with myself, now recovered their several characters and in the landscape revived the expression of an immortal beauty. Trees seemed all at once to be fitly grouped, to sustain new relations to men and to one another. There was somewhat cosmical in the arrangement of nature. O the evening robin, at the close of a New England day! If I could ever find the twig he sits upon! Where does the minstrel really roost? We perceive it is not the bird of the ornithologist that is heard,—the *Turdus migratorius*.

July 27, 1851   After taking the road by Webster's[1] beyond South Marshfield, I walked a long way at noon, hot and thirsty, before I could find a suitable place to sit and eat my dinner,—a place

[1][Daniel Webster's house at Marshfield, Mass.]

where the shade and the sward pleased me. At length I was obliged to put up with a small shade close to the ruts, where the only stream I had seen for some time crossed the road. Here, also, numerous robins came to cool and wash themselves and to drink. They stood in the water up to their bellies, from time to time wetting their wings and tails and also ducking their heads and sprinkling the water over themselves; then they sat on a fence near by to dry. Then a goldfinch came and did the same, accompanied by the less brilliant female. These birds evidently enjoyed their bath greatly, and it seemed indispensable to them.

April 1, 1852 I hear a robin singing in the woods south of Hosmer's, just before sunset. It is a sound associated with New England village life. It brings to my thoughts summer evenings when the children are playing in the yards before the doors and their parents conversing at the open windows. It foretells all this now, before those summer hours are come.

April 11, 1852 The song of a robin on an oak in Hubbard's Grove sounds far off. So I have heard a robin within three feet in a cage in a dark barroom (how unstained by all the filth of that place?) with a kind of ventriloquism so singing that his song sounded far off on the elms. It was more pathetic still for this. The robins are singing now on all hands while the sun is setting. At what expense any valuable work is performed! At the expense of a life! If you do one thing well, what else are you good for in the meanwhile?

April 13, 1852   The robin is the only bird as yet that makes a business of singing, steadily singing,—sings continuously out of pure joy and melody of soul, carols. The jingle of the song sparrow, simple and sweet as it is, is not of sufficient volume nor sufficiently continuous to command and hold attention, and the bluebird's is but a transient warble, from a throat overflowing with azure and serene hopes; but the song of the robin on the elms or oaks, loud and clear and heard afar through the streets of a village, makes a fit conclusion to a spring day. The larks are not yet in sufficient numbers or sufficiently musical. The robin is the prime singer as yet. The blackbird's *conqueree*, when first heard in the spring, is pleasant from the associations it awakens, and is best heard by one boating on the river. It belongs to the stream. The robin is the only bird with whose song the groves can be said to be now *vocal* morning and evening, for, though many other notes are heard, none fill the air like this bird. As yet no other thrushes.

April 21, 1852   On the east side of Ponkawtasset I hear a robin singing cheerily from some perch in the wood, in the midst of the rain, where the scenery is now wild and dreary. His song a singular antagonism and offset to the storm. As if Nature said, "Have faith; these *two* things I can do." It sings with power, like a bird of great faith that sees the bright future through the dark present, to reassure the race of man, like one to whom many talents were given and who will improve its talents. They are sounds to make a dying man live. They sing not their despair. It is a pure, im-mortal melody.

*   *   *

The birds are singing in the rain about the small pond in front, the inquisitive chickadee that has flown all at once to the alders to reconnoitre us, the blackbirds, the song sparrow, telling of ex-panding buds. But above all the robin sings here too, I know not at what distance in the wood. "Did he sing thus in Indian days?" I ask myself; for I have always associated this sound with the village and the clearing, but now I do detect the aboriginal wildness in his strain, and can imagine him a woodland bird, and that he sang thus when there was no civilized ear to hear him, a pure forest melody even like the wood thrush. Every genuine thing retains this wild tone, which no true culture displaces. I heard him even as he might have sounded to the Indian, singing at evening upon the elm above his wigwam, with which was associated in the red man's mind the events of an Indian's life, his childhood. Formerly I had heard in it only those strains which tell of the white man's village life; now I heard those strains which remembered the red man's life, such as fell on the ears of Indian children,—as he sang when these arrow-heads, which the rain has made shine so on the lean stubble-field, were fastened to their shaft. Thus the birds sing round this piece of water, some on the alders which fringe, some farther off and higher up the hills; it is a centre to them.

March 18, 1853   I stand still now to listen if I may hear the note of any new bird, for the sound of my step hinders, and there are so few sounds at this season in a still afternoon like this that you are pretty sure to detect one within a considerable distance. Hark! Did I not hear the note of some bird then? Methinks it could not have been my own breathing through my nose. No, there it is again,—a robin; and we have put the winter so much further behind us. What mate does he call to in these deserted fields? It is, as it were, a scared note as he whisks by, followed by the familiar but still anxious *toot, toot, toot.* He does not sing as yet. There were one or two more fine bird-like tinkling sounds I could not trace home, not to be referred to my breathing.

March 21, 1853   How suddenly the newly arrived birds are dispersed over the whole town! How numerous they must be! Robins are now quite abundant, flying in flocks. One after another flits away before you from the trees, somewhat like grasshoppers in the grass, uttering their notes faintly,—ventriloquizing, in fact. I hear one meditating a bar to be sung anon, which sounds a quarter of a mile off, though he is within two rods. However, they do not yet get to melody. I thank the red-wing for a little bustle and commotion which he makes, trying to people the fields again.

March 31, 1853   The robins sing at the very earliest dawn. I wake with their note ringing in my ear.

April 4, 1853   Last night, a sugaring of snow, which goes off in an hour or two in the rain. Rains all day. . . . The robins sang this morning, nevertheless, and now more than ever hop about boldly in the garden in the rain, with full, broad, light cow-colored breasts.

April 6, 1853   The robin is the singer at present, such is its power and universality, being found both in garden and wood. Morning and evening it does not fail, perched on some elm or the like, and in rainy days it is one long morning or evening. The song sparrow is still more universal but not so powerful. The lark, too, is equally constant, morning and evening, but confined to certain localities, as is the blackbird to some extent. The bluebird, with feebler but not less sweet warbling, helps fill the air, and the phœbe does her part. The tree sparrow, *F. hyemalis*, and fox-colored sparrows make the meadow-sides or gardens where they are flitting vocal, the first with its canary-like twittering, the second with its lively ringing trills or jingle. The third is a very sweet and more powerful singer, which would be memorable if we heard him long enough. The woodpecker's tapping, though not musical, suggests pleasant associations in the cool morning,—is inspiriting, enlivening.

⋆   ⋆   ⋆

The robins, too, now toward sunset, perched on the old apple trees in Tarbell's orchard, twirl forth their evening lays unweariedly.

October 10, 1853   This morning it is very pleasant and warm. There are many small birds in flocks on the elms in Cheney's field, faintly warbling,—robins and purple finches and especially large flocks of small sparrows, which make a business of washing and pruning themselves in the puddles in the road, as if cleaning up after a long flight and the wind of yesterday. The faint suppressed warbling of the robins sounds like a reminiscence of the spring.

March 8, 1855   Stopping in a sunny and sheltered place on a hillock in the woods,—for it was raw in the wind,—I heard the hasty, shuffling, as if frightened, note of a *robin* from a dense birch wood,—a sort of *tche tche tche tche tche*,—and then probably it dashed through the birches; and so they fetch the year about. Just from the South Shore, perchance, it alighted not in the village street, but in this remote birch wood. This sound reminds me of rainy, misty April days in past years. Once or twice before, this afternoon, I thought I heard one and listened, but in vain.

May 4, 1855   A robin sings when I, in the house, cannot distinguish the earliest dawning from the full moonlight. His song first advertised me of the daybreak, when I thought it was night, as I lay looking out into the full moonlight. I heard a robin begin his strain, and yielded the point to him, believing that he was better acquainted with the springs of the day than I,—with the signs of day.

June 2, 1855   Mr. Hoar tells me that Deacon Farrar's son tells him that a white robin has her nest on an apple tree near their house. Her mate is of the usual color. All the family have seen her, but at the last accounts she has not been seen on the nest.

April 16, 1856 The robins sing with a will now. What a burst of melody! It gurgles out of all conduits now; they are choked with it. There is such a tide and rush of song as when a river is straightened between two rocky walls. It seems as if the morning's throat were not large enough to emit all this sound. The robin sings most before six o'clock now. I note where some suddenly cease their song, making a quite remarkable vacuum.

February 27, 1857 Before I opened the window this cold morning, I heard the peep of a robin, that sound so often heard in cheerless or else rainy weather, so often heard first borne on the cutting March wind or through sleet or rain, as if its coming were premature.

October 21, 1857 I see a robin eating prinos[1] berries. Is not the robin the principal berry-eating bird nowadays? There must be more about the barberry bushes in Melvin's Preserve than anywhere.

November 3, 1857 I see on many rocks, etc., the seeds of the barberry, which have been voided by birds,—robins, no doubt, chiefly. How many they must thus scatter over the fields, spreading the barberry far and wide! That has been their business for a month.

March 24, 1858 The chip of the ground-bird[2] resembles that of a robin, *i.e.*, its expression is the same, only fainter, and reminds

[1][Black alder, or winterberry, (*Ilex verticillata*).]
[2]That is, song sparrow.

me that the robin's peep, which sounds like a note of distress, is also a *chip*, or call-note to its kind.

June 3, 1858   They seemed to me wild robins that placed their nests in the spruce up there.[1] I noticed one nest. William Emerson, senior, says they do not breed on Staten Island. They do breed at least at Hudson's Bay. They are certainly a hardy bird, and are at home on this cool mountain-top.

March 7, 1859   The first note which I heard from the robins, far under the hill, was *sveet sveet*, suggesting a certain haste and alarm, and then a rich, hollow, somewhat plaintive *peep* or *peep-eep-eep*, as when in distress with young just flown. When you first see them alighted, they have a haggard, an anxious and hurried, look.

October 5, 1861   This is a rainy or drizzling day at last, and the robins and sparrows are more numerous in the yard and about the house than ever. They swarm on the ground where stood the heap of weeds which was burned yesterday, picking up the seeds which rattled from it. Why should these birds be so much more numerous about the house such a day as this? I think of no other reason than because it is darker and fewer people are moving about to frighten them. Our little mountain-ash is all alive with them. A dozen robins on it at once, busily reaching after and plucking the berries, actually make the whole tree shake. There are also some little birds (I

---

[1][On Mt. Monadnock.]

{ 444 }

think purple finches) with them. A robin will swallow half a dozen berries, at least, in rapid succession before it goes off, and apparently it soon comes back for more.

BLUEBIRD
April 26, 1838

THE BLUEBIRDS

In the midst of the poplar that stands by our door
We planted a bluebird box,
And we hoped before the summer was o'er
A transient pair to coax.

One warm summer's day the bluebirds came
And lighted on our tree,
But at first the wand'rers were not so tame
But they were afraid of me.

They seemed to come from the distant south,
Just over the Walden wood,
And they skimmed it along with open mouth
Close by where the bellows stood.

Warbling they swept round the distant cliff,
And they warbled it over the lea,

And over the blacksmith's shop in a jiff
Did they come warbling to me.

They came and sat on the box's top
Without looking into the hole,
And only from this side to that did they hop,
As 't were a common well-pole.

Methinks I had never seen them before,
Nor indeed had they seen me,
Till I chanced to stand by our back door,
And they came to the poplar tree.

In course of time they built their nest
And reared a happy brood,
And every morn they piped their best
As they flew away to the wood.

Thus wore the summer hours away
To the bluebirds and to me,
And every hour was a summer's day,
So pleasantly lived we.

They were a world within themselves,
And I a world in me,

Up in the tree—the little elves—
With their callow family.

One morn the wind blowed cold and strong,
And the leaves went whirling away;
The birds prepared for their journey long
That raw and gusty day.

Boreas came blust'ring down from the north,
And ruffled their azure smocks,
So they launched them forth, though somewhat loth,
By way of the old Cliff rocks.

Meanwhile the earth jogged steadily on
In her mantle of purest white,
And anon another spring was born
When winter was vanished quite.

And I wandered forth o'er the steamy earth,
And gazed at the mellow sky,
But never before from the hour of my birth
Had I wandered so thoughtfully.

For never before was the earth so still,
And never so mild was the sky,

The river, the fields, the woods, and the hill
Seemed to heave an audible sigh.

I felt that the heavens were all around,
And the earth was all below,
As when in the ears there rushes a sound
Which thrills you from top to toe.

I dreamed that I was a waking thought,
A something I hardly knew,
Not a solid piece, nor an empty nought,
But a drop of morning dew.

'T was the world and I at a game of bo-peep,
As a man would dodge his shadow,
An idea becalmed in eternity's deep,
'Tween Lima and Segraddo.

Anon a faintly warbled note
From out the azure deep
Into my ears did gently float
As is the approach of sleep.

It thrilled but startled not my soul;
Across my mind strange mem'ries gleamed,

As often distant scenes unroll
When we have lately dreamed.

The bluebird had come from the distant South
To his box in the poplar tree,
And he opened wide his slender mouth
On purpose to sing to me.

July 16, 1851   The plaintive, spring-restoring peep of a bluebird is occasionally heard.

October 10, 1851   The air this morning is full of bluebirds, and again it is spring.

March 10, 1852   I see flocks of a dozen bluebirds together. The warble of this bird is innocent and celestial, like its color. Saw a sparrow, perhaps a song sparrow, flitting amid the young oaks where the ground was covered with snow. I think that this is an indication that the ground is quite bare a little further south. Probably the spring birds never fly far over a snow-clad country. A woodchopper tells me he heard a robin this morning.

March 15, 1852   A mild spring day. . . . The air is full of bluebirds. The ground almost entirely bare. The villagers are out in the sun, and every man is happy whose work takes him outdoors. . . . I lean over a rail to hear what is in the air, liquid with the bluebirds' warble.

April 3, 1852   The bluebird carries the sky on his back.

March 10, 1853   What was that sound that came on the softened air? It was the warble of the first bluebird from that scraggy apple orchard yonder. When this is heard, then spring has arrived.

March 18, 1853   I no sooner step out of the house than I hear the bluebirds in the air, and far and near, everywhere except in the woods, throughout the town you may hear them,—the blue curls of their warblings,—harbingers of serene and warm weather, little azure rills of melody trickling here and there from out the air, their short warble trilled in the air reminding of so many corkscrews assaulting and thawing the torpid mass of winter, assisting the ice and snow to melt and the streams to flow.

*   *   *

The bluebird and song sparrow sing immediately on their arrival, and hence deserve to enjoy some preëminence. They give expression to the joy which the season inspires. But the robin and blackbird only peep and chuck at first, commonly, and the lark is silent and flitting. The bluebird at once fills the air with his sweet warbling, and the song sparrow from the top of a rail pours forth his most joyous strain. Both express their delight at the weather which permits them to return to their favorite haunts. They are the more welcome to man for it.

April 5, 1853   The bluebird comes to us bright in his vernal dress as bridegroom. Has he not got new feathers then?

March 11, 1854   Bluebirds' warbling curls in elms.

March 19, 1855 When I reach my landing I hear my first bluebird, somewhere about Cheney's trees by the river. I hear him out of the blue deeps, but do not yet see his blue body. He comes with a warble. Now first generally heard in the village.

April 9, 1856 Meanwhile a bluebird sits on the same oak, three rods off, pluming its wings. I hear faintly the warbling of one, apparently a quarter of a mile off, and am very slow to detect that it is even this one before me, which, in the intervals of pluming itself, is apparently practicing in an incredibly low voice.

May 11, 1856 A bluebird's nest and five eggs in a hollow apple tree three feet from ground near the old bank swallow pit, made with much stubble and dried grass. Can see the bird sitting from without.

July 12, 1856 Hear the plaintive note of young bluebirds, a reviving and gleaming of their blue ray.

September 27, 1856 The bluebird family revisit their box and warble as in spring.

February 18, 1857 I am excited by this wonderful air and go listening for the note of the bluebird or other comer. The very grain of the air seems to have undergone a change and is ready to split into the form of the bluebird's warble. Methinks if it were visible, or I could cast up some fine dust which would betray it, it would take a corresponding shape. The bluebird does not come till the air consents and his wedge will enter easily. The air over these fields is a foundry full of moulds for casting bluebirds' warbles.

Any sound uttered now would take that form, not of the harsh, vibrating, rending scream of the jay, but a softer, flowing, curling warble, like a purling stream or the lobes of flowing sand and clay. Here is the soft air, and the moist expectant apple trees, but not yet the bluebird. They do not quite attain to song.

February 24, 1857 I am surprised to hear the strain of a song sparrow from the riverside, and as I cross from the causeway to the hill, thinking of the bluebird, I that instant hear one's note from deep in the softened air. It is already 40°, and by noon is between 50° and 60°. As the day advances I hear more bluebirds and see their azure flakes settling on the fence-posts. Their short, rich, crispy warble curls through the air. Its grain now lies parallel to the curve of the bluebird's warble, like boards of the same lot.

March 2, 1859 The bluebird which some woodchopper or inspired walker is said to have seen in that sunny interval between the snow-storms is like a speck of clear blue sky seen near the end of a storm, reminding us of an ethereal region and a heaven which we had forgotten. Princes and magistrates are often styled serene, but what is their turbid serenity to that ethereal serenity which the bluebird embodies? His Most Serene Birdship! His soft warble melts in the ear, as the snow is melting in the valleys around. The bluebird comes and with his warble drills the ice and sets free the rivers and ponds and frozen ground. As the sand flows down the slopes a little way, assuming the forms of foliage where the frost comes out of the ground, so this little rill of melody flows a short way down the concave of the sky. The sharp whistle of the black-bird, too, is heard like single sparks or a shower of them shot up from the swamps and seen against the dark winter in the rear.

March 7, 1859 There are few, if any, so coarse and insensible that they are not interested to hear that the bluebird has come. The Irish laborer has learned to distinguish him and report his arrival. It is a part of the news of the season to a lawyer in his office and the mechanic in his shop, as well as to the farmer. One will remember, perchance, to tell you that he saw one a week ago in the next town or county. Citizens just come into the country to live put up a blue-bird box, and record in some kind of journal the date of the first arrival observed,—though it may be rather a late one. The farmer can tell you when he saw the first one, if you ask him within a week.

March 10, 1859 The bluebird on the apple tree, warbling so innocently to inquire if any of its mates are within call,—the angel of the spring! Fair and innocent, yet the offspring of the earth. The color of the sky above and of the subsoil beneath. Suggesting what sweet and innocent melody (terrestrial melody) may have its birth-place between the sky and the ground.

GENERAL

MISCELLANEOUS

March 4, 1840   I learned to-day that my ornithology had done me no service. The birds I heard, which fortunately did not come within the scope of my science, sung as freshly as if it had been the first morning of creation, and had for background to their song an untrodden wilderness, stretching through many a Carolina and Mexico of the soul.

April 25, 1841   A momentous silence reigns always in the woods, and their meaning seems just ripening into expression. But alas! they make no haste. The rush sparrow,[1] Nature's minstrel of serene hours, sings of an immense leisure and duration.

When I hear a robin sing at sunset, I cannot help contrasting the equanimity of Nature with the bustle and impatience of man. We return from the lyceum and caucus with such stir and excite-

---

[1][The field sparrow. See note in Chapter 15.]

ment as if a crisis were at hand; but no natural scene or sound sympathizes with us, for Nature is always silent and unpretending as at the break of day. She but rubs her eyelids.

September 29, 1842 To-day the lark sings again down in the meadow, and the robin peeps, and the bluebirds, old and young, have revisited their box, as if they would fain repeat the summer without the intervention of winter, if Nature would let them.

1850 In all my rambles I have seen no landscape which can make me forget Fair Haven. I still sit on its Cliff in a new spring day, and look over the awakening woods and the river, and hear the new birds sing, with the same delight as ever. It is as sweet a mystery to me as ever what this world is. Fair Haven Lake in the south, with its pine-covered island and its meadows, the hickories putting out fresh young yellowish leaves, and the oaks light-grayish ones, while the oven-bird thrums his sawyer-like strain, and the chewink rustles through the dry leaves or repeats his jingle on a tree-top, and the wood thrush, the genius of the wood, whistles for the first time his clear and thrilling strain,—it sounds as it did the first time I heard it. The sight of these budding woods intoxicates me,—this diet drink.

1850 Now, about the first of September, you will see flocks of small birds forming compact and distinct masses, as if they were not only animated by one spirit but actually held together by some invisible fluid or film, and will hear the sound of their wings rippling or fanning the air as they flow through it, flying, the whole mass, ricochet like a single bird,—or as they flow over the fence. Their mind must operate faster than man's, in proportion as their bodies do.

November 8, 1850 Everything stands silent and expectant. If I listen, I hear only the notes of a chickadee,—our most common and I may say native bird, most identified with our forests,—or perchance the scream of a jay, or perchance from the solemn depths of these woods I hear tolling far away the knell of one departed. Thought rushes in to fill the vacuum. As you walk, however, the partridge still bursts away. The silent, dry, almost leafless, certainly fruitless woods. You wonder what cheer that bird can find in them. The partridge bursts away from the foot of a shrub oak like its own dry fruit, immortal bird! This sound still startles us.

January 7, 1851 The snow is sixteen inches deep at least, but it is a mild and genial afternoon, as if it were the beginning of a January thaw. Take away the snow and it would not be winter but like many days in the fall. The birds acknowledge the difference in the air; the jays are more noisy, and the chickadees are oftener heard.

June 13, 1851 I hear, just as the night sets in, faint notes from time to time from some sparrow (?) falling asleep,—a vesper hymn,—and later, in the woods, the chuckling, rattling sound of some unseen bird on the near trees. The nighthawk booms wide awake.

June 14, 1851 Now the sun is fairly gone, I hear the dreaming frog,[1] and the whip-poor-will from some *darker* wood,—it is not far from eight,—and the cuckoo. The song sparrows sing quite briskly among the willows, as if it were spring again, and the blackbird's harsher note resounds over the meadows, and the veery's comes up from the wood.

★ ★ ★

In Conant's orchard I hear the faint cricket-like song of a sparrow saying its vespers, as if it were a link between the cricket and the bird. The robin sings now, though the moon shines silverly, and the veery jingles its trill.

July 10, 1851 The swallows are improving this short day, twittering as they fly, and the huckleberry-bird[2] repeats his jingling strain, and the song sparrow, more honest than most.

July 12, 1851 I hear that sort of throttled or chuckling note as of a bird flying high, now from this side, then from that.[3] . . . I am startled by the rapid transit of some wild animal across my path, a rabbit or a fox,—or you hardly know if it be not a bird. Looking down from the cliffs, the leaves of the tree-tops shine

---

[1]Toad? [Thoreau afterwards learned that his "dreaming frogs" were toads. In this case it was probably Fowler's toad.]

[2][The field sparrow. See Chapter 15.]

[3][Probably a cuckoo. See Mr. Gerald H. Thayer's account of the nocturnal flights of the black-billed cuckoo in *Bird-Lore*, September–October, 1903, vol. v, pp. 143–145.]

more than ever by day. Here and there a lightning-bug shows his greenish light over the tops of the trees.

As I return through the orchard, a foolish robin bursts away from his perch unnaturally, with the habits of man.

July 13, 1851 I hear, 4 P.M., a pigeon woodpecker on a dead pine near by, uttering a harsh and scolding scream, spying me. The chewink jingles on the tops of the bushes, and the rush sparrow,[1] the vireo, and oven-bird at a distance; and a robin sings, superior to all; and a barking dog has started something on the opposite side of the river; and now the wood thrush surpasses them all.

July 16, 1851 Now, at 4 P.M., I hear the pewee in the woods, and the cuckoo reminds me of some silence among the birds I had not noticed. The vireo (red-eyed?) sings like a robin at even, incessantly,—for I have now turned into Conant's woods. The ovenbird helps fill some pauses. . . . Here comes a small bird with a ricochet flight and a faint twittering note like a messenger from Elysium.

November 9, 1851 Now the leaves are gone the birds' nests are revealed, the brood being fledged and flown. There is a perfect adaptation in the material used in constructing a nest. There is one which I took from a maple on the causeway at Hubbard's Bridge. It is fastened to the twigs by white woolen strings (out of a shawl?), which it has picked up in the road, though it is more than half a

---

[1][The field sparrow. See note in Chapter 15.]

mile from a house; and the sharp eyes of the bird have discovered plenty of horsehairs out of the tail or mane, with which to give it form by their spring; with fine meadow hay for body, and the reddish woolly material which invests the ferns in the spring (apparently) for lining.

March 10, 1852 I was reminded, this morning before I rose, of those undescribed ambrosial mornings of summer which I can remember, when a thousand birds were heard gently twittering and ushering in the light, like the argument to a new canto of an epic and heroic poem. The serenity, the infinite promise, of such a morning! The song or twitter of birds drips from the leaves like dew. Then there was something divine and immortal in our life. When I have waked up on my couch in the woods and seen the day dawning, and heard the twittering of the birds.

April 2, 1852 6 A.M.—The sun is up. The water on the meadows is perfectly smooth and placid, reflecting the hills and clouds and trees. The air is full of the notes of birds,—song sparrows, redwings, robins (singing a strain), bluebirds,—and I hear also a lark,—as if all the earth had burst forth into song. The influence of this April morning has reached them, for they live out-of-doors all the night, and there is no danger that they will oversleep themselves such a morning.

April 4, 1852 P.M.—Going across Wheeler's large field beyond Potter's, saw a large flock of small birds go by, I am not sure what kind, the near ones continually overtaking the foremost, so that the whole flock appeared to roll over as it went forward. When they lit on a tree, they appeared at a distance to clothe it like dead leaves.

April 17, 1852   Gilpin says, "As the wheeling motion of the gull is beautiful, so also is the figured flight of the goose, the duck, and the widgeon; all of which are highly ornamental to coast-views, bays, and estuaries."[1] A flight of ducks adds to the wildness of our wildest river scenery. Undoubtedly the soaring and sailing of the hen-hawk, the red-shouldered buzzard (?), is the most ornamental, graceful, stately, beautiful to contemplate, of all the birds that ordinarily frequent our skies. The eagle is but a rare and casual visitor. The goose, the osprey, the great heron, though interesting, are either transient visitors or rarely seen; they either move through the air as passengers or too exclusively looking for their prey, but the hen-hawk soars like a creature of the air. The flight of martins is interesting in the same way. When I was young and compelled to pass my Sunday in the house without the aid of interesting books, I used to spend many an hour till the wished-for sundown watching the martins soar, from an attic window; and fortunate indeed did I deem myself when a hawk appeared in the heavens, though far toward the horizon against a downy cloud, and I searched for hours till I had found his mate. They, at least, took my thoughts from earthly things.

[1][*Remarks on Forest Scenery.*]

April 23, 1852 Vegetation starts when the earth's axis is sufficiently inclined; *i.e.*, it follows the sun. Insects and all the smaller animals (as well as many larger) follow vegetation. The fishes, the small fry, start probably for this reason; worms come out of the trees; buffaloes finally seek new pastures; water-bugs appear on the water, etc., etc. Next, the large fish and fish hawks, etc., follow the small fry; flycatchers follow the insects and worms. (The granivorous birds, who can depend on the supply of dry seeds of last year, are to some extent independent of the seasons, and can remain through the winter or come early in the spring, and they furnish food for a few birds of prey at that season.) Indians follow the buffaloes; trout, suckers, etc., follow the water-bugs, etc.; reptiles follow vegetation, insects, and worms; birds of prey, the flycatchers, etc. Man follows all, and all follow the sun. The greater or less abundance of food determines migrations. If the buds are deceived and suffer from frost, then are the birds. The great necessary of life for the brute creation is food; next, perhaps, shelter, *i.e.* a suitable climate; thirdly, perhaps, security from foes.

May 3, 1852 It requires so much closer attention to the habits of the birds, that, if for that reason only, I am willing to omit the gun.

May 7, 1852 I think that birds vary their notes considerably with the seasons. When I hear a bird singing, I cannot think of any words that will imitate it. What word can stand in place of a bird's note? You would have to bury [?] it, or surround it with a *chevaux de frise* of accents, and exhaust the art of the musical composer be-sides with your different bars, to represent it, and finally get a bird to sing it, to perform it. It has so little relation to words. The wood thrush[1] says *ah-tully-tully* for one strain. There appear to be one or more little warblers in the woods this morning which are new to the season, about which I am in doubt, myrtle-birds among them. For now, before the leaves, they begin to people the trees in this warm weather. The first wave of summer from the south.

June 4, 1852   The birds sing at dawn. What sounds to be awakened by! If only our sleep, our dreams, are such as to har-monize with the song, the warbling, of the birds, ushering in the day! They appear comparatively silent an hour or two later.

June 25, 1852   I observe that young birds are usually of a duller color and more speckled than old ones, as if for their protec-tion in their tender state. They have not yet the markings (and the beauty) which distinguish their species, and which betray it often, but by their colors are merged in the variety of colors of the season.

July 7, 1852   4 A.M.—The first really foggy morning. Yet be-fore I rise I hear the song of birds from out it, like the bursting of its bubbles with music, the bead on liquid just uncorked. Their song gilds thus the frostwork of the morning. As if the fog were a great sweet froth on the surface of land and water, whose fixed air

---

[1][The hermit thrush?]

escaped, whose bubbles burst with music. The sound of its evap-
oration, the fixed air of the morning just brought from the cellars
of the night escaping. The morning twittering of birds in perfect
harmony with it. . . . The fog condenses into fountains and
streams of music, as into the strain of the bobolink which I hear,
and runs off so. The music of the birds is the tinkling of the rills
that flow from it. I cannot see twenty rods.

July 30, 1852 What a gem is a bird's egg, especially a blue or
a green one, when you see one, broken or whole, in the woods! I
noticed a small blue egg this afternoon washed up by Flint's Pond
and half buried by white sand, and as it lay there, alternately wet
and dry, no color could be fairer, no gem could have a more ad-
vantageous or favorable setting. Probably it was shaken out of
some nest which overhung the water. I frequently meet with broken egg-shells where a crow, perchance, or some other thief has
been marauding. And is not that shell something very precious that
houses that winged life?

August 6, 1852 How different the feeble twittering of the
birds here at sunrise from the full quire of the spring! Only the
wood thrush, a huckleberry-bird or two, or chickadee, the scream
of a flicker or a jay, or the caw of a crow, and commonly only an
alarmed note of a robin. A solitary peawai[1] may be heard, per-

---

[1][Wood pewee.]

chance, or a red-eye, but no thrashers, or catbirds, or oven-birds, or the jingle of the chewink. I hear the ominous twittering of the goldfinch over all.

March 18, 1853   How eagerly the birds of passage penetrate the northern ice, watching for a crack by which to enter! Forthwith the swift ducks will be seen winging their way along the rivers and up the coast. They watch the weather more sedulously than the teamster. All nature is thus forward to move with the revolution of the seasons. Now for some days the birds have been ready by myriads, a flight or two south, to invade our latitudes and, with this milder and serener weather, resume their flight.

★   ★   ★

I came forth expecting to hear new birds, and I am not disappointed. We know well what to count upon. Their coming is more sure than the arrival of the sailing and steaming packets. Almost while I listen for this purpose, I hear the *chuck, chuck* of a blackbird in the sky, whom I cannot detect. So small an object is lost in the wide expanse of the heavens, though no obstacle intervenes. When your eye has detected it, you can follow it well enough, but it is difficult to bring your sight to bear on it, as to direct a telescope to a particular star. How many hawks fly undetected, yet within sight, above our heads! And there's the great gull I came to see, already fishing in front of Bittern Cliff. Now he stoops to the water for his prey, but sluggishly, methinks. He re-

quires a high and perhaps a head wind to make his motions graceful. I see no mate. He must have come up, methinks, before the
storm was over, unless he started when I did. I believe it is only an
easterly wind or storm brings him up.

March 21, 1853   Morning along the river.

The air full of song sparrows,—*swedit swedit swedit* and then a
rapid jingle or trill, holding up its head without fear of me, the innocent, humble bird, or one pursuing another through the alders
by the waterside. Why are the early birds found most along the
water? These song sparrows are now first heard *commonly.* The
blackbirds, too, create some melody. And the bluebirds, how
sweet their warble in the soft air, heard over the water! The robin
is heard further off, and seen flying rapidly, hurriedly through the
orchard. And now the elms suddenly ring with the *chill-lill-lill* and
canary-like notes of the *Fringilla hyemalis,* which fill the air more
than those of any bird yet,—a little strange they sound because
they do not tarry to breed with us,—a ringing sound.

March 22, 1853   Already I hear from the railroad the plaintive
strain of a lark or two. They sit now conspicuous on the bare russet
ground. The tinkling bubbles of the song sparrow are wafted from
distant fence-posts,—little rills of song that begin to flow and tinkle as soon as the frost is out of the ground. The blackbird tries to
sing, as it were with a bone in his throat, or to whistle and sing at
once. Whither so fast, the restless creature,—*chuck, chuck,* at every
rod, and now and then *whistle-ter-ee?* The *chill-lill* of the blue snow-

birds is heard again. A partridge goes off on Fair Haven Hill-side with a sudden whir like the wad of a six-pounder, keeping just level with the tops of the sprouts. These birds and quails go off like a report.

April 16, 1853 Birds loosen and expand their feathers and look larger in the rain.

May 4, 1853 The woods and paths next them now ring with the silver jingle of the field sparrow, the medley of the brown thrasher, the honest *qui vive* of the chewink, or his jingle from the top of a low copse tree, while his mate scratches in the dry leaves beneath; the black and white creeper is hopping along the oak boughs, head downward, pausing from time to time to utter its note like a fine, delicate saw-sharpening; and ever and anon rises clear over all the smooth, rich melody of the wood thrush.

May 10, 1853 There is now a multiplicity of sounds, in which the few faint spring ones are drowned. The birds are in full blast, singing, warbling, chirping, humming. Yet we do not receive more ideas through our ears than before. The storms and ducks of spring have swept by and left us to the repose of summer, the farmers to the ignoble pursuits of planting and hoeing corn and potatoes. The summer is not bracing, as when you hear the note of the jay in the cool air of October from the rustling chestnut woods.

June 16, 1853 Before 4 A.M., or sunrise, the sound of chip-birds and robins and bluebirds, etc., fills the air and is incessant. It is a crowing on the roost, methinks, as the cock crows before he goes abroad. They do not sing deliberately as at eve, but greet the morning with incessant twitter. Even the crickets seem to join the concert. Yet I think it is not the same every morning, though it may be fair. An hour or two later it is comparative silence. The awakening of the birds, a tumultuous twittering.

November 8, 1853 Birds generally wear the russet dress of nature at this season. They have their fall no less than the plants; the bright tints depart from their foliage or feathers, and they flit past like withered leaves in rustling flocks. The sparrow is a withered leaf.

December 5, 1853 Saw and heard a downy woodpecker on an apple tree. Have not many winter birds, like this and the chickadee, a sharp note like tinkling glass or icicles? The *chip* of the tree sparrow, also, and the whistle of the shrike, are they not wintry in the same way? And the sonorous hooting owl? But not so the jay and *Fringilla linaria*, and still less the crow.

February 14, 1854 In Stow's wood, by the Deep Cut, hear the *gnah gnah* of the white-breasted, black-capped nuthatch. I went up the bank and stood by the fence. A little family of titmice gathered about me, searching for their food both on the ground and on the trees, with great industry and intentness, and now and then pursuing each other. There were two nuthatches at least, talking to each other. One hung with his head down on a large pitch pine, pecking the bark for a long time,—leaden blue above, with a black cap and white breast. It uttered almost constantly a faint but sharp *quivet* or creak, difficult to trace home, which appeared to be answered by a baser and louder *gnah gnah* from the other. A downy woodpecker also, with the red spot on his hind head and his cassock open behind, showing his white robe, kept up an incessant loud tapping on another pitch pine. All at once an active little brown creeper makes its appearance, a small, rather slender bird, with a long tail and sparrow-colored back, and white beneath. It commences at the bottom of a tree and glides up very rapidly, then suddenly darts to the bottom of a new tree and repeats the same movement, not resting long in one place or on one tree. These birds are all feeding and flitting along together, but the chickadees are the most numerous and the most confiding. I observe that three of the four thus associated, *viz.* the chickadee, nuthatch, and woodpecker, have black crowns,—at least the first two, very conspicuous black caps. I cannot but think that this sprightly association and readiness to burst into song has to do with the prospect of spring,—more light and warmth and thawing weather. The titmice keep up an incessant faint tinkling *tchip*; now and then one utters a lively *day day day*, and once or twice one commenced a gurgling strain quite novel, startling, and springlike.

March 1, 1854   As for the birds of the past winter: I have seen but three hawks,—one early in the winter and two lately; have heard the hooting owl pretty often late in the afternoon. Crows have not been numerous, but their cawing was heard chiefly in pleasanter mornings. Blue jays have blown the trumpet of winter as usual, but they, as all birds, are most lively in spring-like days. The chickadees have been the *prevailing* bird. The partridge common enough. One ditcher tells me that he saw two robins in Moore's Swamp a month ago. I have not seen a quail, though a few have been killed in the thaws. Four or five downy woodpeckers. The white-breasted nuthatch four or five times. Tree sparrows one or more at a time, oftener than any bird that comes to us from the north. Two pigeon woodpeckers, I think, lately. One dead shrike, and perhaps one or two live ones. Have heard of two white owls,— one about Thanksgiving time and one in midwinter. One short-eared owl in December. Several flocks of snow buntings for a week in the severest storm, and in December, last past. One grebe in Walden just before it froze completely. And two brown creepers once in middle of February. Channing says he saw a little olivaceous-green bird lately. I have not seen an *F. linaria*, nor a pine grosbeak, nor an *F. hyemalis* this winter, though the first was the prevailing bird last winter.

March 12, 1854 All these birds do their warbling especially in the still, sunny hours after sunrise, as rivers twinkle at their sources. Now is the time to be abroad and hear them, as you detect the slightest ripple in smooth water. As with tinkling sounds the sources of streams burst their icy fetters, so the rills of music begin to flow and swell the general quire of spring.

May 10, 1854   In Boston yesterday an ornithologist said significantly, "If you held the bird in your hand—;" but I would rather hold it in my affections.

August 10, 1854   The tinkling notes of goldfinches and bobolinks which we hear nowadays are of one character and peculiar to the season. They are not voluminous flowers, but rather nuts, of sound,—ripened seeds of sound. It is the tinkling of ripened grains in Nature's basket. It is like the sparkle on water,—a sound produced by friction on the crisped air.

April 6, 1855   The banks of the river are alive with song sparrows and tree sparrows. They now sing in advance of vegetation, as the flowers will blossom,—those slight tinkling, twittering sounds called the singing of birds; they have come to enliven the bare twigs before the buds show any signs of starting.

May 3, 1855   Humphrey Buttrick, one of eight who alone returned from Texas out of twenty-four, says he can find woodcock's eggs; now knows of several nests; had seen them setting with snow around them; and that Melvin has seen partridges' eggs some days ago. He has seen crows building this year. Found in a hen-hawk's nest once the legs of a cat. Has known of several goshawks' nests (or what he calls some kind of eagle; Garfield called it the Cape eagle); one in a shrub oak, with eggs.[1] Last year his dog caught seven black ducks so far grown that he got sixty cents a pair for them; takes a pretty active dog to catch such. He frequently finds or hears of them. Knew of a nest this year. Also finds wood ducks' nests. Has very often seen partridges drum close to him. Has watched one for an hour. They strike the body with their wings. He shot a white-headed eagle from Carlisle Bridge. It fell in the

---

[1][There are no authentic records of the nesting of the goshawk in Massachusetts.]

water, and his dog was glad to let it alone. He suggested that my fish hawks found pouts in holes made by ice.

May 17, 1855   Waked up at 2.30 by the peep of robins, which were aroused by a fire at the pail-factory about two miles west. I hear that the air was full of birds singing thereabouts. It rained gently at the same time, though not steadily.

August 5, 1855   8 P.M.—On river to see swallows.

At this hour the robins fly to high, thick oaks (as this swamp white oak) to roost for the night. The wings of the chimney swallows flying near me make a whistling sound like a duck's. Is not this peculiar among the swallows? They flutter much for want of tail. I see martins about. Now many swallows in the twilight, after circling eight feet high, come back two or three hundred feet high and then go down the river.

September 15, 1855   Three weeks ago saw many brown thrashers, catbirds, robins, etc., on wild cherries. They are worth raising for the birds about you, though objectionable on account of caterpillars.

October 22, 1855   Birds are certainly afraid of man. They [allow] all other creatures,—cows and horses, etc.,—excepting only one or two kinds, birds or beasts of prey, to come near them, but not man. What does this fact signify? Does it not signify that man, too, is a beast of prey to them? Is he, then, a true lord of creation, whose subjects are afraid of him, and with reason? They know very well that he is not humane, as he pretends to be.

December 11, 1855   Standing there, though in this *bare* November landscape, I am reminded of the incredible phenomenon of small birds in winter,—that ere long, amid the cold powdery snow, as it were a fruit of the season, will come twittering a flock of delicate crimson-tinged birds, lesser redpolls, to sport and feed on the seeds and buds now just ripe for them on the sunny side of a wood, shaking down the powdery snow there in their cheerful social feeding, as if it were high midsummer to them. These crimson aerial creatures have wings which would bear them quickly to the regions of summer, but here is all the summer they want. What a rich contrast! tropical colors, crimson breasts, on cold white snow! Such etherealness, such delicacy in their forms, such ripeness in their colors, in this stern and barren season! It is as surprising as if you were to find a brilliant crimson flower which flourished amid snows. They greet the chopper and the hunter in their furs. Their Maker gave them the last touch and launched them forth the day of the Great Snow.[1] He made this bitter, imprisoning cold before which man quails, but He made at the same time these warm and glowing creatures to twitter and be at home in it. He said not only, Let there be linnets in winter, but linnets of rich plumage and pleasing twitter, bearing summer in their natures. The snow will be three feet deep, the ice will be two feet thick, and last night, per-

---

[1][The "Great Snow" to which Thoreau refers several times in his *Journal* and in *Walden* occurred in 1780, as we learn from the entry for March 28, 1856.]

chance, the mercury sank to thirty degrees below zero. All the fountains of nature seem to be sealed up. The traveller is frozen on his way. But under the edge of yonder birch wood will be a little flock of crimson-breasted lesser redpolls, busily feeding on the seeds of the birch and shaking down the powdery snow! As if a flower were created to be now in bloom, a peach to be now first fully ripe on its stem. I am struck by the perfect confidence and success of nature. There is no question about the existence of these delicate creatures, their adaptedness to their circumstances. There is super-added superfluous paintings and adornments, a crystalline, jewel-like health and soundness, like the colors reflected from ice-crystals.

When some rare northern bird like the pine grosbeak is seen thus far south in the winter, he does not suggest poverty, but dazzles us with his beauty. There is in them a warmth akin to the warmth that melts the icicle. Think of these brilliant, warm-colored, and richly warbling birds, birds of paradise, dainty-footed, downy-clad, in the midst of a New England, a Canadian winter. The woods and fields, now somewhat solitary, being deserted by their more tender summer residents, are now frequented by these rich but delicately tinted and hardy northern immigrants of the air. Here is no imperfection to be suggested. The winter, with its snow and ice, is not an evil to be corrected. It is as it was designed and made to be, for the artist has had leisure to add beauty to use. My acquaintances, angels from the north. I had a vision thus prospectively of these birds as I stood in the swamps. I saw this familiar—too *familiar*—fact at a different angle, and I was charmed and haunted by it. But I could only attain to be thrilled and enchanted, as by the sound of a strain of music dying away. I had seen into paradisiac regions, with their air and sky, and I was no longer wholly or merely a denizen of this vulgar earth. Yet had I hardly a foothold there. I was only sure that I was charmed, and no mistake. It is only necessary to behold thus the least fact or phenomenon, however familiar, from a point a hair's breadth aside from our habitual path or routine, to be overcome, enchanted by its beauty and significance. Only what we have touched and worn is trivial,—our scurf, repetition, tradition, conformity. To perceive freshly, with fresh senses, is to be inspired. Great winter itself looked like a precious gem, reflecting rainbow colors from one angle.

December 21, 1855   Going to the post-office at 9 A.M. this very pleasant morning, I hear and see tree sparrows on Wheildon's pines, and just beyond scare a downy woodpecker and a brown creeper in company, from near the base of a small elm within three feet of me. The former dashes off with a loud rippling of the wing, and the creeper flits across the street to the base of another small elm, whither I follow. At first he hides behind the base, but ere long works his way upward and comes in sight. He is a gray-brown, a low curve from point of beak to end of tail, resting flat against the tree.

December 30, 1855   He who would study birds' nests must look for them in November and in winter as well as in midsummer, for then the trees are bare and he can see them, and the swamps and streams are frozen and he can approach new kinds. He will often be surprised to find how many have haunted where he little suspected, and will receive many hints accordingly, which he can act upon in the summer. I am surprised to find many new ones (*i.e.* not new species) in groves which I had examined several times with particular care in the summer.

January 18, 1856   Observed some of those little hard galls on the high blueberry pecked or eaten into by some bird (or *possibly* mouse), for the little white grubs which lie curled up in them. What entomologists the birds are! Most men do not suspect that there are grubs in them, and how secure the latter seem under these thick, dry shells! Yet there is no secret but it is confided to some one.

February 4, 1856   I have often wondered how red cedars could have sprung up in some pastures which I knew to be miles distant from the nearest fruit-bearing cedar, but it now occurs to me that these and barberries, etc., may be planted by the crows, and probably other birds.

February 8, 1856   E. Garfield says there were many quails here last fall, but that they are suffering now. One night as he was spearing on Conant's cranberry meadow, just north the pond, his dog caught a sheldrake in the water by the shore. Some days ago he saw what he thought a hawk, as white as snow, fly over the pond, but it *may* have been a white owl (which last he never saw).[1] He sometimes sees a hen-hawk in the winter, but never a partridge or other small hawk at this season. Speaks again of that large speckled hawk he killed once, which some called a "Cape eagle." Had a humbird's nest behind their house last summer, and was amused to see the bird drive off other birds; would pursue a robin and alight on his back; let none come near. I. Garfield saw one's nest on a horizontal branch of a white pine near the Charles Miles house, about seven feet from ground. E. Garfield spoke of the wren's nest as not uncommon, hung in the grass of the meadows, and how swiftly and easily the bird would run through a winrow of hay.

April 9, 1856 The air is full of birds, and as I go down the causeway, I distinguish the seringo note. You have only to come forth each morning to be surely advertised of each newcomer into these broad meadows. Many a larger animal might be concealed, but a cunning ear detects the arrival of each new species of bird. These birds give evidence that they prefer the fields of New England to all other climes, deserting for them the warm and fertile south. Here is their paradise. It is here they express the most happiness by song and action. Though these spring mornings may often be frosty and rude, they are exactly tempered to their constitutions, and call forth the sweetest strains.

[1]Was it a gyrfalcon?

June 6, 1856   How well suited the lining of a bird's nest, not only for the comfort of the young, but to keep the eggs from breaking! Fine elastic grass stems or root-fibres, pine-needles, or hair, or the like. These tender and brittle things which you can hardly carry in cotton lie there without harm.

February 20, 1857   What is the relation between a bird and the ear that appreciates its melody, to whom, perchance, it is more charming and significant than to any else? Certainly they are intimately related, and the one was made for the other. It is a natural fact. If I were to discover that a certain kind of stone by the pond-shore was affected, say partially disintegrated, by a particular natural sound, as of a bird or insect, I see that one could not be completely described without describing the other. I am that rock by the pond-side.

September 7, 1857   Returning to my boat, at the white maple, I see a small round flock of birds, perhaps blackbirds, dart through the air, as thick as a charge of shot,—now comparatively thin, with regular intervals of sky between them, like the holes in the strainer of a watering-pot, now dense and dark, as if closing up their ranks when they roll over one another and stoop downward.

March 17, 1858   Sitting under the handsome scarlet oak beyond the hill, I hear a faint note far in the wood which reminds me of the robin. Again I hear it; it is he,—an occasional peep. These notes of the earliest birds seem to invite forth vegetation. No doubt the plants concealed in the earth hear them and rejoice. They wait for this assurance.

March 18, 1858 How much more habitable a few birds make the fields! At the end of winter, when the fields are bare and there is nothing to relieve the monotony of the withered vegetation, our life seems reduced to its lowest terms. But let a bluebird come and warble over them, and what a change! The note of the first blue-bird in the air answers to the purling rill of melted snow beneath. It is eminently soft and soothing, and, as surely as the thermome-ter, indicates a higher temperature. It is the accent of the south wind, its vernacular. It is modulated by the south wind. The song sparrow is more sprightly, mingling its notes with the rustling of the brash along the watersides, but it is at the same time more *ter-rene* than the bluebird. The first woodpecker comes screaming into the empty house and throws open doors and windows wide, call-ing out each of them to let the neighbors know of its return. But heard further off it is very suggestive of ineffable associations which cannot be distinctly recalled,—of long-drawn summer hours,—and thus it, also, has the effect of music. I was not aware that the capacity to hear the woodpecker had slumbered within me so long. When the blackbird gets to a *conqueree* he seems to be dreaming of the sprays that are to be and on which he is to perch. The robin does not come singing, but utters a somewhat anxious or inquisitive peep at first. The song sparrow is immediately most at home of any that I have named. I see this afternoon as many as a dozen bluebirds on the warm side of a wood.

★ ★ ★

Each new year is a surprise to us. We find that we had virtually forgotten the note of each bird, and when we hear it again it is remembered like a dream, reminding us of a previous state of existence. How happens it that the associations it awakens are always pleasing, never saddening; reminiscences of our sanest hours? The voice of nature is always encouraging.

May 10, 1858 It is remarkable how many new birds have come all at once to-day. The hollow-sounding note of the ovenbird is heard from the depth of the wood. The warbling vireo cheers the elms with a strain for which they must have pined. The trees, in respect to these new arrivers, have been so many empty music-halls. The oriole is seen darting like a bright flash with clear whistle from one tree-top to another over the street. The very catbird's mew in the copse harmonizes with the bare twigs, as it were shaming them into life and verdure, and soon he mounts upon a tree and is a new creature. Toward night the wood thrush ennobles the wood and the world with his strain.

June 7, 1858 It is evidence enough against crows and hawks and owls, proving their propensity to rob birds' nests of eggs and young, that smaller birds pursue them so often. You do not need the testimony of so many farmers' boys when you can see and hear

the small birds daily crying "Thief and murder" after these spoil-
ers. What does it signify, the kingbird, blackbird, swallow, etc.,
etc., pursuing a crow? They say plainly enough: "I know you of
old, you villain; you want to devour my eggs or young. I have
often caught you at it, and I'll publish you now." And probably the
crow pursuing the fish hawk and eagle proves that the latter sometimes devour their young.

June 16, 1858   No doubt thousands of birds' nests have been
destroyed by the flood,—blackbirds', bobolinks', song sparrows',
etc. I see a robin's nest high above the water with the young just
dead and the old bird in the water, apparently killed by the abundance of rain, and afterward I see a fresh song sparrow's nest which
has been flooded and destroyed.

July 16, 1858   About the mountains were wilder and rarer
birds, more or less arctic, like the vegetation. I did not even *hear* the
robin on them, and when I had left them a few miles behind, it was
a great change and surprise to hear the lark, the wood pewee, the
robin, and the bobolink (for the last had not done singing). On the
mountains, especially at Tuckerman's Ravine, the notes even of familiar birds sounded strange to me. I hardly knew the wood thrush
and veery and oven-bird at first. They sing differently there.[1] In
two instances,—going down the Mt. Jefferson road and along the

---

[1][His wood thrush and veery of Tuckerman's Ravine were probably the olive-
backed thrush and Bicknell's thrush, respectively.]

road in the Franconia Notch,—I started an *F. hyemalis* within two feet, close to the roadside, but looked in vain for a nest. They alight and sit thus close. I doubt if the chipping sparrow is found about the mountains.

March 7, 1859 It is a good plan to go to some old orchard on the south side of a hill, sit down, and listen, especially in the morning when all is still. You can thus often hear the distant warble of some bluebird lately arrived, which, if you had been walking, would not have been audible to you. As I walk, these first mild spring days, with my coat thrown open, stepping over tinkling rills of melting snow, excited by the sight of the bare ground, especially the reddish subsoil where it is exposed by a cutting, and by the few green radical leaves, I stand still, shut my eyes, and listen from time to time, in order to hear the note of some bird of passage just arrived.

April 8, 1859 When the question of the protection of birds comes up, the legislatures regard only a low use and never a high use; the best-disposed legislators employ one, perchance, only to examine their crops and see how many grubs or cherries they contain, and never to study their dispositions, or the beauty of their plumage, or listen and report on the sweetness of their song. The legislature will preserve a bird professedly not because it is a beautiful creature, but because it is a good scavenger or the like. This, at least, is the defense set up. It is as if the question were whether some celebrated singer of the human race—some Jenny Lind or another—did more harm or good, should be destroyed, or not, and therefore a committee should be appointed, not to listen to her singing at all, but to examine the contents of her stomach and see if she devoured anything which was injurious to the farmers and gardeners, or which they cannot spare.

September 1, 1859 If you would study the birds now, go where their food is, *i.e.* the berries, especially to the wild black cherries, elder-berries, poke berries, mountain-ash berries, and ere long the barberries, and for pigeons the acorns. In the sprout-land behind Britton's Camp, I came to a small black cherry full of fruit, and then, for the first time for a long while, I see and hear cherry-birds—their shrill and fine seringo[1]—and the note of robins, which of late are scarce. We sit near the tree and listen to the now unusual sounds of these birds, and from time to time one or two come dashing from out the sky toward this tree, till, seeing us, they whirl, disappointed, and perhaps alight on some neighboring twigs and wait till we are gone. The cherry-birds and robins seem to know the locality of every wild cherry in the town. You are as sure to find them on them now, as bees and butterflies on the this-tles. If we stay long, they go off with a fling, to some other cherry tree, which they know of but we do not. The neighborhood of a wild cherry full of fruit is now, for the notes of birds, a little spring

---

[1][Thoreau's word for a note of the quality of the cedar waxwing's. See Chapter 15.]

come back again, and when, a mile or two from this, I was pluck-ing a basketful of elder-berries (for which it was rather early yet), there too, to my surprise, I came on a flock of golden robins and of bluebirds, apparently feeding on them. Excepting the vaccin-iums, now past prime and drying up, the cherries and elder-berries are the two prevailing fruits now. We had remarked on the general scarcity and silence of the birds, but when we came to the localities of these fruits, there again we found the berry-eating birds assem-bled,—young (?) orioles and bluebirds at the elder-berries.

November 11, 1859 Also, October 24th, riding home from Acton, I saw the withered leaves blown from an oak by the road-side dashing off, gyrating, and surging upward into the air, so ex-actly like a flock of birds sporting with one another that, for a min-ute at least, I could not be sure they were not birds; and it suggested how far the motions of birds, like those of these leaves, might be determined by currents of air, *i.e.*, how far the bird learns to con-form to such currents.

January 5, 1860 How much the snow reveals! I see where the downy woodpecker has worked lately by the chips of bark and rot-ten wood scattered over the snow, though I rarely see him in the winter. Once to-day, however, I hear his sharp voice, even like a woodchuck's. Also I have occasionally seen where (probably) a flock of goldfinches in the morning had settled on a hemlock's top, by the snow strewn with scales, literally blackened or darkened with them for a rod. And now, about the hill in front of Smith's, I see where the quails have run along the roadside, and can count the number of the bevy better than if I saw them. Are they not peculiar in this, as compared with partridges,—that they run in company, while at this season I see but [one] or two partridges together?

January 22, 1860 Birds are commonly very rare in the winter. They are much more common at some times than at others. I see more tree sparrows in the beginning of the winter (especially when snow is falling) than in the course of it. I think that by observation I could tell in what kind of weather afterward these were most to be seen. Crows come about houses and streets in very cold weather and deep snows, and they are heard cawing in pleasant, thawing winter weather, and their note is then a pulse by which you feel the quality of the air, *i.e.*, when cocks crow. For the most part, lesser redpolls and pine grosbeaks do not appear at all. Snow buntings are very wandering. They were quite numerous a month ago, and now seem to have quit the town. They seem to ramble about the country at will.

January 29, 1860 Not only the Indian, but many wild birds and quadrupeds and insects, welcomed the apple tree to these shores. As it grew apace, the bluebird, robin, cherry-bird, king-bird, and many more came with a rush and built their nests in it, and so became orchard-birds. The woodpecker found such a savory morsel under its bark that he perforated it in a ring quite round the tree, a thing he had never done before. It did not take the partridge long to find out how sweet its buds were, and every winter day she flew and still flies from the wood to pluck them, much to the farmer's sorrow. The rabbit too was not slow to learn the taste of its twigs and bark. The owl crept into the first one that became hollow, and fairly hooted with delight, finding it just the place for him. He settled down into it, and has remained there ever since. The lackey caterpillar saddled her eggs on the very first twig that was formed, and it has since divided her affections with the wild cherry; and the canker-worm also in a measure abandoned the elm to feed on it. And when the fruit was ripe, the squirrel half carried, half rolled, it to his hole, and even the musquash crept up the bank and greedily devoured it; and when it was frozen and thawed, the crow and jay did not disdain to peck it. And the beautiful wood duck, having made up her mind to stay a while longer with us, has concluded that there is no better place for her too.

August 28, 1860   There was no prolonged melody of birds on the summit of Monadnock. They for the most part emitted sounds there more in harmony with the silent rocks,—a faint chipping or *chink*ing, often somewhat as of two stones struck together.

September 1, 1860   See how artfully the seed of a cherry is placed in order that a bird may be compelled to transport it. It is placed in the very midst of a tempting pericarp, so that the creature that would devour a cherry must take a stone into its mouth. The bird is bribed with the pericarp to take the stone with it and do this little service for Nature. Cherries are especially birds' food, and many kinds are called birds' cherry, and unless we plant the seeds occasionally, I shall think the birds have the best right to them. Thus a bird's wing is added to the cherry-stone which was wing-less, and it does not wait for winds to transport it.

October 7, 1860 Rice[1] says that when a boy, playing with darts with his brother Israel, one of them sent up his dart when a flock of crows was going over. One of the crows followed it down to the earth, picked it up, and flew off with it a quarter of a mile before it dropped it. He has observed that young wood ducks swim faster than the old, which is a fortunate provision, for they can thus retreat and hide in the weeds while their parents fly off. He says that you must shoot the little dipper as soon as it comes up,—before the water is fairly off its eyes,—else it will dive at the flash.

[1][Reuben Rice, of Concord.]

Twenty-Three

DOMESTIC BIRDS

DUCKS

April 7, 1853 Approach near to Simon Brown's ducks, on river. They are continually bobbing their heads under water in a shallow part of the meadow, more under water than above. I infer that the wild employ themselves likewise. You are most struck with the apparent ease with which they glide away,—not seeing the motion of their feet,—as by their wills.

June 29 1856 A man by the riverside[1] told us that he had two young ducks which he let out to seek their food along the riverside at low tide that morning. At length he noticed that one remained stationary amid the grass or salt weeds and something prevented its following the other. He went to its rescue and found its foot shut tightly in a quahog's shell amid the grass which the tide had left. He took up all together, carried to his house, and his wife opened the shell with a knife, released the duck, and cooked the quahog.

[1][In New Bedford, where Thoreau was visiting Mr. Daniel Ricketson.]

DOMESTIC FOWL

July 11, 1851   And now, at half-past 10 o'clock, I hear the cockerels crow in Hubbard's barns, and morning is already anticipated. It is the feathered, wakeful thought in us that anticipates the following day. This sound is wonderfully exhilarating at all times. These birds are worth far more to me for their crowing and cackling than for their drumsticks and eggs. How singular the connection of the hen with the man,—that she leaves her eggs in his barns always! She is a domestic fowl, though still a little shyish of him. I cannot help looking at the whole as an experiment still and wondering that in each case it succeeds. There is no doubt at last but hens may be kept. They will put their eggs in your barn by a tacit agreement. They will not wander far from your yard.

July 19, 1851   I see that hens, too, follow the cows feeding near the house, like the cow troopial, and for the same object. They cannot so well scare up insects for themselves. This is the dog the cowbird uses to start up its insect game.

July 22, 1851   I hear the cockerels crow through it,[1] and the rich crow of young roosters, that sound indicative of the bravest, rudest health, hoarse without cold, hoarse with rude health. That crow is all-nature-compelling; famine and pestilence flee before it.

January 15, 1852   It is good to see Minott's hens pecking and scratching the ground. What never-failing health they suggest!

[1][Fog.]

Even the sick hen is so naturally sick,—like a green leaf turning to brown. No wonder men love to have hens about them and hear their creaking note. They are even laying eggs from time to time still,—the undespairing race!

June 17, 1852 I hear the universal cock-crowing with surprise and pleasure, as if I never heard it before. What a tough fellow! How native to the earth! Neither wet nor dry, cold nor warm, kills him.

July 6, 1852 When the hen hatches ducks they do not mind her clucking. They lead the hen. Chickens and ducks are well set on the earth. What great legs they have! This part is early developed. A perfect Antæus is a young duck in this respect, deriving a steady stream of health and strength, for he rarely gets off it, ready either for land or water. Nature is not on her last legs yet. A chick's stout legs! If they were a little larger they would injure the globe's tender organization with their scratching. Then, for digestion, consider their crops and what they put into them in the course of a day! Consider how well fitted to endure the fatigue of a day's excursion. A young chick will run all day in pursuit of grasshoppers and occasionally vary its exercise by scratching, go to bed at night with a protuberant crop, and get up early in the morning ready for a new start.

July 25, 1852 As I came along, the whole earth resounded with the crowing of cocks, from the eastern unto the western horizon, and as I passed a yard, I saw a white rooster on the topmost rail of a fence pouring forth his challenges for destiny to come on. This salutation was travelling round the world; some six hours since had resounded through England, France, and Spain; then the sun passed over a belt of silence where the Atlantic flows, except a clarion here and there from some cooped-up cock upon the waves, till greeted with a general all-hail along the Atlantic shore.

April 2, 1853 The farmers are trembling for their poultry nowadays. I heard the scream of hens, and a tumult among their mistresses (at Dugan's), calling them and scaring away the hawk, yesterday. They say they do not lose by hawks in midsummer. White quotes Linnæus as saying of hawks, "Paciscuntur inducias cum avibus, quamdiu cuculus cuculat," but White doubts it.[1]

June 2, 1853 The birds are wide awake, as if knowing that this fog presages a fair day. I ascend Nawshawtuct from the north side. I am aware that I yield to the same influence which inspires the birds and the cockerels, whose hoarse courage I hear now vaunted. So men should crow in the morning. I would crow like chanticleer in the morning, with all the lustiness that the new day imparts, without thinking of the evening, when I and all of us shall go to roost,—with all the humility of the cock, that takes his perch upon the highest rail and wakes the country with his clarion. Shall not men be inspired as much as cockerels?

[1][Gilbert White, *Natural History of Selborne*, letter of Sept. 13, 1774, to Daines Barrington. "They make a truce with the birds as long as the cuckoo sings."]

November 23, 1853   The cocks are the only birds I hear, but they are a host. They crow as freshly and bravely as ever, while poets go down the stream, degenerate into science and prose.

October 19, 1855   Therien tells me, when I ask if he has seen or heard any large birds lately, that he heard a cock crow this morning, a wild one, in the woods. It seems a dozen fowls (chickens) were lost out of the cars here a fortnight ago. Poland has caught some, and they have one at the shanty, but this cock, at least, is still abroad and can't be caught. If they could survive the winter, I suppose we should have had wild hens before now.

July 25, 1856   The haymakers getting in the hay from Hubbard's meadow tell me the cock says we are going to have a long spell of dry weather or else very wet. "Well, there's some difference between them," I answer; "how do you know it?" "I just heard a cock crow at noon, and that's a sure sign it will either be very dry or very wet."

December 4, 1856   Sophia says that just before I came home Min[1] caught a mouse and was playing with it in the yard. It had got away from her once or twice, and she had caught it again; and now it was stealing off again, as she lay complacently watching it with her paws tucked under her, when her friend Riordan's stout but solitary cock stepped up inquisitively, looked down at it with one eye, turning his head, then picked it up by the tail and gave it two or

---

[1][The Thoreaus' cat.]

three whacks on the ground, and giving it a dexterous toss into the air, caught it in its open mouth, and it went head foremost and alive down his capacious throat in the twinkling of an eye, never again to be seen in this world, Min, all the while, with paws comfortably tucked under her, looking on unconcerned. What matters it one mouse more or less to her? The cock walked off amid the currant bushes, stretched his neck up, and gulped once or twice, and the deed was accomplished, and then he crowed lustily in celebration of the exploit. It might be set down among the *gesta* (if not *digesta*) *Gallorum.* There were several human witnesses. It is a question whether Min ever understood where that mouse went to.

February 4, 1857 Minott says that Dr. Heywood used to have a crazy hen (and he, too, has had one). She went about by herself uttering a peevish *craw craw*, and did not lay. One day he was going along on the narrow peninsula of Goose Pond looking for ducks, away in Walden Woods a mile and a half from Heywood's, when he met this very hen, which passed close by him, uttering as usual a faint *craw craw*. He knew her perfectly well, and says that he was never so surprised at anything in his life. How she had escaped the foxes and hawks was more than he knew.

February 8, 1847 Riordan's solitary cock, standing on such an icy snow-heap, feels the influence of the softened air, and the steam from patches of bare ground here and there, and has found his voice again. The warm air has thawed the music in his throat, and he crows lustily and unweariedly, his voice rising to the last.

{ 493 }

April 26, 1857 Riordan's cock follows close after me while spading in the garden, and hens commonly follow the gardener and ploughman, just as cowbirds the cattle in a pasture.

September 30, 1857 Talked with Minott, who was sitting, as usual, in his wood-shed. His hen and chickens, finding it cold these nights on the trees behind the house, had begun last night to roost in the shed, and one by one walked or hopped up a ladder within a foot of his shoulder to the loft above. He sits there so much like a fixture that they do not regard him. It has got to be so cool, then, that tender chickens seek a shelter at night; but I saw the hens at Clark's (the R. Brown house) were still going to roost in the apple trees.

October 1, 1858 Let a full-grown but young cock stand near you. How full of life he is, from the tip of his bill through his trembling wattles and comb and his bright eye to the extremity of his clean toes! How alert and restless, listening to every sound and watching every motion! How various his notes, from the finest and shrillest alarum as a hawk sails over, surpassing the most accomplished violinist on the short strings, to a hoarse and terrene voice or cluck! He has a word for every occasion,—for the dog that rushes past, and partlet cackling in the barn. And then how, elevating himself and flapping his wings, he gathers impetus and air and launches forth that world-renowned ear-piercing strain! not a vulgar note of defiance, but the mere effervescence of life, like the bursting of a bubble in a wine-cup. Is any gem so bright as his eye?

August 6, 1860 I heard a cock crow very shrilly and distinctly early in the evening of the 8th.[1] This was the most distinct sound from the lower world that I heard up there at any time, not excepting even the railroad whistle, which was louder. It reached my ear perfectly, to each note and curl,—from some submontane cock. We also heard at this hour an occasional bleat from a sheep in some mountain pasture, and a lowing of a cow. And at last we saw a light here and there in a farmhouse window. We heard no sound of man except the railroad whistle and, on Sunday, a church-bell. Heard no dog that I remember. Therefore I should say that, of all the sounds of the farmhouse, the crowing of the cock could be heard furthest or most distinctly under these circumstances. It seemed to wind its way through the layers of air as a sharp gimlet through soft wood, and reached our ears with amusing distinctness.

DOMESTIC PIGEON

April 16, 1855 I am startled sometimes these mornings to hear the sound of doves alighting on the roof just over my head; they come down so hard upon it, as if one had thrown a heavy stick on to it, and I wonder it does not injure their organizations. Their legs must be cushioned in their sockets to save them from the shock?

[1][In camp on the summit of Mt. Monadnock.]

PARROT

May 21, 1857   I saw yesterday a parrot exceedingly frightened in its cage at a window. It rushed to the bars and struggled to get out. A piece of board had been thrown from the window above to the ground, which probably the parrot's instinct had mistaken for a hawk. Their eyes are very open to danger from above.

INDEX TO PASSAGES RELATING
TO BIRDS IN THOREAU'S WORKS
EXCLUSIVE OF THE JOURNAL

C. C.   Cape Cod.
Exc.   Excursions.
M. W.   The Maine Woods.
Misc.   Miscellanies.
Riv   Riverside Edition.
Walden   Walden, or Life in the Woods.
Wal.   Walden Edition.
Week   A Week on the Concord and Merrimack Rivers.

References in parentheses are to passages taken from the Journal (and appearing in this book) but usually somewhat revised.

Bittern, *Riv.*: Week, 21; Exc., 137. *Wal.*: Week, 17; Exc., 111.
Blackbirds, *Riv.*: Week, 514. *Wal.*: Week, 417.
Bluebird, *Riv.*: Exc., 136. *Wal.*: Exc., 110.
Bunting, Black-throated, *Riv.*: C. C., 156. *Wal.*: C. C., 131.
Chickadee, *Riv.*: Walden, 426; M. W., 130, 144; Exc., 138. *Wal.*: Walden, 304; M. W., 108, 118; Exc., 112.

Coots, sea, *Riv.*: C. C., 134, 135. *Wal.*: C. C., 113, 114.

Crow, *Riv.*: Exc., 139. *Wal.*: Exc., 113.

"Dipper," *Riv.*: M. W., 226, 227. *Wal.*: M. W., 184.

Duck, domestic, *Riv.*: C. C., (100, 101). *Wal.*: C. C., (86).

Duck, Wood, *Riv.*: Exc., 328. *Wal.*: Exc., 268.

Ducks, wild, *Riv.*: Week, 6; Walden, 385; Exc., 135. *Wal.*: Week, 5; Walden, 274, 275; Exc., 110.

Eagle, Bald, *Riv.*: M. W., 35, 36, 384. *Wal.*: M. W., 30, 309.

Flicker, *Riv.*: Exc., (137). *Wal.*: Exc., (111).

Flycatcher, Olive-sided, *Riv.*: M. W., 226. *Wal.*: M. W., 183.

Fowl, domestic, *Riv.*: Walden, 199, 200; Exc., 301, 302; Misc., 360, 361. *Wal.*: Walden, 140, 141; Exc., 246, 411, 412.

General and Miscellaneous, *Riv.*: Week, 70, 71, 208, 293, 419; Walden, 135, 330, 478, 479; M. W., 143, 144, 178; C. C., 204, 222; Exc., 134–140, 182, 218, (230), (360, 361). *Wal.*: Week, 56, 57, 167, 236, 237, 339; Walden, 95, 234, 342; M. W., 118, 146, 184; C. C., 170, 184, 185; Exc., 108–114, 149, 179, (187, 188), (293, 294).

Goldfinch, American, *Riv.*: Exc., 139. *Wal.*: Exc., 113.

Goose, Canada, *Riv.*: Walden, 385, 421, (482, 483). *Wal.*: Walden, 274, 275, 300, (345).

Grouse, Ruffed, *Riv.*: Walden, 352–354, 427, 435; Exc., 134. *Wal.*: Walden, 250–252, 304, 305, 310, 311; Exc., 109.

Gulls, *Riv.*: C. C., 83, 84, 104, 105, 306. *Wal.*: C. C., 71, 72, 89, 253.

Hawk, Fish, *Riv.*: M. W., 178; Exc., 136, 137. *Wal.*: M. W., 146; Exc., 110, 111.

Hawk, Marsh, *Riv.*: Walden, 479. *Wal.*: Walden, 342.

Hawks, *Riv.*: Walden, 487, 488; M. W., 298. *Wal.*: Walden, 348, 349; M. W., 240, 241.

Hen-hawks, *Riv.*: Walden, 248. *Wal.*: Walden, 176.

Heron, Great Blue, *Riv.*: Week, 514. *Wal.*: Week, 416, 417.

Heron, Green, *Riv.*: Week, 309, 310, (311). *Wal.*: Week, 249, (250).

Jay, Blue, *Riv.*: Walden, 425, 426; Exc., 138, 243, 244 *Wal.*: Walden, 303, 304; Exc., 112, 199.

Jay, Canada, *Riv.*: M. W., 293. *Wal.*: M. W., 237.

Loon, *Riv.*: Walden, 363–368 (mostly from Journal); M. W., 225, 251, 307, 308, 362, 377; Exc., 140. *Wal.*: Walden, 258–262; M. W., 182, 203, 247, 248, 291, 303, 304; Exc., 114.

Merganser, American, *Riv.*: M. W., 224, 225, 340, 343, 384, 385. *Wal.*: M. W., 182, 274, 276, 309.

Nighthawk, *Riv.*: Walden, 247, 248. *Wal.*: Walden, 175, 176.

Owl, Barred, *Riv.*: Walden, 411, 412. *Wal.*: Walden, 293.

Owl, Great Horned, *Riv.*: Walden (196, 197), 420, 421; M. W., 384 *Wal.*: Walden, (138, 139), 300, 301; M. W., 309.

Owl, Screech, *Riv.*: Walden, (194, 195). *Wal.*: Walden, (138).

Owls, *Riv.*: Week, 70. *Wal.*: Week, 56.

Phalarope, *Riv.*: C. C., 134. *Wal.*: C. C., 113.

Phœbe, *Riv.*: Walden, 491; Exc., 134 note, 138. *Wal.*: Walden, 351; Exc., 109 note, 112.

Pigeon, Passenger, *Riv.*: Week, 292; Walden, (179), 248. *Wal.*: Week, 235, 236; Walden, (127), 176.

Plover, Piping, *Riv.*: C. C., 82, 134, 222. *Wal.*: C. C., 71, 113, 185.

Plover, Upland, *Riv.*: C. C., 156, 196. *Wal.*: C. C., 131, 132, 164.

Robin, *Riv.*: Walden, (481); Exc., 134. *Wal.*: Walden, (344); Exc., 109.

Sandpiper, Spotted, *Riv.*: M. W., 178, 225. *Wal.*: M. W., 146, 182.

Shrike, *Riv.*: Exc., 134. *Wal.*: Exc., 109.

Snipe, *Riv.*: Exc., 140. *Wal.*: Exc., 113.

Sparrow, Song, *Riv.*: Walden, (480). *Wal.*: Walden, (343).

Sparrow, White-throated, *Riv.*: M. W., 263, 264, 308. *Wal.*: M. W., 213, 214, 248, 249.

Swallow, Bank, *Riv.*: C. C., 196. *Wal.*: C. C., 164.

Tern (Mackerel Gull), *Riv.*: C. C., 82. *Wal.*: C. C., 71.

Thrasher, Brown, *Riv.*: Walden, 246, 247. *Wal.*: Walden, 175.
Thrush, "wood," *Riv.*: M. W., 229, 376. *Wal.*: M. W., 186, 303.
Veery, *Riv.*: Exc., 138. *Wal.*: Exc., 112.
Vireo, *Riv.*: Exc., 138. *Wal.*: Exc., 112.
Whip-poor-will, *Riv.*: Walden, 194. *Wal.*: Walden, 137.
Woodcock, *Riv.*: Walden, 355. *Wal.*: Walden, 252, 253.
Woodpecker, Pileated ("red-headed"), *Riv.*: M. W., 384. *Wal.*: M. W., 309.

Hosmer, Abel, 128
Hosmer, Joseph, 203
Hosmer, Luther, 374
Hubbard, Charles, 278
Hubbard, Cyrus, 101
Hubbard, Ebby, 118, 265
Huckleberry-bird. *See* Sparrow, Field
Hummingbird, Ruby-throated, 46,
  237–239, 249, 477

Indians, 395, 439
Indigo-bird, **358**

Jay, Blue, 179–180, **252–257**, 417, 421,
  452, 456, 466, 467, 469
Jones, Josh, 265–266
Junco, Slate-colored (Slate-colored
  Snowbird, *Fringilla hyemalis*), 184
  and n, 294, 311 and n, **339–344**,
  360–364, 410, 441, 465–466, 482

Kingbird, 138, 156, **240–244**
Kingfisher, Belted, **213–214**
Kinglet, Ruby-crowned (Ruby-
  crested Wren), 127n, 259, **424–425**

Lark. *See* Meadowlark
Lark, Shore, **250–252**
Lightning-bug, 458
Linaria. *See* Redpoll, Lesser
Lind, Jenny, 422n, 482

Linnaeus, 491
Loon, **4–8**, 15
Loon, Red-throated, **8**
Loring, Mr. (of Concord), 60

MacGillivray, William, 148, 149, 150,
  194n
Man, birds' fear of, 472
Mann, Horace, Jr., 77 and n, 87, 272
Marshfield, Mass., 436 and n
Martin, Purple, **369**, 460
Meadow-Hen. *See* Rail, Virginia
Meadowlark (Lark), **285–286**, 340,
  438, 441, 450, 465
Melvin, George, 42 and n, 117, 201,
  311, 321, 471
Merganser, American (Sheldrake,
  Goosander), 16, 17 and n, **21–39**,
  52, 55, 56, 82, 476
Merganser, Red-breasted, 36 and n
Merriam, Joe, 42
Miles, Charles, 477
Miles, Martial, 139 and n, 189, 270
Milkweed, 282, 394–395
Minot's Ledge, 20
Minott, George, 40–41, 42, 62 and n,
  71, 76 and n, 127–128, 131, 185, 264
  and n, 265, 338, 349, 350, 378–379,
  489, 493, 494
Mockingbird, **407**
Moore, J. B., 55